GUY STANDING

Basic Income:
And How We Can Make It Happen

A PELICAN INTRODUCTION

PELICAN
an imprint of
PENGUIN BOOKS

PELICAN BOOKS

UK | USA | Canada | Ireland | Australia
India | New Zealand | South Africa

Penguin Books is part of the Penguin Random House
group of companies whose addresses can be found at
global.penguinrandomhouse.com.

Penguin
Random House
UK

First published 2017

Text copyright © Guy Standing, 2017

The moral right of the author has been asserted

Book design by Matthew Young
Set in 10/14.664 pt FreightText Pro
Typeset by Jouve (UK), Milton Keynes
Printed in Great Britain by Clays Ltd, Elcograf S.p.A.

A CIP catalogue record for this book is
available from the British Library

ISBN: 978-0-141-98548-0

MIX
Paper from
responsible sources
FSC® C018179

Penguin Random House is committed to a
sustainable future for our business, our readers
and our planet. This book is made from Forest
Stewardship Council® certified paper.

www.greenpenguin.co.uk

Contents

'It is from the champions of the impossible
rather than the slaves of the possible
that evolution draws its creative force.'

BARBARA WOOTTON

PREFACE

Since at least Thomas More's *Utopia* of 1516, many thinkers have flirted with the idea of a basic income – everybody in society receiving a regular amount of income as a right. Some have recoiled at the effrontery of the idea; some have mocked it, as fantasy and a threat to civilization – albeit most unlikely to come about; some have pushed it into the 'dream, brother' recesses of the mind; some have grown tiresome in their enthusiasm. The gamut of sentiments and reactions has been impressively wide.

However, only in the 1980s was an international network set up to promote debate around the issue. The Basic Income European Network (BIEN) was formally established in September 1986 by a small group of economists, philosophers and other social scientists from western Europe, meeting in Louvain-la-Neuve, Belgium. This was symbolic; *Utopia*, the first vision of a society with a publicly financed basic income, was originally published in Louvain (Leuven in Flemish). I was one of those founder members, and came up with the name. As well as being an acronym, BIEN played on the French word meaning 'well', hinting at the well-being we believe basic income could bring about.

Gradually, as more people joined from outside Europe, it

became appropriate to rename the organization. In 2004 the E in BIEN was converted from 'European' to 'Earth'. Nevertheless, until quite recently, the idea that a basic income should be paid to all as a right drew little attention from mainstream commentators, academics or politicians. Honourable exceptions included Michel Rocard, a former French Prime Minister, and Bishop Desmond Tutu, winner of the Nobel Peace Prize, who both addressed BIEN congresses. Then came the financial crash of 2007–8, which threatened the global economy, since when there has been a huge surge of interest.

Nevertheless, please indulge me in a note of appreciation for those who, through the activities of BIEN, kept the idea alive during the doldrum years and whose research and writing helped to shape thinking and fill in the policy gaps. From the outset, we sought to ensure that every political hue could be represented, within limits of respect for gender equality, racial equality and free and democratic societies.

Indeed, there have always been tensions between those who have taken a libertarian approach and those who have been more egalitarian, and between those who see a basic income as a 'stand-alone' policy and those who see it as part of a progressive political strategy. Yet this 'broad church' approach has been key to the success of BIEN as it has built the knowledge base required for when it can be said with conviction that 'this is an idea whose time has come'.

A Political Imperative?

The growing interest in basic income partly reflects a recognition that current economic and social policies are producing unsustainable inequalities and injustices. The twentieth-century income distribution system has broken down, as globalization has swept forward, as 'neo-liberal' economics has done its work, and as the technological revolution has facilitated transformative changes in labour markets. One outcome has been a growing 'precariat', consisting of millions of people facing unstable, insecure labour, a lack of occupational identity, declining and increasingly volatile real wages, loss of benefits and chronic indebtedness.

The shares of national income going to 'capital' and 'labour' used to be roughly stable; that old consensus has gone. We are in a Second Gilded Age, in which more and more income is going to a minority of 'rentiers' who are thriving from the proceeds of property – physical, financial and 'intellectual'. This has no moral or economic justification. And the inequities are multiplying, as is the resentment. The mixture of anxiety, anomie, alienation and anger is creating a 'perfect storm', enabling populist politicians to play on fears in order to build support for agendas that have echoes of the ugly aftermath of the First Gilded Age.

Unless a new income distribution system can be constructed – or at least the firm beginnings of one – the drift to the far right, which underpinned Brexit and the triumph of Donald Trump in 2016, will only grow stronger. I would argue that, as the anchor of a more egalitarian and more emancipatory system, basic income has become a political imperative, which is one of the reasons for writing this book.

About the Book

The book is intended to guide the reader through the arguments for and against the introduction of a basic income as a right, paid in cash (or equivalent) to all individuals regardless of age, gender, marital status, work status and work history. It draws on thirty years of research, advocacy and social activism by many people, and especially on the growth of BIEN, its sixteen international congresses and the hundreds of papers presented at them, up to and including the congress in Seoul in July 2016. As far as possible, I have given references and sources that interested readers can go to for more elaborated discussion.

However, the intention here is to provide an introduction and a reflective guide to the issues. In what follows, I consider what is meant by basic income and discuss the three main perspectives – justice, freedom and security – that have been used to justify it, as well as the economic rationale. I also deal with the various objections that have been made to it, especially on affordability and the impact on labour supply, and look at the practical and political challenges of implementation.

It is hoped that the book will be of use to politicians and policymakers as well as to what are sometimes rather patronizingly called 'lay readers'. The simple call to 'give everybody a basic income' is actually more complex than it sounds, and many people have strong opinions formed without evidence or considered reflection. So readers are urged to approach this book with as open a mind as possible.

As a founder member of BIEN and currently its honorary co-president, I am an unapologetic supporter of basic income. However, I have endeavoured to 'give the devil the best tunes' (well, let us pretend!), so that readers can weigh the arguments for themselves. The purpose is, and should be, to encourage a dispassionate *conversation*, rather than a dialogue of the deaf. It is up to those who are in the political arena to take the conversation forward into action.

How to give politicians inclined to support a basic income the courage to say it out loud and work for it? I, for one, have grown tired of hearing prominent politicians say in private that they support basic income but do not know how to 'come out'. I would like to think that the arguments in this book, underlined by the events of 2016, will help to strengthen their collective backbone.

CHAPTER 1

Basic Income – Its Meaning and Historical Origins

'The easiest way out is through the door.
Why do so few use this method?'
CONFUCIUS

We need to start by defining what is meant by a basic income. Although there are a number of variants, which will be discussed in due course, a basic income can be defined as a modest amount of money paid unconditionally to individuals on a regular basis (for example, monthly). It is often called a universal basic income (UBI) because it is intended to be paid to all.

This deceptively simple definition nevertheless needs unpacking.

The Essentials

WHAT IS MEANT BY 'BASIC'?

The term 'basic' causes a lot of confusion. At the least, it means an amount that would enable someone to survive *in extremis*, in the society they live in. It could be more. However, the underlying purpose is to provide basic economic security, not total security or affluence. Total security would be neither feasible nor desirable.

Deciding what constitutes basic security is a challenge, but intuitively it should be easy to understand. Basic security in terms of being able to obtain enough to eat and a place to live, an opportunity to learn and access to medical care surely constitutes what any 'good society' should provide, equally and as certainly as it can. Most advocates of a basic income believe it should be provided as a 'right', meaning that it cannot be withdrawn at will. This issue is discussed further in Chapter 3.

Some argue that the basic income should be sufficient to ensure 'participation in society'. As a definition, this seems both unnecessary and too vague. However, it reflects a laudable wish for all to have adequate resources to enable them, in words associated with Alexis de Tocqueville, to go forth in society as citizens with equal status. A sensible pragmatic position is that the level of a basic income should be sufficient to advance in that direction.

So, how high should the basic income be? Some advocates believe it should be set at the highest amount that is sustainable, and as close as possible to an 'above-poverty' level. This is the libertarian view, discussed in Chapter 3, which is often accompanied by claims that a basic income could then replace all state benefits and welfare services.

Others, including this writer, believe that a basic income could start at a low level and be built up gradually, determined by the size of a fund set up for the purpose and the level and change in national income. Whatever level is set, however, a basic income need not – and should not – be a calculated means of dismantling the welfare state.

WHAT IS MEANT BY 'UNIVERSAL'?

In an ideal world, we might want every human being to have equal basic income security. But 'universal' here means that a basic income would be paid to everyone usually resident in a given community, province or country. The basic income would not, strictly speaking, be a 'citizenship income', as it is sometimes referred to, because non-resident citizens would not qualify. Conversely, in-migrants could be required to be legal residents for a defined period (or, in the case of foreigners, have achieved permanent residence status) before qualifying to receive the basic income. This is a political matter to be decided by democratic means.

WHAT IS MEANT BY 'PAID TO INDIVIDUALS'?

The basic income would be paid to each individual as an individual, regardless of marital, family or household status. Thus it would not favour or discriminate against any type of household arrangement. And, unlike benefits paid according to 'family status', there would be no presumption of automatic sharing of income within a household, let alone equal sharing, which is often not the case.

The basic income should also be *uniform*, that is, paid equally to every adult, whatever their circumstances. Some existing state benefits, being family-based, in effect give members of large households a lower amount, assuming economies of scale within families. A basic income makes no such assumption and so avoids unintended discrimination.

Most (but not all) proponents of a basic income also advocate paying a lower amount to children, usually specifying that the child's basic income should be paid to the mother or a surrogate for the mother. And many propose paying supplements for pensioners, for the frail elderly and for those with disabilities, to compensate for their higher costs of living and their relatively low probability of earning extra income. Thus 'equality' can be interpreted as equality of basic living standard.

WHAT IS MEANT BY 'UNCONDITIONALLY'?

The important claim that the basic income should be provided by the state *unconditionally* has three aspects. First, there would be no *income* conditions, that is, no means testing. People would not have to prove they have an income below a certain amount, or that this was not their 'fault' or 'responsibility'; such tests are much more arbitrary and inequitable than commonly presumed.

Second, there would be no *spending* conditions; the basic income would be paid without direction or restriction on what, when or how recipients spent the money. This distinguishes basic income from benefits in kind, or vouchers or cash cards, that can only be spent on specific items and are thus inherently paternalistic. A basic income allows people to determine their own spending priorities.

Third, there would be no *behavioural* conditions, requiring people to behave in certain ways and not others, such as taking jobs or particular types of job, or being willing to do so, in order to qualify for the basic income. This is what both advocates and critics of basic income usually mean when they refer to basic income as an 'unconditional' payment.

WHAT IS MEANT BY 'REGULAR'?

The basic income would be paid at regular intervals, the usual suggestion being monthly, though it could be more frequent or less. Importantly, the amount each month would be similar and paid automatically, without form filling, queuing and so on. Predictability is a crucial component of basic security. Unlike most other forms of state benefit, basic income would be both guaranteed and known in advance.

It would also be *non-withdrawable*. In other words, basic income should be a right that, like other fundamental rights such as the right to liberty, cannot be taken away except by due process of law. (Some basic income advocates propose suspending payments to prisoners, but other options could include using the basic income to help defray the costs of upkeep in prison, payment of the basic income to another family member or even the banking of payments to await release, easing subsequent reintegration into society.) It should also be *non-repayable*. Sometimes the term 'non-foreclosable' is used, to signify that the basic income could not be seized for non-payment of debts. It should be an economic right to basic income security.

A Warning

A stable and predictable basic income, paid come rain come shine, is thus different from a *minimum income guarantee*, which tops up low incomes to a given level, usually requiring complex means tests. And it is different from a *negative income tax* or *tax credits*, which are withdrawn as income rises.

Nevertheless, these variants are often referred to in the same breath as basic income, and they do have in common the idea that everyone should have some sort of basic income security. While this book reserves the term 'basic income' for schemes that conform to the definition given at the start of the chapter, readers should be aware (and beware) that commentators often confound these diverse approaches under the 'basic income' label. Sometimes this may be done mischievously; more usually, it is a sign that they do not know what they are talking about.

Basic Income v. Basic Capital Grants

It is important to distinguish between a basic income (modest amounts paid regularly) and basic capital grants (larger amounts paid as a single lump sum). It has been said that a basic capital grant aims to produce 'capitalism with equal starts', which permits market-driven inequalities, whereas a basic income aims for 'capitalism with baseline income maintenance'.[1]

Advocates of a basic capital grant typically envisage a one-off payment given to everybody on reaching a certain age, such as twenty-one. Bruce Ackerman and Anne Alstott, the two principal contemporary proponents, have called this a 'stakeholder grant'.[2] Elsewhere, I have called it a 'coming-of-age grant', a COAG.[3]

In a variant known as a 'baby bond', introduced by Britain's New Labour government, parents were given a voucher for £250 or more at the birth of a child, to invest in a trust fund that paid out at age eighteen. That scheme was abolished by the coalition government of 2010–15, before the first recipients reached adulthood, so there could be no evaluation of its impact prior to the decision to end it.

The main criticism of one-off capital grants is the

'weakness-of-will' effect. Someone receiving a large lump sum, especially at age eighteen or twenty-one, might be tempted to make risky investments or might squander the money, ending up with nothing. There is also a timing issue, since one age cohort may receive the grant when investment values are rising, another when opportunities are scarce or more risky. The advice of an expert (or perhaps a 'nudge' by a government-appointed adviser) may have poor results for one person and good ones for another at a different time. In effect, the capital grant leaves too much to chance.

It would be difficult to refuse help for people if, for whatever reason, they subsequently fell upon hard times. But this would also create a moral hazard, since expectation of further financial support if the money was lost could tempt some recipients into more reckless decisions. By contrast, a modest amount paid as a regular basic income would not encourage excessive risk-taking, and would have the added advantage of allowing people to learn over time how to handle money if they had not been able to do so previously.

The Roots of Basic Income

Several candidates jostle for pride of place as the originator of the idea that the state should provide all its citizens with a basic income. Sir Thomas More, in his fictional vision of the island of *Utopia* (literally, 'no place'), published in Latin in 1516, is commonly identified as the first to picture a society with a basic income.

However, there is a case for going much further back, to Pericles and Ephialtes, who in 461 BC triumphed as leaders of the 'plebeians' in ancient Athens. It was Ephialtes, in fact, who initiated democratic reforms that involved paying citizens for jury service. Shortly afterwards, he was assassinated (allegedly by his political opponents), and Pericles, his second-in-command, then took over. So, although it was hardly the ideal omen, we could say that Ephialtes was the true originator of the basic income, or at least the 'citizen's income' variant.

The essence of ancient Greek democracy was that the citizens were expected to participate in the *polis*, the political life of the city. Pericles instituted a sort of basic income grant that rewarded them for their time and was intended to enable the plebs – the contemporary equivalent of the precariat – to take part. The payment was not conditional on actual participation, which was nevertheless seen as a moral duty. Sadly, this enlightened system of deliberative democracy, facilitated by the basic income, was overthrown by an oligarchic coup in 411 BC. The road was blocked for a very long time.

The medieval roots of basic income can be found in the epochal Charter of the Forest, which was issued alongside the Magna Carta in 1217. (Although the original Charter of Liberties of June 1215 is often referred to as the Magna Carta, it was not given that name until a shorter version was issued in 1217 after certain sections were moved to and elaborated in the forest charter.) The Charter of the Forest asserted the rights of the common man to subsistence and to what were called *estovars*, the means of subsistence in the commons. In the thirteenth century, every church was required to read out the Charter to congregations four times a year. One remarkable feature inserted in the revised Magna Carta was the right granted to widows to 'reasonable *estovar* of common'. Every widow had the right to a basic income, in the form of the right to take food, fuel and housing materials from the commons.

It was nevertheless Thomas More who first depicted what a society with a basic income might look like. In a novel justification that is not without modern parallels,[4] he saw basic income as a better way to reduce thievery than hanging, then the usual punishment. One of his characters says:

> No penalty on earth will stop people from stealing if it is their only way of getting food . . . Instead of inflicting these horrible punishments, it would be far more to the point to provide everyone with some means of livelihood, so that nobody is under the frightful necessity of becoming first a thief and then a corpse.

Ten years later, a Spanish-Flemish scholar and friend of More, Johannes Vives, submitted a detailed proposal to the Mayor of Bruges for ensuring a minimum subsistence for all the city's residents; this led to a brief trial of the idea in the town of Ypres. For this reason, some credit Vives with being the first to initiate something like a basic income. But in his model the assistance (food) was targeted on the poor only. Vives was also a proponent of 'workfare', making the poor labour in return. Still, More, Vives and others helped to legitimize the idea of publicly funded and publicly provided poor relief, rather than reliance on discretionary charity by the Church or the rich.

In the centuries after More, a few other thinkers followed

in his footsteps. In France, for example, Montesquieu's *Spirit of the Laws* of 1748 asserted, 'The State owes all its citizens a secure subsistence, food, suitable clothes and a way of life that does not damage their health.' Later, the Marquis de Condorcet, an enlightened man for his time and place, argued for something similar. The guillotine that ended his life in 1794 again symbolized a road not followed.

However, perhaps the most influential advocate in the early phase was Thomas Paine, the great republican and author of *The Rights of Man*. The key assertion was not in his widely distributed pamphlet *Common Sense* (1776) that inspired the American War of Independence, a copy of which was said to be in every cabin in America, but in the core of his seminal essay 'Agrarian Justice', written in 1795.[5] There he proposed what might be called a 'coming-of-age' capital grant as well as a basic income for the elderly, both remarkably innovative proposals for his time.

Paine's radical contemporary in England, Thomas Spence, also argued for a basic income as a natural right, as a matter of justice. He envisaged a sort of 'social dividend' derived from land rents paid into parish funds, with the proceeds distributed equally between all inhabitants on a quarterly basis.

In the nineteenth century, a few writers toyed with some version of a basic income. In continental Europe, French, Dutch and Belgian thinkers were prominent in this phase, notably the socialists Charles Fourier, Joseph Charlier, and François Huet, who in 1853 advocated an unconditional transfer to all young adults, funded by taxes on inheritance and gifts. But they were to be marginalized in the burst of communist fervour and the paternalism of social democracy.

Across the Atlantic, contributors included the flamboyant Henry George, whose book *Progress and Poverty* (1879) sold millions and whose influence was widespread and prolonged. Another influential publication was Edward Bellamy's novel *Looking Backward!* (1888), describing in detail a United States in the year 2000 that credited all citizens with an equal income.

In Britain, William Morris's radical futuristic novel, *News from Nowhere* (1890), written in part in reaction to Bellamy's book, envisaged a cooperative craft-based society in an England of 1956. The novel itself was too earnest to be regarded as great literature, but Morris captured something special in portraying a society where, with a basic income granted by the state, people pursued work as creative activity, not as labour for bosses. It was a vision of work soon to be lost in the dour 'labourism' of both socialists and communists in the early decades of the twentieth century, which made income and benefits dependent on jobs.

What might be regarded as the *second wave* of proponents came in the wake of the First World War, in the writings of Bertrand Russell, Mabel and Dennis Milner, Bertram Pickard, G. D. H. Cole and the disciples of Henry George.[6] Walter van Trier wrote an engaging doctoral dissertation identifying the Milners as the pioneers of a basic income (which they called a 'state bonus') as practical policy.[7] Shortly after them, writing in the 1920s, came British engineer C. H. Douglas, founder of the 'social credit' movement and the first proponent inspired by a technological vision of a widening divide between economic output and workers' incomes and purchasing power. He was to have a bevy of like-minded thinkers in the twenty-first century.

As a general principle, Russell stated the aim of basic income clearly:

> [T]he plan we are advocating amounts essentially to this: that a certain small income, sufficient for necessaries, should be secured to all, whether they work or not, and that a larger income – as much larger as might be warranted by the total amount of commodities produced – should be given to those who are willing to engage in some work which the community recognizes as useful . . . When education is finished, no one should be *compelled* to work, and those who choose not to work should receive a bare livelihood, and be left completely free.[8]

Russell's statement was one of many similar calls in a very charged social context, a time of economic misery following the carnage of the Great War of 1914–18, which had decimated the industrial working class of Europe. But the Labour Party, which discussed the ideas of basic income and state bonuses at its annual conference in 1920, formally rejected them the following year. It was a missed opportunity to advance a different form of society.

Subsequently, there were a few lone voices in the United States, most notably Senator Huey Long. In Britain, the various related proposals figured peripherally in the debates on the formation of the welfare state, notably in the early work of James Meade and Juliet Rhys-Williams (1943), which was taken forward by her son Brandon after he became a

Conservative MP. But the 'labourist' version of the welfare state prevailed, tying income and benefits to the performance of paid labour, and the basic income road was not taken, again.

The Frankfurt School psychoanalyst Erich Fromm advocated a 'universal subsistence guarantee' in a famous 1955 book, *The Sane Society*, and in a later essay, 'The Psychological Aspects of the Guaranteed Income'. But the labourist welfare state was then in its ascendancy and his voice and that of others went unheeded.

What might be called the *third wave* came in the 1960s, predominantly in the United States, at a time of rising concern over 'structural' and 'technological' unemployment. This was famously associated with the 1972 proposal by President Richard Nixon for a Family Assistance Plan, a form of negative income tax. He refused to use the term 'guaranteed annual income', and it would be an exaggeration to see Nixon as a convert to the basic income cause. He believed in supporting 'the working poor', by which was meant those in low-paid jobs, ignoring the many forms of unpaid work.

Nevertheless, the measure was an advance in the basic income direction. It passed in the House of Representatives but died in the Senate, despite overwhelming support in public opinion polls. Ironically, the reform was killed by Democrats, some on the specious grounds that the proposed amount was not enough. It was yet another instance of a road not taken. The era of tax credits emerged in its stead.

Earlier, in 1968, an astonishing 1,200 economists from 150 universities had signed a petition in favour of a negative income tax. And, although forgotten for many years, in 1967, shortly before he was assassinated, Martin Luther King wrote as follows:

> I am now convinced that the simplest approach will prove to be the most effective – the solution to poverty is to abolish it directly by a now widely discussed measure: the guaranteed income . . . New forms of work that enhance the social good will have to be devised for those for whom traditional jobs are not available . . . a host of positive psychological changes inevitably will result from widespread economic security. The dignity of the individual will flourish when the decisions concerning his life are in his own hands, when he has the assurance that his income is stable and certain, and when he knows that he has the means to seek self-improvement.[9]

There were many other advocates around this time, though most seem to have supported a means-tested guaranteed minimum income. They included a string of Nobel Prize-winning economists – James Meade, Friedrich Hayek, Milton Friedman, Jan Tinbergen, James Tobin, Paul Samuelson and Gunnar Myrdal. The idea was also supported by other prominent economists, such as J. K. Galbraith, and by sociologists, most notably New York Senator Daniel Patrick Moynihan, who, although a Democrat, had a strong influence on Nixon's proposed Family Assistance Plan.[10]

The *fourth wave* could be said to have started in a quiet way with the establishment of the Basic Income European (now Earth) Network (BIEN) in 1986. After attracting a steady stream of converts, the wave gathered real momentum in the wake of the financial crash of 2007–8. Since then a wide range of economists and commentators have come out in support of some variant or another of basic income, often associated with fears of technological unemployment, growing inequality and high unemployment.

Supporters in this fourth wave include: Nobel Prize winners James Buchanan, Herbert Simon, Angus Deaton, Christopher Pissarides and Joseph Stiglitz; academics Tony Atkinson, Robert Skidelsky and Robert Reich, former Secretary of Labour under Bill Clinton; prominent economic journalists Sam Brittan and Martin Wolf; and leading figures in the BIEN movement, such as German sociologist Claus Offe and the Belgian philosopher Philippe van Parijs.

Latterly, the idea has been taken up by Silicon Valley luminaries and venture capitalists, some putting up money for the cause, as we shall see. They include Robin Chase, co-founder of Zipcar, Sam Altman, head of the start-up incubator Y Combinator, Albert Wenger, a prominent venture capitalist, Chris Hughes, co-founder of Facebook, Elon Musk, founder of SolarCity, Tesla and SpaceX, Marc Benioff, CEO of Salesforce, Pierre Omidyar, founder of eBay, and Eric Schmidt, Executive Chairman of Alphabet, Google's parent.

Some people have rejected basic income on the rather crude reasoning that support from this quarter means it must be wrong! All that can be said at this stage is that the breadth of support, from across the political spectrum, from business executives to trade union leaders to social activists, and across all disciplines of the social sciences, promises a more robust movement than at any time in the past.

Looking back at the four waves of advocacy, the first, disjointed wave can be characterized as responses to the conflictual emergence of industrial capitalism, imagining a way to adjust society to preserve communities and the values of 'work' against advancing proletarian 'labour'. The impetus for the second wave was primarily social justice, the need to right the wrongs of the First World War and the decimation of the working class. But it was crushed by the juggernaut of universal labourism espoused by social democrats, communists and Fabian socialists.

The third wave reflected the fear of technological unemployment and faded as that fear receded. The fourth wave has been spurred by the emergence of mass insecurity and rising inequality as well as by concerns about labour displacement by robotics, automation and artificial intelligence. Basic income now appears to be more deeply embedded in public debate, helped by the realization on the left that labourism has run its course, and on the right that chronic insecurity and inequality have made the market economy increasingly unstable and unsustainable.

What's in a Name?

Many names have been given to the essential idea over the centuries, yet the various alternatives have distinctive connotations.

Basic income. This has the virtue of simplicity and familiarity. It differs from 'minimum income', a term usually denoting means-tested schemes, where the state ostensibly guarantees the poor some income if they can prove they are poor and 'deserving' in some way. And it differs from 'guaranteed annual income', a term that has figured prominently in debates in Canada and the US, which seems to signify a means-tested income guarantee, a form of negative income tax. Basic income also differs from the 'minimum wage', a statutory amount usually expressed as an hourly rate, that employers are meant to pay to those in jobs.

Basic income grant (BIG). The BIG is a popular way to refer to basic income in southern Africa. In the US, USBIG stands for the US Basic Income Guarantee Network.

Universal basic income (UBI). This term, widely used in North America and Europe, conveys the idea that basic income would be paid equally to every individual regardless of family or financial status.

Unconditional basic income. Some campaigners have attached the word 'unconditional', intended to make clear that no spending, income or behavioural conditions would be set on entitlement. However, it is not quite true that there would be no conditions of any kind. Most obviously, to qualify, someone would have to be (legally) resident in the community or country covered by the basic income scheme. So the word 'unconditional' may cause more confusion than clarification.

Citizen's income or *citizenship income*. Probably the third most common name, this suggests that all citizens of a country are entitled to a basic income, and that only citizens are entitled. That is doubly problematical. Almost all basic income proposals exclude citizens living abroad and most include long-term legal residents, even if they have not taken out citizenship. So, again, the term is not correct in the literal sense, even though it does convey the notion of basic income as a citizenship right. A newly popular variant is *citizen's basic income*.

Participation income/grant. This concept, discussed in more detail later, is most associated with Tony Atkinson, a long-time advocate. It shares several features of a basic income – it would be universal, paid to individuals in cash on a regular basis – but it imposes the condition that they do some economic activity in return. By setting a behavioural condition, it fails the definition of basic income in a crucial respect.

Social dividend or *dividends-for-all*. The term 'social dividend', favoured by this writer, has an honourable pedigree and captures a key justification of basic income, that it is a return on society's investment and wealth accumulation (see Chapter 2).

State bonus. This term, used by the Milners and Pickard, for example, was popular in the early decades of the twentieth century. It has a certain appeal, conveying the idea of a social payment derived from the state.

Demogrant. Springing into prominence in the US in the late 1960s, this term was briefly adopted, though later dropped, by Democrat Senator George McGovern during his unsuccessful presidential campaign. It remains an attractive name, suggesting a link between 'democracy' and 'grants'.

Freedom grant. This was the name proposed by the writer for a basic income grant (BIG) advocated in South Africa after Nelson Mandela became the country's first post-apartheid president.[11] Sadly, the International Monetary Fund and the then South African finance minister opposed the BIG, since when inequality and chronic insecurity have persisted and grown.

Stabilization grant. This term, another proposed by the

writer, refers to a form of basic income, or a component of it, that would vary with the economic cycle, rising in recessions to encourage spending and falling in better times. This idea is discussed further in Chapter 5.

Stakeholder grant. This is a rebranding of the idea of capital grants, involving a single lump sum paid to individuals on reaching adulthood. The fundamental difference between capital and income grants is the weakness-of-will factor mentioned earlier. But capital grants share with basic income the principles that payments would be universal, unconditional, individual and non-withdrawable.

Among this plethora of terms for the essential idea, the two favoured by the writer are 'basic income' and 'social dividend'. Each has an advantage the other lacks, as should become clear in the course of the following chapters.

Before continuing, it is important to stress once again that introducing a basic income does not imply the automatic or necessary abolition of all or most other existing state benefits, contrary to what some commentators contend.[12] It should be seen rather as a desirable floor of a new income distribution system, whether or not it replaces other state benefits. Basic income is not 'welfare' by another name; it is income.

Basic Income as Social Justice

'Distribution should undo excess,
And each man have enough.'

SHAKESPEARE, *KING LEAR*

What is the ethical or philosophical justification for a basic income? A fundamental claim is that it is an instrument of social justice that reflects the intrinsically social or collective character of society's wealth. In the writer's view, social justice is the most important rationale for moving towards basic income as an economic right, although it is complementary to the other two major rationales, namely freedom and economic security.

Regrettably, much public debate on basic income has focused on it as an alternative form of social protection to existing policies, and therefore much of the discussion has been on so-called 'consequential' aspects, such as the alleged effect on labour and work. The authentic justification lies elsewhere, beginning with social justice.

Social Inheritance – Thomas Paine and Social Dividends

The social justice perspective is linked to the intuitively reasonable claim that society's wealth is collective in character; our incomes and wealth today are due far more to the efforts and achievements of past generations than to anything we may do ourselves. Consider the oft-quoted words by Thomas Paine in his 'Agrarian Justice', written in the winter of 1795 and sent to the Directory of the French Republic in 1796:

> It is a position not to be controverted that the earth, in its natural, uncultivated state was, and ever would have continued to be, the common property of the human race . . . it is the value of the improvement only, and not the earth itself, that is in individual property. Every proprietor, therefore, of cultivated land, owes to the community a ground-rent (for I know of no better term to express the idea) for the land which he holds; and it is from this ground-rent that the fund proposed in this plan is to issue.[1]

His plan derived from this reasoning was remarkably clear and radical, bearing in mind the social and political turmoil in France and the United States where he was writing. The proposal was:

> To create a National Fund, out of which there shall be paid to every person, when arrived at the age of twenty-one years, the sum of fifteen pounds sterling, as a compensation in part, for the loss of his or her natural inheritance, by the introduction of the system of landed property. And also, the sum of ten pounds per annum, during life, to every person now living, of the age of fifty years, and to all others as they shall arrive at that age.[2]

Paine also recommended that 'the blind and lame' should receive regular payments on the same basis as the elderly. He cannot be faulted for specifying what was in effect a capital grant for others rather than a regular basic income, since the latter would have been impractical with the administrative structures of the time. And he went on to justify his call for universalism:

> It is proposed that the payments . . . be made to every person, rich or poor. It is best to make it so, to prevent invidious distinctions. It is also right it should be so, because it is in lieu of the natural inheritance, which, as a right, belongs to every man, over and above the property he may have created, or inherited from those who did. Such persons as do not choose to receive it can throw it into the common fund.[3]

We can see in this the nucleus of the 'social dividend' approach to basic income. And in words that deserve to ring in the ears of all contemporary politicians and commentators, Paine went on a few pages later to state emphatically: 'It is not charity but a right, not bounty but justice, that I am pleading for . . . I care not how affluent some may be, provided that none be miserable in consequence of it.'[4]

A basic income can thus be conceived as a social dividend paid from the collective wealth of society created and maintained by our ancestors and as a shared return on the commons and natural resources that belong to all. This reasoning supports basic income as social justice rather than as a response to poverty per se, and contrasts with the system of entitlements based on direct contributions that was to emerge in social insurance schemes in the nineteenth and twentieth centuries.

The Libertarian Debate

The contemporary philosophical literature on social justice has been dominated by a debate between 'right' and 'left' libertarians. Both are based on the argument that every individual has or should have self-ownership, and thus owes no *duty* of service to others, except through their own voluntary action. However, the two factions differ in their attitude to nature, 'natural resources' and 'property'.

A right-wing perspective starts from the presumption that, to begin with, nature, natural resources and land in particular, are owned by no one and can be privately appropriated by the first to claim them, without the prior consent of, or payment to, other members of society. A left libertarian perspective starts from the premise that nature in its natural state is 'the commons', owned by all, and that private appropriation is only justifiable if the public have consented through democratic channels and are compensated.

The Legacy of Henry George

Henry George has been an influential figure ever since he burst upon the American scene in the late nineteenth century. His most famous book, *Progress and Poverty*, sold over three million copies almost immediately after it was published in 1879, and more than 100,000 people flocked to his funeral after he died from a stroke during an election campaign in New York.[5]

George argued that land was the common inheritance of

all, and all should share the rental income derived from it. He proposed a land rent levy on all private land, with the surplus distributed directly to the public, claiming that this 'single tax' could replace all other taxes including those on labour and production. Many have since used his reasoning to call for a basic income paid from land taxes. While George took a left libertarian view on the collective ownership of land, his approach has especially pleased right-wing libertarians because relying on a land tax rather than personal income and consumption taxes is consistent with their idea of freedom.

George recognized that vast wealth was derived from economic rents, not only from possession of land but also from ownership of other natural resources and of 'intellectual property' such as patents, which he opposed as illegitimate. Rental income from these other sources has exploded in recent decades.[6] As discussed further in Chapter 7, extending George's argument, a levy on all forms of rent could help finance a basic income.

The Middlesbrough Tale

The social justice rationale can be illustrated by the example of Middlesbrough, a decayed industrial town in north-east England.[7] A nondescript hamlet in the 1820s, within a decade of the discovery of iron ore nearby, Middlesbrough and the surrounding Teesside area had become the hub of the industrial revolution and a hub of the British Empire. It was the site of the country's first ironworks, later branching out into steel and chemicals. The Golden Gate Bridge in San

Francisco was built with steel from Middlesbrough; Sydney Harbour Bridge was too, as was much of the Indian railway system. On a gate in the town is emblazoned: 'Born of iron, made of steel.'

Yet today, Middlesbrough's old town hall stands derelict on a hill, surrounded by wasteland and weeds. Abandoned homes, concrete blocks where their windows once were, litter the dilapidated housing estates studied by Tracy Shildrick and colleagues.[8] Some 140,000 people continue to live in the town, many reluctant to move, to give up their roots. They suffer the cruelty of history.

Much of the wealth of people now living in more affluent parts of the country was generated by those nineteenth- and twentieth-century workers in Teesside. Why should they have lives so much more comfortable and secure than the descendants of those who created the country's wealth and power in the first place?

Thinking of Middlesbrough, and places like it in industrial societies everywhere, should remind us of Paine's argument. Communities producing wealth that is enjoyed by others may subsequently suffer deindustrialization and impoverishment, whereas those who gained from their productive efforts may continue to flourish, often through inherited wealth and privilege. A basic income can thus be seen as a transfer of part of our collective inheritance to people in less privileged communities. Sharing the inherited wealth created by those ironworkers and their successors is a matter of inter-generational social justice.

The standard objection to the social dividend rationale for a basic income is that no individual has a right to a share of inherited social wealth because they have done nothing to 'deserve' it. In that case, following the same logic, private inheritance should also be abolished. If private inheritance is allowed, then the principle of social inheritance should be too.

The Rentier Economy

Our inherited wealth does not only consist of land and physical assets, but intangible assets as well, including financial assets and 'intellectual property'. Intangible assets also generate economic rents derived from natural or contrived scarcity, enabling companies and individuals to gain income simply by virtue of possession. In the case of intellectual property, the state creates and enforces regulations and laws that have generated vast rental incomes from patents, copyrights, brands and the like.

Thomas Jefferson, in 1813, described ideas as natural public goods, since communicating an idea to someone else does not deprive the originator of it. He added that patents brought 'more embarrassment than advantage to society'. Yet the modern state has strengthened patent protection, granting a tiny minority a monopoly income for twenty years, while copyright can last up to ninety-five years.[9] This rental income is augmented by large government subsidies, mostly in the form of tax breaks, without any obligation to give back to society.

Many patented inventions are derived from publicly subsidized research. So why should an individual or single corporation gain all the income? A basic income would be a means of sharing the gains across society. After all, society made the income possible. And the public bears much of the risk for which intellectual property rights are supposedly created. Making the modern situation even more unjust, in a global economic system the enriched person or corporation can easily channel the income abroad, so avoiding or evading taxes on income gained from society's generosity.

In that context, consider the extraordinary wealth, and cumulative income derived from it, of Microsoft's Bill Gates, consistently one of the richest men in the world, who was worth over $80 billion at the end of 2016. His personal technical contribution built on a stream of inventions and ideas of others, yet he has gained most of the income attributable to those inventions and ideas as well as his own. And that income in turn is based on the lengthy monopoly he enjoys on Microsoft software and other products, thanks to patent and copyright rules that were vastly strengthened globally by the World Trade Organization in 1995. He was thus helped to gain his fortune by state and international regulations, rather than by his individual endeavour alone. His income is based largely not on 'merit' or 'hard work' but on artificial rules privileging a particular way of gaining income.

More often than not, individual wealth owes more to luck, laws and regulations, inheritance or fortunate timing than to individual brilliance. Leaving aside fortunes criminally obtained, many people have become rich through the commercial plunder of the commons that belong to all, and through rental income derived from the commercialization and privatization of public services and amenities. This is further justification for taxing rental income to give everybody a social dividend, a share of socially created wealth.

Philippe van Parijs has presented another variant of the rentier argument. He argues that having a job is a privilege in an economy with high unemployment, which justifies an 'employment rent' (a tax) to help fund a basic income for all.[10] This seems rather a sweeping generalization, since many if not most jobs are anything but a privilege. However, certain jobs and occupations, notably those that restrict entry, could be said to obtain rental income, which would add to the justice rationalization.

Sharing rental income derived from ownership of assets, including so-called 'intellectual property', could be regarded as a left libertarian justification for basic income, paid out as social dividends.[11] It would amount to saying that a modest share for everybody would be socially just.

A Policy Principle for Social Justice

One way to judge any social policy involves a variant of the social justice principle enunciated by John Rawls in his influential *Theory of Justice*.[12] His 'Difference Principle' specifies that justice is served only if the policy improves the position of the least advantaged. I have dubbed a variant of this the 'Security Difference Principle', according to which a social policy or institutional change should be regarded as socially just only if it improves the security of the most insecure groups in society.

The general relevance of 'security' is considered in Chapter 4. But if the Security Difference Principle is accepted, a basic income would certainly satisfy it. And if moving to a basic income made some people temporarily worse off in economic security terms – for example, if it replaced a scheme that was well targeted on those most in need – it would be socially just to compensate the losers so that no group lost out.

Rawls advocated 'justice as fairness', arguing that 'the most reasonable principles of justice are those everyone would accept and agree to from a fair position'. So another way of looking at justice principles is to ask people what they think is fair. Following a long debate between Rawls and his critic John Harsanyi, who felt that most people would opt for a utilitarian approach that would maximize average income, psychologists came up with an ingenious and since much-replicated way of asking people directly, in what has been dubbed 'experimental ethics'.

In an important series of experiments conducted initially in Canada, Poland and the US, groups of people with different backgrounds and values were asked to prioritize one principle of income distribution from four possible rules, behind a 'veil of ignorance' on where they themselves would be in the spectrum of income distribution.[13] The rules were:

> Maximizing the floor income, expressed as 'The most
>   just distribution of income is that which maximizes
>   the floor or lowest income in society.'
> Maximizing the average income.
> Maximizing the average with a floor constraint.
> Maximizing the average with a range constraint.

Essentially, to simplify a complex analysis, the researchers asked respondents which option they preferred, after they had the meaning of each option carefully explained to them. A majority in all cases chose one of the options with a floor constraint, effectively a basic income.

The experiments then became even more interesting with the introduction of small-group discussions. After several hours of this 'deliberative democracy', the proportion opting for the floor 'basic income' rose significantly. It was overwhelmingly the preferred justice option of all groups.

A large-scale research programme directed by the writer at the International Labour Organization gave the same options in surveys covering many thousands of people in a wide range of developing nations and 'transition' countries of central and eastern Europe.[14] Respondents were asked whether they 'agreed strongly', 'agreed', 'disagreed', 'disagreed strongly' or were 'unsure' about each of the income rules. In every country, the most strongly supported option was the income floor principle; women were slightly more inclined than men to agree strongly with it.

Empirical approaches thus bolster the 'justice' case for a basic income. While such exercises are not infallible, they do suggest that this is a promising route to take.

Tax Justice

A classic liberal position is that the structure of taxation and benefits in society should be 'fair'. People disagree on what that means in practice. But most would accept that, behind a 'veil of ignorance' of where they themselves would be in the distribution of outcomes in society, those on low incomes should not be taxed more than those on high incomes.

Yet this 'justice as fairness' requirement is abused in all countries. One reason is that governments have shifted social security systems towards means-tested social assistance. In Britain, Germany and most other industrialized countries, people going from low state benefits into low-wage jobs, which may well be the only jobs on offer, can face marginal 'tax' rates of over 80 per cent as benefits are withdrawn. This is much higher than tax rates for medium- or high-income earners. Contrast that with a system where the social protection floor was an untaxed (and non-withdrawable) basic income, with all income above the floor being taxed at a standard rate, perhaps with higher rates on higher income bands. That would have a claim to be tax justice.

Another reason for tax unfairness is the taxation of different sources of income at different rates, mainly favouring the more affluent. It is surely a matter of social justice that all sources of income should be taxed in a similar manner. In particular, the tax rate on earnings from labour should not be higher than the tax rates on income from property or investments. Yet in practice, in most societies, taxes on property and profits are much lower than those on earnings.

A basic income system would help to rectify that discrepancy. Marginal and average rates of income tax on labour would decline, while still leaving room for taxes on unearned income to rise, so equalizing rates for all sources of income. That would also help finance a basic income, making it more affordable.

The Demographics of Justice

Would a basic income foster social justice between men and women, across all age groups, and for those with disabilities or impairments that are treated as disabilities in a modern market economy? There is a rich literature on these issues, which I will not attempt to summarize. The short answer is 'not by itself'. But it would help, especially if combined with anti-discrimination measures and mechanisms to strengthen the individual and collective voice of disadvantaged groups.

The first reason for this claim is that a basic income would be paid *individually*. It would not go only to someone designated or self-designated as 'household head' or 'family head', or to a family or household where interpersonal power relations are rarely equal. An individualized basic income would not overcome all the structured inequalities within households or families, but it would reduce financial dependence and provide a way of checking on the fair allocation of monetary resources, because each person would know how much they were due.

A second reason is that a basic income would be *universal* and *uniform* (equal for each person in a household, or for each adult). By contrast, a means-tested benefit would exclude a financially deprived woman in an above-poverty household. The same applies, often more forcefully, to household members with disabilities and the dependent elderly. An individual universal payment would be fairer.

A third reason is that a basic income would be *unconditional*. Behavioural conditionality is not only morally questionable, but is inherently more onerous on some people than on others and is thus unjust. This has been clearly demonstrated by conditional cash transfer schemes, widely adopted in Latin America and elsewhere, which commonly pay grants to low-income mothers provided their children go to school and receive health check-ups. Such schemes are much favoured by the 'libertarian paternalists' whose 'nudge' agenda has been influential in policy making, especially in the US and Britain (see Chapter 3). Yet these conditions almost invariably impose obligations on women as mothers that are not imposed on men, in practice if not in theory, constituting an unfair burden that is both time-using and psychologically stressful.

In terms of interpersonal justice, therefore, a basic income would be beneficial, whatever else might be said for or against it.

The Ecological Imperative

Humanity and the planet face an impending ecological catastrophe in the threat posed by climate change. Already we are seeing disappearing species, shrinking icecaps, rising seas, expanding deserts, extremes of rain and drought, and storms, cyclones and hurricanes of unprecedented destructive power. And many other forms of environmental pollution, linked to industrialization and urbanization, are putting health and well-being at risk. If we have a sense of intergenerational justice and a care for the natural wonders of the world, we need to act urgently to avert disaster.

What has this to do with basic income? Probably most

significantly, a basic income would encourage people to shift some of their time from resource-depleting labour activities to resource-preserving 'reproductive' activities such as caring or voluntary work. This is discussed further in Chapter 8 on work and labour. However, there are also justice issues involved.

Environmental pollution is a regressive phenomenon, since the rich can find ways of insulating themselves from bad air, dirty water, loss of green spaces and so on. Moreover, much pollution results from production and activities that benefit the more affluent – air transport, car ownership, air conditioning, consumer goods of all kinds, to take some obvious examples. A basic income could be construed, in part, as partial compensation for pollution costs imposed on us, as a matter of social justice.

Conversely, a basic income could be seen as compensation for those adversely affected by environmental protection measures. A basic income would make it easier for governments to impose taxes on polluting activities that might affect livelihoods or have a regressive impact by raising prices for goods bought by low-income households. For instance, hefty carbon taxes would deter fossil fuel use and thus reduce greenhouse gas emissions and mitigate climate change as well as reduce air pollution. Introducing a carbon tax would surely be easier politically if the tax take went towards providing a basic income that would compensate those on low incomes, miners and others who would lose income-earning opportunities.

The basic income case is especially strong in relation to the removal of fossil fuel subsidies. Across the world, in rich countries and in poor, governments have long used subsidies as a way of reducing poverty, by keeping down the price of fuel. This has encouraged more consumption, and more wasteful use, of fossil fuels. Moreover, fuel subsidies are regressive, since the rich consume more and thus gain more from the subsidies. But governments have been reluctant to reduce or eliminate the subsidies for fear of alienating voters. Indeed, a number of countries that have tried to reduce fuel subsidies have backed down in the face of angry popular demonstrations.

A basic income could resolve this impasse, as the Iranian example shows (see Chapter 10). If subsidies on fossil fuels were removed, fuel prices would rise. However, the vast amount of money governments spend on those subsidies could then be redirected to finance 'green dividends', paid equally to everybody. This compensation would be progressive; people using more fossil fuels would pay more, while the dividend would be worth more to those with low incomes, in relation both to spending on fossil fuels and to income. If, in addition to removing subsidies, fossil fuels were taxed to cover 'externalities' (costs not factored into the market price, such as illness and deaths from air and water pollution), these taxes too could be redirected to top up green dividends. In this double way, low-income citizens would be economically better off. And all would benefit from reduced use of fossil fuels in terms of less pollution, improved health and a better ecological future for the planet.

Some advocates, such as climate scientist James Hansen, have argued that 100 per cent of carbon tax revenues should be given out as equal green dividends.[15] Others have suggested that companies using fossil fuels for production should be compensated with part of the money collected, at least for a period in which to convert to other sources of energy. Either way, here is a source of funding a basic income, a way of building up the financial base for payment, and justifiable on social justice principles.

This adds up to a formidable case for a basic income system as a valuable weapon in the struggle against environmental degradation, which is also a fight for inter-generational justice. However, the main ecological argument is that a basic income would give people a modest inducement to do valuable forms of work that would help reproduce and strengthen family and community life. It would enable the relatively poor to engage in society and would appeal to what John Berger, in his book *Pig Earth*, called 'the culture of survival' rather than 'the culture of progress', the drive for consumption and the accumulation of wealth.

The Strengthening of Citizenship

As a universal right derived from the collective wealth of society, a basic income would strengthen the sense of common citizenship. This can be linked to what might be called the communitarian case for basic income. It would express a moral obligation we have to one another as human beings and would help bind communities together.

Amitai Etzioni, a leading communitarian, has argued that the more people see themselves as part of a social community, the more they will favour reallocations of wealth. A universal basic income would strengthen that sense of community.

There is a wider argument. Societies consisting of people of roughly equal social status tend to be more democratic and tolerant. A basic income system would be an expression of that equality, fostering social solidarity and common citizenship.

Religious Rationales

Is there a religious justification for a basic income? Religious arguments justifying basic income should be contrasted with the 'religification' of social policy. All religions give a role to charity. But too often their leaders are just moralistic, differentiating the 'deserving' and 'undeserving', and laying emphasis on the poor's duty to labour in return for any charity they receive. Fortunately, that is by no means the only religious perspective.

It is worth recalling that the most prominent advocates of basic income in the post-1918 'first wave' were young Quakers (the Milners and Pickard mentioned in Chapter 1). They adhered to the principle that every human being has an equal right to 'the primal necessities of life'.

Succinct Christian rationales for basic income have been presented by Malcolm Torry and by Torsten Meireis, who takes a Lutheran view in seeing a basic income as enabling people to pursue their 'calling'.[16] The Christian perspective is that, to be faithful to the doctrine preached by Jesus, every Christian should try to shape society to reflect what would be desired in the Kingdom of God, thereby creating societies that are expressions of hope for the Kingdom's coming.

In that context, a basic income would be a reflection of God's grace, which is universal. Malcolm Torry draws an analogy with giving blood, done freely in Britain and many other countries, without the donor and recipient knowing each other. It is a gift without reciprocity or judgement of the worthiness of either party. The Christian view also holds that all wealth is God's gift and should be intended for the common good, not for enriching a few to the exclusion of the majority. Recognizing the reality that the gift is not shared as God intended, a basic income would entail the fortunate sharing with the majority.[17]

In a 2015 Encyclical Letter, Pope Francis wrote: 'The earth is essentially a shared inheritance, whose fruits are meant to benefit everyone.'[18] He went on to uphold the principle of inter-generational equity, arguing that 'Each community can take from the bounty of the earth whatever it needs for subsistence, but it also has the duty to protect the earth and to ensure its fruitfulness for the coming generations.'

The Christian argument for basic income stands in sharp contrast to the class-based perspective voiced most stridently by Boris Johnson, then Mayor of London, in 2013. He used the analogy of a shaken packet of cornflakes in which the best rise to the top, arguing that those with above-average genetic endowments were entitled to greater economic rewards. A Christian riposte would surely be that as such endowments are the gift of God and are unequally bestowed, those most blessed should be most taxed, and those least blessed should be entitled to compensation. (Left libertarians make a similar case, seeing genetic endowments as 'natural resources' subject to redistribution.)

Other religions also have their way of depicting charity as justice. In Judaism, the word *tzedakah*, commonly used to signify charity, refers to the religious obligation to do what is right and just. Zakat, one of the five pillars of Islam, requires followers to build a society without poverty. There is also a commitment in the Koran to give to others *unconditionally*. Chinese Confucianism, Buddhism and Daoism all support the belief that every human being deserves equal respect and care.

A basic income may thus be justified in religious terms. But religious beliefs should not be used to incentivize, reward or penalize individuals, or to separate the 'deserving' from the 'undeserving' poor. Then religion surely loses its moral compass. Fortunately, there are theologians who recognize that danger and focus on the aspects of grace and humanity.

Concluding Reflections

According to what is called a 'radical democratic' perspective, everybody should receive a basic income to affirm their status as equal members of a political entity, not as part of a needy group dependent on the state. In return for acceding to the prevailing rules of economic life, which always privilege some groups over others, every citizen would be entitled to a share of the economic surplus.

Basic income is also a matter of state *altruism*. Altruism fosters altruism in those who benefit from it, whereas mean-spiritedness by the state acting in our name fosters mean-spiritedness in its citizens. We collectively want to be fair. The state acting justly will tend to induce its citizens to behave in like manner.

This is not being naive. Not everyone will reciprocate altruism. But moral suasion is the soft power of any good society committed to social justice. That sense of altruism should not have been jettisoned as cavalierly as it has been by those who have built a welfare edifice of means tests, behaviour tests, sanctions and intrusive prying. Has that done anything worthwhile, other than spread injustice in its wake?

Basic Income and Freedom

'The real function of government being to maintain conditions of life in which morality shall be possible, and morality consisting of the disinterested performance of self-imposed duties, paternal government does its best to make it impossible by narrowing the room for the self-imposition of duties and for the play of disinterested motives.'

T. H. GREEN, 1879

Almost all proponents of basic income claim that it would enhance and give substance to freedom. This is the second major justification for a basic income. But what is freedom? By way of introduction, it can be argued that in the twentieth century the political left gave too little attention to the enhancement of individual freedom, while the political right gave freedom a libertarian slant that went against a very important historical tradition, that of 'republican' freedom.

The standard liberal and libertarian version is that liberty involves freedom from constraint (negative liberty) and freedom to act (positive liberty). This view is often linked to the political philosophy of utilitarianism, a perspective that has dominated recent political strategies of the centre right and left. Utilitarianism aims to promote the happiness of the majority (often summed up as 'the greatest happiness of the greatest number'), which has the obvious danger of allowing politicians to care too little about making the minority miserable.[1]

Classic liberals, exemplified by T. H. Green opposite, as well as libertarians, have long been united in their opposition to paternalism of all sorts, and above all to what is best described as state paternalism, except regarding children and

49

the mentally frail. But intellectual consistency has not been a virtue of modern politicians, on the left as well as the right. Many have implicitly or explicitly embraced a dangerous hybrid known as 'libertarian paternalism', which 'steers' or 'nudges' people to 'make the right choice'. Today it may be a bigger threat to freedom than outright authoritarianism, because it is so invidious and manipulative. The implications are considered later in this chapter.

A basic income can be described as a basic economic right that is a necessary condition for liberal notions of freedom. It is what is known as a basic liberty upon which other basic liberties depend – freedom of speech, freedom of thought, freedom of religion and freedom to associate. But a basic income fits differently into libertarian and republican notions of freedom.

The Libertarian Perspective

Libertarians believe in 'a small state', on the grounds that the state, by which they mean government, infringes on individual liberty. A pure libertarian shares with the communist and anarchist the desire for the state to 'wither away'. Government is necessarily intrusive and must collect taxes, which are seen as limiting individual freedom.

Consequently, it may seem strange that many libertarians have come to espouse a basic income provided by government. But they do so with the argument that this is the next best thing to having government withdraw from social policy altogether, often ruefully admitting that a libertarian 'utopia' is politically impossible. Such libertarians include Robert

Nozick and Charles Murray on the political right, and Philippe van Parijs, who calls his version 'real libertarianism', and Karl Widerquist on the left.[2]

Van Parijs' view that a basic income would enable people to choose to do what they wished to do has been criticized on the grounds that it does not prioritize essential freedoms, fails to recognize that some have more difficulty than others in converting income into freedom, and promotes freedom without responsibility.[3] Widerquist's thesis is that basic income provides 'freedom as effective control self-ownership', the effective power to accept or refuse cooperation with other willing people.

Those in the right libertarian tradition who have recently argued in favour of a basic income include Michael Tanner of the Cato Institute and Matt Zwolinski, who draws on the work of the late Nobel Prize-winning economist James Buchanan.[4] But perhaps the most prominent advocate has been Charles Murray, who in 2014 summarized his nominally libertarian argument as follows:

> The society is too rich to stand aside and say, 'We aren't going to do anything for people in need.' I understand that; I accept that; I sympathize with it. What I want is a grand compromise between the left and the right. We on the right say, 'We will give you huge government, in terms of the amount of money we spend. You give us small government, in terms of the ability of government to mess around with people's lives. So you have a system whereby every month, a check goes into an electronic bank account for everybody over the age of 21, which they can use as they see fit. They

can get together with other people and then combine their resources. But they live their own lives. We put their lives back in their hands . . . my real goal with all of this is to revive civil society. Here's what I mean by that. You have a guy who gets a check every month, alright. He is dissolute; he drinks it up and he's got 10 days to go before the next check comes in and he's destitute. He now has to go to friends, relatives, neighbours or the Salvation Army, and say, 'I really need to survive.' He will get help. But under a guaranteed basic income, he can no longer portray himself as a victim who's helpless to do anything about it. And you've got to set up feedback loops where people say, 'Okay, we're not going to let you starve on the streets. But it's time for you to get your act together. And don't tell us that you can't do it because we know you've got another check coming in in a couple of days.'[5]

Elsewhere, Murray has asserted that 'the welfare state is self-destructing'.[6] He is controversial, and detested by many on the political left, for his unsavoury views on race, culture and so on. But his reasoning on this should be considered on its own merits. Where he errs is in leaping from the image of the irresponsible drunk or gambler to saying that *all* welfare schemes should be abolished, to be replaced by a basic income.

Had Murray concentrated only on those schemes that compromise individual freedom, that would have been more challenging. For undoubtedly many modern welfare schemes do impinge on freedom, usually very deliberately. Doing away with those would enhance freedom. But many public services also enhance freedom. A public health service, for instance, can restore the ability to act freely to someone who falls ill or has an accident. Similarly, benefits and services for the disabled, and requirements for public amenities, help to create a society in which there is equal freedom for all.

For right libertarians, a basic income would be ideal 'if we scrap all existing welfare programmes',[7] a delightful prospect in their eyes, partly because it would facilitate lower taxes. Typical of this position, in mid-2016, former New Mexico Governor Gary Johnson (and erstwhile libertarian US presidential candidate) came out in favour of a basic income, saying it would save 'bureaucratic costs'.[8]

Proceeding on this rationale, right libertarians should see a trade-off between the *level* of basic income and the extent to which other welfare schemes should be scrapped. But a basic income could not replace schemes that seek to rectify or compensate for brute ill-luck or disadvantages that cannot be attributed to 'free choice'. Someone with a disability cannot be blamed for their extra costs of living or needs. Needs-based supplements, in terms of monetary benefits or public services, should always be preserved.

Another avowed libertarian, Matt Zwolinski, advocating what he called a basic income guarantee (BIG), noted that US federal welfare programmes cost over $668 billion annually, spread over at least 126 programmes. To that must be added state and local welfare spending of $284 billion, totalling almost $1 trillion every year or over $20,000 for every poor person.[9] Meanwhile, benefit phase-out rules, varying from programme to programme, implied high marginal tax rates for those trying to move from benefits to low-paying jobs.

Zwolinski asserted, 'No libertarian would wish for a BIG as an addition to the currently existing welfare state.' This is probably unfair to left libertarians, but captures the essence of the right libertarian position, that basic income would be a freedom-enhancing alternative to the intrusive government-driven welfare state.

On the political non-libertarian left, revulsion towards the libertarian rationale has been so intense that many have rejected the idea of a basic income altogether, choosing to see it as a ruse to dismantle the welfare state. While many libertarians do have that objective, this antipathy to basic income is based on emotion rather than reason, since most contemporary advocates of a basic income believe in public social services and needs-based welfare benefits as well.

Nevertheless, the fact that prominent libertarians propose a basic income as a straight alternative to all public welfare has prompted a spirited debate within the BIEN community, to the point that the 16th international congress in Seoul passed a resolution stating that payment of a basic income should not put the welfare state in jeopardy. This recognizes the political pitfall of seeing basic income as a panacea.

Some other libertarians object to a basic income on the grounds that, to be at a level high enough to replace all welfare schemes, provide for a person's most basic needs and protect the freedom of the vulnerable, it would have to involve much higher taxes, which, in their view, would infringe the freedom of taxpaying citizens.

In arguing for what he called a 'consequential' libertarian case for basic income, Zwolinski recognized this trade-off:

'The idea is that a basic income can help protect the freedom of certain vulnerable people. But I recognize that a basic income that's large and broad enough to do that might have to be funded by taxes that violate the freedom of others. So we are trading off freedom for freedom.'[10]

Although this line of reasoning can be rebutted in various ways, the simplest retort is that unless the state protects the basic freedoms of its most vulnerable members, they will be inclined to hit back by violating the freedoms of those intensifying their vulnerability. If libertarians succeeded in creating such a minimalist social state that the vulnerable were left bereft of hope, they should not be surprised if the resentment led to some retributive justice.

The Danger of Libertarian Paternalism

Many libertarians reveal themselves as little more than moralistic conservatives. Thus Charles Murray sees a basic income as encouraging 'better' behaviour and a revival of 'civic culture'. This is a paternalistic argument, not one about freedom. But he is not as explicit as the new breed of libertarian paternalists, who lean on 'behavioural economics' and 'nudge theory' to justify giving a very prominent role to government to steer or nudge people to make 'the right choices'. They have been highly influential, to the extent that one of the authors of *Nudge*, the seminal book on the subject, became principal regulator in Barack Obama's White House, while the other became an adviser to the British Prime Minister.[11]

Libertarian paternalism has become a dominant mode of

policy making in the globalization era, advocated and implemented by those calling themselves liberals (as in the case of Britain's Liberal Democrats when they were in the coalition government) and by social democrats, as well as by conservatives. Its vision of 'right' and 'wrong' is rooted in the political philosophy of utilitarianism, drawing heavily on the writings of Jeremy Bentham (1748–1832). In particular, libertarian paternalism derives from Bentham's 'panopticon', a prison design enabling prisoners to be watched by a guard at all times and their behaviour monitored. Bentham's idea was to give prisoners apparent free choice, while knowing they would be punished if they made the 'wrong' choice.

The authors of *Nudge* used the same words and phrases as Bentham, without mentioning his name or the panopticon. No doubt they were well-intentioned. Most paternalists mean well. But today, more than ever, the state can rely on subliminal and other devices, including incentives, sanctions and time-using obstacles, to induce people to act in one way rather than another. That growing power of the state, aided by an army of intrusive paternalistic psychologists and behavioural economists, will surely be welcomed by authoritarians. It is a powerful new reason for supporting basic income.

Freedom is incompatible with libertarian paternalism. To consider just one of the many objections, what if the choice to which people are steered turns out to be the wrong choice, either for the individual making it or in general? Who is then liable for the cost, especially if the person was unaware of being barged into that choice?

Pension schemes in many countries are a classic illustration of what can go wrong. To take a recent example, there were angry protests in 2016 over Chile's privatized pension system, after the typical payout turned out to be half the 70 per cent of final salary people were told to expect on retirement. The contribution rate was set too low, fees charged by the fund managers were exorbitant, and many people missed years of contribution because of childcare responsibilities, unemployment or informal jobs. Reforms to the system will be of little use to those already retired on a pittance.

There is a crude Darwinian ethos that underpins all forms of libertarianism, which libertarian paternalism fails to overcome. Libertarianism ultimately shows no respect for the freedom of the weak and vulnerable, which means most of us at various stages of our lives. Libertarians may see a rationale for basic income, but they cannot legitimize it as a pretext to abandon public social services based on solidaristic principles.

Republican Freedom

The prevailing utilitarianism and the liberal perspective equate freedom with non-interference. The 'republican' variant is that freedom must mean non-domination. Stemming from Aristotle, republican freedom requires freedom from *potential* domination as well as from *actual* domination by figures, institutions or processes of unaccountable domination.[12] In other words, to the extent that authority figures or institutions could, if they wished, 'arbitrarily interfere' with a person's ability to act or think (or develop), republican freedom is compromised.[13] This view is linked to the argument, derived in part from the philosophy of Jean-Jacques Rousseau, that the very existence of property can destroy or compromise such freedom. After all, if a few families own all the land, to talk of everyone having freedom would be absurd.

Robust republican freedom could be said to exist if everyone in society could avoid or escape from unwanted interference, and also from the rational *fear* of it. To be free, a person must be free of the will of others. If I fear rationally and reasonably that, were I to offend someone, my freedom would be lost, I am not free.

By contrast with libertarianism, which sees all government as compromising freedom, republican freedom requires and depends on government. But it must be government that is democratically accountable and geared to the promotion of full freedom, defined primarily as the ability of the most vulnerable in society to avoid domination. Republican freedom also requires government to ensure that the choices of the powerful cannot block others from making choices themselves. If everything is based on competition and 'competitiveness', then automatically freedom is limited, because there must be losers, and lots of them. It is inconceivable to have a free society if it is based solely on rewards to individual competitiveness.

To be free in the republican sense, people must have adequate resources enabling them to make reasonable choices, whatever the preferences and opinions of others. And full freedom requires that others are *aware* of this freedom and thus cannot look down on someone in pity or contempt.

Freedom must mean neutrality towards individual decision making, not a carefully constructed, devious, non-transparent edifice of devices to induce norm-driven behaviour, however benevolent the intention. This clearly justifies a basic income, and combats the pernicious notion of the beggar, a 'stigmatized petitioner'.

Part of the republican tradition, associated with Hannah Arendt as well as Aristotle, also embraces the idea of 'associational freedom' – the ability and opportunity to act in concert as a group. Associational freedom has been under relentless attack by the neo-liberal state, for the simple reason that 'associations' can be portrayed as opposed to market forces and as distorting them. A republic is conceivable only if everybody is in the company of equally self-confident people free of existential fear. This is the position of Katja Kipping, a leading MP in the *Die Linke* political party in Germany.[14]

In the republican tradition, freedom is disclosed, or even discovered, in the togetherness of people deliberating and acting in concert. This depends vitally on the dignity of possible involvement, the status of equals, which Alexis de Tocqueville so memorably depicted as the essence of early American democracy (sadly lost now).

For a classical liberal, freedom is essentially domestic in character. It is the liberty of the consumer, choosing between options, buying this rather than that, taking this job rather than that one, choosing this charismatic politician rather than the other. Republican freedom goes beyond this: we are free because we can act together, politically. This is a good standpoint to combat the excesses of libertarianism, particularly its modern variant of libertarian paternalism.[15]

Both republican and associational freedom have another dimension which has been given less attention. It is also necessary to curb the power and influence of the powerful. Freedom is jeopardized if a plutocracy or elite can shape public discourses and decisions by manipulative devices over which they have control, including the media.

Whatever variant of freedom is espoused, a basic income would enhance it. However, in the liberal tradition a basic income would be both necessary *and* sufficient, if judged high enough to meet basic needs. In the republican tradition, however, basic income would be necessary but not sufficient; other institutions and policies would be needed properly to advance freedom.

A basic income would strengthen the following prosaic or day-to-day freedoms:

— the freedom to refuse a job that is onerous, boring, low-paying or just nasty;
— the freedom to accept a job that is none of the above but which could not be accepted if financial necessity dictated;
— the freedom to stay in a job that pays less than previously or that has become more financially insecure;
— the freedom to start a small-scale business venture, which is risky but potentially rewarding;
— the freedom to do care work for a relative or friend, or voluntary work in and for the community, that might not be feasible if financial necessity required long hours of paid labour;
— the freedom to do creative work and activities of all kinds;

— the freedom to risk learning new skills or competences;
— the freedom from bureaucratic interference, prying and coercion;
— the freedom to form relationships and perhaps set up 'home' with someone, often precluded today by financial insecurity;
— the freedom to leave a relationship that has turned sour or abusive;
— the freedom to have a child;
— the freedom to be lazy once in a while, a vital freedom to which we will return.

Would alternative social policies do as well on any of these counts? At the very least, a social protection policy should be neutral on behavioural freedom, not moralistic, directive, coercive or punitive. The drift to means-tested benefits around the world runs counter to any notion of freedom. A basic income would do the reverse.

Policy Principles for Freedom

Two general principles should be applied to any social policy, especially those pitched as alternatives to an unconditional basic income. The first is:

The Paternalism Test Principle. A social policy is unjust if it imposes controls on some groups that are not imposed on the most free groups in society.

Policies that dictate what a person can do or that steer people to behave in certain ways rather than other (legal) ways clearly violate this principle. Many politicians who proclaim their belief in freedom nevertheless support policies that involve telling the 'poor' what they may or may not do. The rationalization of libertarian paternalism – undemocratically built into the modern structures of social policy – is that the deliberate steering or nudging of people to take certain options rather than others is 'for their own good' or in their best interests.

This is amoral, since the 'nudgers' do not put their money where their proverbial mouth is. If they argue that a decision they steer people towards is for the best, then they and not the steered should take responsibility for the outcome if things do not work out. The recipients should be compensated by the state. That does not happen.

The second general freedom and social justice principle is slightly more complex:

The Rights-not-Charity Principle. A social policy is just only if it advances the rights or freedom of the recipient or target person rather than the discretion or power of the provider.

A basic income passes such a test, whereas any social benefit that requires actual or potential recipients to satisfy behavioural conditions does not. All the conditions for entitlement invented by politicians or civil servants are partly arbitrary, and most are capable of several interpretations. Too often discretionary power is left to a local-level bureaucrat, and the needy person is left in no doubt that they are a 'supplicant'.

The Right to Have Rights

'If you believe you are a citizen of the
world, you are a citizen of nowhere.'

THERESA MAY, BRITISH PRIME MINISTER,
OCTOBER 2016

Who has the right to have rights? A citizen is conventionally
defined as someone who has rights, and this can be at any
level of community. The United Nations *Universal Declaration
of Human Rights* of 1948 and the *International Covenant on
Economic, Social and Cultural Rights* of 1966 established once
and for all that everybody everywhere has rights. In that
quip, Theresa May was profoundly wrong. As citizens of the
world, we all have human rights.

However, there are layers of rights: some are universal,
some are established by and within the state, some hold for
regions or for associations that grant rights and privileges to
members. At country level, all rights worthy of the name
began life as demands against the state. And many start as
'claim rights', demands that society should move *towards*
realizing them, and not away from doing so. Basic income is
one such claim right.

The practical question is: Who should have the right to a
basic income? This is partly an ethical question, partly a practical, pragmatic one. In an ideal world, in some utopian
future, we might happily say that everybody, wherever they
might be, should have the right to a basic income. But for the
present, our eyes must be focused on the state and in

particular the nation, the country, where social policy is still crafted and implemented.

A typical starting point is to say that every citizen should have the right to a basic income. But should this right be extended to citizens living and working abroad? Most advocates adjust the eligibility rule to mean every citizen usually resident in the country. What does 'usually' mean? Clear practical rules have to be established, for example, that citizens must regard the country as their permanent home, or be resident for at least six months in any year. No rule will be ideal, or less than somewhat arbitrary.

More difficult are eligibility rules for non-citizens who are usually resident in the country. It would be unfair to exclude legal residents but, again, the right would have to be defined pragmatically, for example, once someone had lived legally in the country for at least two years or had acquired permanent residence status.

Ideally, the basic income should be permanent, established as a constitutional right. However, arguing that, once established, this right could never be taken away could become an obstacle to political acceptance of basic income. It would deter experiments, or its introduction on a provisional or piecemeal basis, subject to changes in eligibility, level or other rules. It would not be wise at the outset to rule out democratic decisions on policy, or even introduction of a short-term basic income, say, for five years. Purists might object that a short-term basic income would not be a *right*. But it would have the status of a right within the specified time-frame since, during that period, nobody could have their basic income arbitrarily taken away. That said, in principle, basic income should be established as a life-long commitment by the state, subject to democratic adjustment.

Another feature of a right is that it is *non-withdrawable*, that is, it cannot be taken away without due process of law. A rarely emphasized aspect is that a basic income could not be seized in payment of debt. That would set it apart from some means-tested benefits, which can be reduced to help pay off debts to the state.

Why Basic Income's Emancipatory Value Exceeds Its Monetary Value

'Oh, the little more, and how much it is!

And the little less, and what worlds away!'

ROBERT BROWNING

Between 2010 and 2013 the writer was involved in a large-scale basic income pilot in Madhya Pradesh, India, which gave a small basic income to all 6,000 residents of nine villages.[16] Other similar villages were chosen as controls for evaluation of the pilot. It soon became clear that the positive impact was far greater than could have been anticipated from the amount of the basic income itself. A fundamental reason was that, in those communities and families, money itself was a scarce commodity.

If a needed commodity is scarce, or hard to obtain, its price tends to rise. People with little income or savings to fall back on are often forced to borrow at short notice to pay for daily necessities or unexpected costs (medical bills, for example), typically at very high rates of interest. They must also often surrender something as security. And they cannot put money into longer-term higher-return savings, because they need to keep to hand what little they have to meet day-to-day and sudden contingencies.

In these circumstances, a basic income, paid without fail to all family members and to all neighbours, acts as a sort of guarantee against default, enabling people to borrow more cheaply, whether from moneylenders or their neighbours. This is not the case with subsidized goods or services (the main form of support for the poor in India), or with means-tested or behaviour-tested conditional benefits, which by definition can be refused or withdrawn and, in any case, do not go to everyone. A basic income, with its certainty (or near so), lowers the cost of living for recipients and the community, because it gives scope for collective action at times of individual stress. An amount paid as a basic income is thus worth more than a similar amount paid on a means-tested basis.

In the Indian basic income pilots, those receiving the basic income were more likely than others to reduce their debt and were more likely to save, even when they were still indebted, because they realized the value of monetary liquidity.[17] This liquidity also enabled individuals and families to be more strategic in their decision making, enabling some to borrow at much lower interest rates and acquire small equipment, seeds and fertilizer when needed.

The emancipatory value of the basic income did not stop there. Landlords and moneylenders (often the same people) had taken advantage of the traditional shortage of money to put low-income villagers into debt bondage. Instead of paying off long-standing loans with money, they had to provide labour as and when the landlord wished. Often this deprived the smallholders of vitally needed time on their own small farms in harvest periods, further intensifying their poverty. It was wonderful to see some trapped in debt bondage gradually collect enough money from their basic income, and that of relatives and friends, to buy their freedom.

The emancipatory value was not merely financial. In one village, when the pilot began, all the young women wore veils and the photographs needed for their identity cards, required to receive the basic income, had to be taken in a hut out of sight of men. When, a few months later, the writer visited that village with a colleague from the research team, we observed that none of the young women was wearing a veil. On asking why that was, one young woman explained that, before, they had to do as their elders told them; now that they had their own money, they could decide for themselves.

Having the basic income countered a form of cultural domination and helped embolden them, strengthening their cultural rights. Lifting the veil, of their own volition, allowed them to participate more freely in village life. They could pass 'the eyeball test', the ability to look others in the face without having to give in to their will. That is vital for republican freedom.

The Necessity of Voice

As mentioned earlier, for republican freedom, a basic income would be a necessary condition, but not a sufficient one. It is emancipatory, but it is not a panacea. There is also the necessity of Voice, of agency. My view has long been that the two 'meta-securities' are basic income security and Voice security; without affordable access to individual and collective representation, a person with basic income would remain vulnerable to unaccountable domination, to loss of republican freedom. But Voice should also include constraints on the power of the plutocracy and elite, which are necessary to ensure basic security for all.

In this context, it was one of the stranger aspects of debate around basic income in the twentieth century that trade union leaders were among the most vehemently opposed. Although some leading union thinkers have latterly come out in favour, this institutionalized hostility has persisted. Some of the opposition has stemmed, at least ostensibly, from a belief that a basic income would allow employers to pay lower wages.

I will come to this argument in a later chapter. But a more disturbing reason for the opposition, privately expressed by prominent union leaders, is the view that, if workers had basic income, they would not see the need to join trade unions. That is a sad reflection of the union leaders' confidence. In fact, as psychological studies have shown, people who have basic security are *more* likely, not less, to join bodies representing their interests.

Finally, basic income is an instrument of democratization, since all citizens need assured access to resources to make rights meaningful.[18] A basic income would help establish individual self-government and equal self-respect. Early advocates of democracy conceived democratization as the universalization of freedom, equality and independence, the last being based on the 'natural freedom' principle enunciated by John Locke. It states that, to be free, someone should be able to act without having to ask for consent and without fear of retribution, unless doing harm to others.

This sense of independence, central to emancipation, surely depends on having a right to subsistence. As one of the founders of the US Constitution, Alexander Hamilton, put it in 1788: 'A power over a man's subsistence amounts to a power over his will.'

While a basic income would promote real freedom, the assurance of republican or *full* freedom requires agency. This can only come from access to institutions and mechanisms that provide Voice, collectively and individually, particularly whenever we are exposed to vulnerability and adversity. Basic income may not be sufficient for full freedom, but it is essential.

Reducing Poverty, Inequality and Insecurity

'Everyone has the right to a standard of living adequate for the health and well-being of himself and his family, including food, clothing, housing and medical care and the necessary social services, and the right to security in the event of unemployment, sickness, disability, widowhood, old age or other lack of livelihood in circumstances beyond his control.'

UNITED NATIONS, *UNIVERSAL DECLARATION OF HUMAN RIGHTS*, ARTICLE 25

The most common claim in favour of a basic income is that it would be the most effective way to reduce poverty, simply because it would be the most direct and transparent way, with relatively low administrative costs. A related, but not identical, claim is that it would be a good way of providing basic economic *security*. This is important because in today's market-oriented global capitalism, the predominant source of insecurity is economic *uncertainty*, and uncertainty, as opposed to risk, defies conventional forms of insurance.

It should be recognized at the outset that a badly designed or poorly implemented basic income system could leave people worse off than under existing social protection schemes. But this is by no means an inherent feature of basic income.

Poverty

While globalization has been associated with a decline in absolute poverty worldwide, as emerging market economies have gradually raised living standards, in many countries the poverty *rate* – the share of people living in poverty – has risen. Moreover, globalization and the austerity policies widely adopted since the crash of 2007–8 have plunged millions more in industrialized countries into *absolute* poverty.

In the US, supposedly the richest country in the world, one and a half million families, including three million children, are struggling with per capita cash incomes of less than $2 a day.[1] And, as Nobel Laureate economist Angus Deaton and Anne Case have demonstrated, America has seen a rising tide of 'deaths of despair', through suicides, overdoses of prescription and illegal drugs, alcohol abuse and so on.[2] In Europe and Japan, the picture is similar, if not quite so bad.

On present trends, income poverty shows no sign of disappearing in the near or medium-term future, despite the obvious fact that in income terms the world is wealthier than at any time in history. Within nominally rich countries, absolute and relative poverty have grown in the twenty-first century, not fallen, while the number of homeless has hit new records. This is a powerful indictment of all governments.

Globalization and policies of market flexibility, combined with the technological revolution unleashed by or associated with globalization, have also produced a growing precariat, consisting of millions of people everywhere living in chronic insecurity and losing all forms of rights.[3] Even if economic growth were to pick up, which seems unlikely, the precariat would not gain economically.

It certainly has not done so in the first two decades of this century. In a relative sense, the precariat almost certainly loses from growth, because the gains from the sort of growth that is occurring go disproportionately if not entirely to the plutocracy, elite and salariat.[4]

To compound the challenge, the old recipe of job

creation – 'work is the best route out of poverty' – is increasingly wrong and even counter-productive. Governments may be able to boost the number of jobs by rolling back labour protections in order to make labour markets more flexible, but in doing so they make many more people more economically insecure. And that makes many more people angry, ready to curse the politicians who go down that road.

Increasingly, jobs being generated in much of the world, including all rich industrialized countries, are not a reliable route out of poverty. In real terms, taking account of price inflation, average wages in developed countries have stagnated for more than three decades and can be expected to continue to do so. For those in the precariat, wages have been falling in real terms and have become more volatile; one mishap, mistake or accident would throw them into real poverty.

However hard they work, a growing proportion of those in relative poverty and economic insecurity will be unable to escape. Tax credits and statutory minimum wages that have been enlarged steadily have failed to arrest the upward trend. It is the income distribution *system* that has broken down.

UNIVERSALISM AND TRANSPARENCY

Unlike most alternatives, a basic income is a way of reducing poverty without stigmatizing the recipients and making them supplicants. As numerous studies have shown, the stigma attached to means-tested targeted welfare means that many people in real need do not apply for assistance, from pride, fear or ignorance. It is shameful that politicians persist in supporting such schemes when the inherent defects are well known.

The contrast with a universalistic scheme was brought out in the Canadian Mincome experiment in Dauphin, Manitoba (see Chapter 11).[5] Many people on low incomes, including the unemployed, did not apply for standard 'welfare' because of stigma, but gladly took the unconditional minimum income payments that blurred distinctions between low-wage workers, the unemployed and recipients of social assistance.

Respondents to questions about the experiment said they welcomed the Mincome payments because they made them feel independent and enabled them to work while avoiding the invasive and degrading procedures associated with means-tested welfare. As one man said, these gave 'a bad image to the family'. Another said Mincome 'trusts Canadians and leaves a man or woman their pride'.

Because it is universal and unconditional, a basic income also avoids the standard utilitarian device of distinguishing between the 'deserving' and 'undeserving' poor, a device deployed by moralistic politicians that is arbitrary, inequitable and ridiculously expensive to apply.

The elimination of social stigma should be regarded as a high-priority desirable objective. Stigma should not be used deliberately as a means of reducing the cost of state benefits by deterring needy people from applying for them. And social policymakers should cease unedifying practices of categorizing people as deserving or undeserving.

OVERCOMING POVERTY AND PRECARITY TRAPS

One reason why a basic income would be the most effective way of reducing poverty is that it would overcome 'poverty traps' and would reduce 'precarity traps'. In Britain, for example, someone on low state benefits faces what is in effect a marginal tax rate of 80 per cent or more in going from benefits into a low-paying job. That is the official calculation; when the costs of working such as transport, childcare and so on are taken into account, the rate is higher.

In many continental European countries, including Denmark, Finland and Germany, the marginal tax rate is higher still. If the middle classes faced such high marginal rates of tax there would be riots! It is widely accepted that any tax rate above 40 per cent induces high-income earners to find ways of avoiding or evading taxes. Yet commentators refer to impoverished people who 'stay on benefits', and who do not take low-wage jobs in circumstances where they would face double that rate, as 'scroungers' or worse.

Libertarians, both right and left, recognize that a basic income paid regardless of work status or other income would remove the poverty trap inherent in existing welfare schemes. In so doing, it would *increase* the incentive to take relatively low-wage jobs, or undertake inherently risky own-account economic activity.

Besides poverty traps, delays in paying benefits to those who become entitled also act as a disincentive to take short-term or casual jobs. The reason is best described as a 'precarity trap'. The complexity of modern means-tested and conditional benefits means that when a person becomes entitled to a benefit, it is rarely paid immediately. In addition, many people may be unsure whether they are entitled to assistance. Applicants must use up a lot of time, energy and limited confidence, filling in lengthy forms and answering

intrusive questions. Then they need to keep demonstrating
that they satisfy some demeaning condition to continue
receiving the benefits.

These pitfalls, stigma and discouragement lead to low
take-up rates that some defenders of the system eagerly and
wilfully depict as proving that people who do not apply do
not need or deserve the benefits. But for those who do eventually obtain benefits, the fear of losing them and having to
start all over again acts as a deterrent to taking casual, short-
term low-paying jobs.

Consider this testimony from a British man receiving disability benefit:

> There was a time a number of years ago when my health
> improved spontaneously. Half of my brain sought to grab
> life by the horns and get out in to the working world as
> soon as I could. The other half stood terrified by the
> bureaucratic difficulties endemic in the system; difficulties
> that forced you to either relinquish your crucial income in
> the hope of being able to replace it, or lie to the
> Department of Work and Pensions. As it happened, I did
> manage to work for a short while, only to have to push
> myself far too hard to replace the benefit lost, leading to a
> relapse from which I have never recovered.[6]

A basic income paid as a *right* would remove the worst poverty trap and this precarity trap. It would reduce the moral
hazard entailed by existing social assistance schemes, that
people do not do what they would otherwise wish to do (for
example, taking a job). It would also reduce the immoral
hazard of entering the shadow or black economy instead,

because the disincentives to entering the legal tax-paying economy are excessive.

That said, should basic income be touted as a way of *eradicating* poverty? This would leave the way open to the counterattack that in practical terms the initial amount paid out would do no such thing. If it were set at a level that tried to do so, the fiscal jolt would be too great to appeal to the popular or political imaginations.

However, if properly designed, a basic income should reduce the *incidence* of poverty, the number of people living in relative poverty, as well as the *depth* of poverty of anybody in or near the poverty line, whatever that might be. A basic income will not eradicate poverty. No policy by itself ever will. But it should reduce the threat of poverty, faced by all those hovering just above it.

For example, the British think-tank Compass has calculated the impact as of 2015–16 of a transitional universal basic income system that would keep most existing welfare benefits but give every adult £71 a week, pensioners £51 (on top of the basic state pension) and children £59. Sixty per cent of those in the bottom fifth of the income distribution would gain by more than a fifth and child poverty would be nearly halved.[7] Of course, these figures are merely illustrative, but they do suggest that the scope for reducing poverty is considerable with even modest basic incomes.

Do the Poor Spend Wisely?

One objection to a basic income is the claim that income-poor people will squander it on 'private bads', either out of ignorance or weakness of will (they cannot resist doing so, due to bad habits or addiction) or because of 'bad character'. Some critics go further, suggesting that needing state benefits is indicative of all those traits. Yet the evidence runs in the opposite direction.

The experience of cash transfer programmes and basic income pilots is that, for the most part, the money is spent on 'private goods', such as food for children, healthcare and schooling. What is more, studies have shown that, contrary to popular prejudice, receipt of a basic income or cash transfer leads to *reduced* spending on drugs, alcohol and tobacco, which can be seen as 'therapy bads' (or 'compensatory bads') for alleviating a difficult and hopeless situation.

Four examples are worth reflection. In Liberia, a group of alcoholics, addicts and petty criminals were recruited from the slums, and each given the equivalent of US$200, with no conditions attached. Three years later, they were interviewed to find out what they had used the money for. The answer was mainly for food, clothing and medicine. As one of the researchers wondered, if such people did not squander a basic income grant, who would?[8]

Another study, reported by *The Economist*, took place in the City of London, known as the Square Mile, where a 'hidden legion of homeless people' emerges in the evening.[9] Broadway, a charity, identified 338 of them, most of whom had spent over a year living on the streets. It singled out the longest-term rough sleepers, those who had been on the streets for over four years, asked what they needed to change their lives and gave it to them. The average outlay was £794. Of the thirteen who engaged, eleven had moved off the streets within a year. None said they wanted the money for drink, drugs or gambling. Several told researchers that they cooperated because they were offered control over their lives, rather than, in their eyes, being bullied into hostels. And the cost was a fraction of the £26,000 estimated to be spent annually on each homeless person, in health, police and prison bills.

A third study, in the US, found that compared with the widely admired early pre-education programmes, such as Head Start, cash transfers to families had an even greater positive effect on child education.[10] Financial security was crucial, in reducing stress and enabling parents to spend more time with their children, reading to them, taking them to museums and the like.

A final study comes from Utah, a conservative part of the United States, where an inspirational policy was launched of giving homeless people permanent housing rather than the long-standing practice of temporary shelter. The initial cost seemed high, but it turned out to save much more. The stability provided enabled people to reintegrate themselves in society, saving the authorities a wide range of expenditures on remedying addictions, depression and so on. The policy has since been copied in hundreds of American cities. As the chief executive of the National Association of Homelessness put it, 'It's intuitive, in a way. People do better when they have stability.'[11]

Too often, observers and commentators presume the poor are 'stupid', irrational or incapable of making rational decisions. Some enlightened experiments have shown that they just have fewer resources. No doubt, trust will sometimes disappoint. But it is a good principle to guide social policy. Moreover, we all *need* the freedom to make some poor decisions (though preferably not calamitous ones) in order to learn from them and experiment. Without the freedom to make 'mistakes', people cannot learn to take control of their lives successfully.

Inequality and Equity

Gross income and wealth inequality is bad for society, bad for the economy and, most of all, bad for those at the lower end of the income and wealth spectrum. Inequality has been growing in most countries in recent decades and, in many, inequality is greater than at any time since statistics began to be collected. There is also strong evidence that high and rising inequality impedes economic growth (which of itself is not necessarily a bad thing, but which is conventionally treated as so) and impairs sustainable development.

Would universal basic income tend to reduce income inequality? In one sense, it should do so. An equal amount given to everybody represents a higher proportion for those on low incomes. But a note of caution is in order here, because the impact on inequality would depend on how a basic income was introduced and funded.

Some prominent economists have asserted that a basic income would worsen rather than reduce inequality – witness these remarks by Jason Furman, Chairman of the Council of Economic Advisers under US President Barack Obama:

Replacing our current antipoverty programs with UBI would in any realistic design make the distribution of income worse, not better. Our tax and transfer system is largely targeted towards those in the lower half of the income distribution, which means that it works to reduce both poverty and income inequality. Replacing part or all of that system with a universal cash grant, which would go to all Americans regardless of income, would mean that relatively less of the system was targeted towards those at the bottom – increasing, not decreasing, income inequality.[12]

Furman's statement is based on some tendentious assumptions. First, a basic income does not have to 'replace' anti-poverty programmes. Most proponents of basic income do not advocate the abolition of all or most anti-poverty schemes, particularly those that address special needs such as disability, illness and frailty. Second, even accepting the claim – which is dubious – that existing schemes are 'largely targeted', that would still leave a lot that Furman himself admits are not targeted. Third, there are the well-known perverse effects of targeting via means testing and behaviour testing, which induce or oblige people to act contrary to their best interests – for instance, putting them through useless training or job-search programmes when they could be doing something more worthwhile.

In any case, social policy spending is not well targeted in the United States any more than in other countries. Meanwhile, huge expenditures go on tax breaks and other forms of subsidy that are perversely targeted in going mainly to the affluent. Why did the imagination of the Chairman of the Council of Economic Advisers not stretch to 'replacing' some of these with a basic income? Furman has erected a very flimsy straw man.

A better way of approaching the inequality issue is to say that a basic income is needed because the twentieth-century income distribution system has broken down. The share of national income going to labour has declined and is most unlikely to rise again. Because of globalization and techno-logical change, a rising proportion of jobs will involve wages and earnings that will not enable people to rise above pov-erty or to step on a ladder of opportunity for upward social mobility. A new income distribution system needs to be con-structed, in which basic income must figure.

In that context, consider the following statement:

> The pie is growing bigger; there is no guarantee that everyone will benefit if we leave the market alone. In fact, if anything, we think that not everyone will benefit if we leave the market alone. So we need to develop a new system of redistribution, new policies that will redistribute from those that the market would have rewarded in favour of those that the market would have left behind. Having a universal minimum income is one of those ways. In fact, it is one I am very much in favour of, as long as we know how to apply it without taking away the incentive to work at the lower end of the market.[13]

This was the rationale given by Sir Christopher Pissarides, who received the Nobel Prize in Economics in 2010. I would quibble only with his use of the word 'redistribution' rather than 'distribution' and with his last point, since it is the existing system of means testing that has taken away the incentive to labour, due to poverty traps and precarity traps. A basic income would increase that incentive.

INTERPERSONAL EQUITY

Inequity arises when a person with certain characteristics is systematically disadvantaged by direct or indirect forms of discrimination. It is probably fair to say that identity-based inequity has been reduced in many parts of the world, paradoxically at a time of growing income and wealth inequality. Changes in legislation and social attitudes have reduced discrimination relating to many forms of disability, race and ethnicity, gender, sexual preferences, and diverse relationships and partnerships. But there is still a long way to go to ensure equality in all these respects.

A system founded on a basic income would help in that long march. An equal amount paid to everybody is worth more to those who have less opportunity to earn additional income. But it would make sense to build a tiered system, in which supplements could and should be paid to those with extra costs of living or with known lower opportunity incomes, paid in effect to compensate for market-induced inequities.

THE INEQUALITY OF KEY ASSETS

There is another complementary way of looking at the relationship between basic income and inequality. Inequality in today's world is not just about money incomes. It reflects unequal access to the other key assets of a good life – security (both physical and economic), quality time, quality space, education and knowledge, and financial capital.[14]

Security is the pivotal key asset, which is probably even more unequally distributed than income or wealth as conventionally defined and measured. The rich can buy physical security, and have almost total economic security. Someone in the precariat or with low and uncertain income has no security at all. A basic income would rectify that chronic inequality.

Similarly, the inequality of control over time is vast. The upper echelons of the income and wealth spectrum can have complete control of their time, paying others to do tasks they do not wish to do. By contrast, the precariat has little or no control over time. Even if it did not do so fully or adequately, a basic income would allow people more control over the allocation of their time, for example, by reducing the financial pressure to work long or unsocial hours at the expense of family and community life. These are real inequalities that matter to everybody.

Economic Security – the Menace of Uncertainty

'Insecurity is worse than poverty'
CONFUCIUS

Another strong rationale for basic income is that it would provide basic security, would do so *continuously* and would do so better than any alternative. Aristotle famously claimed that only the insecure man is free. But without basic security people cannot function rationally, or be expected to do so, whereas if they are too secure they can become careless and indolent. Confucius and Aristotle surely had different degrees of insecurity in mind.

That aside, a basic income is arguably more justified by the need for economic security than by a desire to eradicate poverty. Martin Luther King captured several aspects of this rather well in his 1967 book, *Where Do We Go from Here?*

> [A] host of positive psychological changes inevitably will result from widespread economic security. The dignity of the individual will flourish when the decisions concerning his life are in his own hands, when he has the assurance that his income is stable and certain, and when he knows that he has the means to seek self-improvement. Personal conflicts between husband, wife and children will diminish when the unjust measurement of human worth on a scale of dollars is eliminated.[15]

Twentieth-century welfare states tried to reduce certain risks of insecurity with contributory insurance schemes. In an industrial economy, the probability of so-called 'contingency risks', such as illness, workplace accidents, unemployment and disability, could be estimated actuarially. A system of social insurance could be constructed that worked reasonably well for the majority.

In a predominantly 'tertiary' economy, in which more people are in and out of temporary, part-time and casual jobs and are doing a lot of unpaid job-related work outside fixed hours and workplaces, this route to providing basic security has broken down. The contributory basis has been eroded, fewer people are covered, and the inherent problem of 'immoral hazards' (concealing income or circumstances to obtain or maintain benefits) has led governments to respond to perceptions of abuse by becoming more intrusive and punitive, thereby weakening the legitimacy of the system.

However, the most important reason for the degradation of the social insurance model is that today's economic insecurity is profoundly different, at least in its structure, from that prevailing in the mid-twentieth century. Now, there is chronic insecurity that is characterized mainly by uncertainty. As economists understand it, this is different from risk. Uncertainty is about 'unknown unknowns'.

Uncertainty undermines resilience – the ability to cope with, compensate for and recover from shocks (unchosen adverse events) and hazards (normal life-cycle events that bring costs and risks, such as marriage, birth of a child, or death). No one can be sure of their interests or how to realize them, or know what best to do if an adverse outcome materializes, perhaps because there is no such 'best'. Whereas risks are insurable because they can be quantified, uncertainty cannot be. A basic income would provide a modicum of ex ante security, reducing the stress of uncertainty and the probability that a shock or hazard would precipitate a financial crisis for the person or family.

Nearly half of all US households would not be able to lay their hands on $400 for an emergency without borrowing or selling something, or would not be able to come up with the money at all, according to surveys by the US Federal Reserve Board.[16] For what that means in practice, take this example.

Getting a tire replaced seems easy to me. I'd just go to the nearest tire place and get it fixed. But Jayleene was living from paycheck to paycheck and didn't have $110 to spare. She couldn't get to work, and her boss fired her. She couldn't make her rent and was soon out on the street – all because she needed $110 at the right time. Jayleene told me her story during my volunteer shift at a soup kitchen. Her experience was the final straw that convinced me to support the idea of providing a basic income.[17]

A basic income would provide more universal security than the social insurance schemes associated with William Beveridge and Otto von Bismarck; they fail to reach the growing number of people, in and close to the precariat, who cannot build up adequate contribution records, and face uncertain and volatile earnings. And a basic income would improve security more effectively than current means-tested schemes, which are directed at the poor only. These do not provide ex ante security because they themselves are zones of uncertainty, as shown by extensive disentitlement, low take-up rates, and the associated stigma that deters people from applying for benefits to which they are entitled.

There is much more systemic economic insecurity today than in the heyday of welfare states that operated on the basis of closed economies, steady technological change and industrial employment. In an open globalizing economy, we are confronted by unpredictable decisions affecting us taken elsewhere in the world over which we have no possible means of control, including decisions directly affecting employment and production in our neighbourhood. Their impact is exacerbated by disruptive technological changes as well as labour market policies that have deliberately sacrificed labour-based security in exchange for flexibility for employers.

The result has been to shift and increase risks and the costs of adverse outcomes onto workers and citizens. Moreover, pervasive low wages mean that people are more likely to be living on the edge of unsustainable debt, reducing their ability to cope with adverse shocks or hazards. And their ability to recover from shocks and hazards has diminished because channels of social mobility have been restricted by changing labour markets, as well as by the impact of globalization and technology.

Reforms to social protection systems over the past two decades have intensified rather than mitigated insecurity, magnifying uncertainty and degrading resilience. The shift to means testing, behaviour testing, sanctions and delays increases the exposure to uncertainty. Few people know for sure whether they will be entitled to receive or continue to receive benefits and services to which they think they are entitled. A new direction is needed.

A basic income, being universal, unconditional and institutionally assured, would provide a sense of psychological security that no means-tested, behaviour-tested or non-universal system of benefits could. Psychological security helps to sustain mental stability. Parents will convey that to their children, children will convey it to their friends.

Risk-taking, Resilience and Mental Bandwidth

Neo-liberals and libertarians pay little respect to state-provided basic security. But basic security is a human need. Recent research has shown that lack of basic security impairs mental as well as physical health, triggers various psychological disorders and reduces short-term intelligence, or 'mental bandwidth'.[18] When people lack, or fear they will lack, something essential such as money or food, preoccupation with daily hassles uses up much of their mental energy. They become worse at problem solving and make worse decisions. Insecurity also leads to lower self-esteem, blunting aspirations for themselves and those around them.[19]

It is thus to be expected that chronically insecure people may not act wisely or make sensible or optimal decisions, particularly in terms of strategic or longer-term planning. Asserting that only people who behave responsibly and 'well' should receive social benefits and assistance is putting the problem the wrong way around.

The impact of a basic income on mental health would include what are called 'relational effects', inducing more balanced and relaxed interpersonal relationships once financial stress is reduced. A study of children in Cherokee tribal families who received regular payments from the reservation's casino earnings found that parents argued less (mainly because they were less likely to argue over money) while children suffered less from anxiety and behavioural disorders, did better at school and were less likely to drift into crime.[20]

A basic income would also strengthen personal resilience. Nassim Taleb has developed the idea of 'anti-fragility' in relation to coping with the shock of rare events, which he calls 'black swans'.[21] In his view, it is a mistake to try too hard to avoid shocks; an efficient economic system requires moderate volatility and disruption (perhaps coming from technological change) coupled with mechanisms that prepare people to deal with shocks.

For instance, someone with a seemingly secure job in a large firm may easily develop a sense of dependency, so that the sudden loss of that job can be a major shock, with devastating psychological and financial outcomes. By contrast, someone in a less secure job can, paradoxically, be less vulnerable to a similar shock. Moderate insecurity prepares people for shocks, enabling them to cope and recover better. But the key word here is moderate. Basic security increases resilience.

Psychologists thus have a distinctive take on basic income, providing evidence that the assurance of basic security is beneficial for mental health and rational decision making.

Giving people security also has instrumental value by increasing their willingness to take collective action.[22] For example, people with basic security are less fearful of threats of intimidation if they join a union.[23] That makes common sense. If true, a basic income would strengthen real unionization, which should have some positive effect on wages. While this might alarm the political right, the upside is that economically secure people make more reasonable bargaining counterparts.

Achieving a strong sense of personal agency and basic income security are interdependent. You cannot have one without the other. Today, many people lack both.

Towards a 'Good Society'

If society pretends to *formal* equality of status amidst gross real inequalities of power, status and property ownership, the ground is laid for active resentment. Perceptions of inadequacy, humiliation, envy, alienation and anomie generate unhealthy political impulses, fuelling support for the politicians who best promise to 'turn the clock back'. This should not surprise the economic winners of the age, who have supported the steady strengthening of property rights, the extraordinary growth of the subsidy state geared to their interests, and a regime of tax cuts for capital, profits and rentiers.

In that context, a basic income – even the promise of moving in its direction – would offer a sensible prospect of reducing poverty, insecurity and inequality. It would signal an end to the winner-takes-all mentality and system.

It is too much to expect that a basic income would *eradicate* poverty. It could go a long way towards that aim but should be regarded both more modestly and more ambitiously. If properly designed and implemented it could reduce both poverty and inequality, particularly if combined with other social policies including supplements for people, such as those with disabilities, who face structural extra costs of living.

A basic income would also not remove all forms of economic insecurity. However, it could give many more people basic security and a sense of belonging to their communities. These are desirable properties of any society that could be regarded as 'good'.

Basic income is not ultimately about eradicating income poverty, however worthy that aim. It is about other worthy objectives – social justice, freedom, equality and security. These would all be enhanced whatever the level of basic income, although the higher the level the greater the effect would be.

Constructing a basic income system is also about altering mindsets, about having the security to balance our desire to create a good life for ourselves, our families and communities, with the necessity of preserving the sustenance and beauties of the natural world. Security is a precious asset. It should be a goal of everyone who genuinely wants to build a good society rather than one that facilitates the aggrandizement of a privileged elite who knowingly gain from the insecurities of others. Wanting others to have what you want takes courage. That is what basic income is about.

The Economic Arguments

Although, in the view of the writer, the primary justifications for basic income are social justice, freedom and security, a basic income system would also have a number of economic advantages. These include higher, more sustainable, economic growth, a stabilizing impact on the economic cycle, and protection against possible large-scale unemployment as a result of disruptive technological change.

Economic Growth

What would be the implications of a basic income for economic growth? While growth per se should not necessarily be regarded as wholly beneficial, a universal basic income system would have several positive effects. Additional money flowing into the economy would raise aggregate demand and thereby propel economic growth, as long as there were no serious supply constraints. Even if basic income only substituted for other public spending, it would still boost demand because it would increase the purchasing power of those on low incomes, who have a higher propensity than the affluent to spend any money they receive.

For the same reason, a basic income could also lessen the

balance of payments constraint associated with stimulating aggregate demand. People on higher incomes tend to buy more imported goods (and imported services such as foreign travel) than those on lower incomes. The growth stimulated by basic income would thus be less likely to cause unsustainable balance of payments deficits, because more of the extra spending would go on *local* goods and services, rather than on 'luxury' imports.

One counter-argument is that, if the basic income were additional money, it would be inflationary. This objection will be dealt with in more detail in the next chapter, but it suffices to say here that it reflects 'one-handed' economic reasoning. That is because increased demand resulting from additional money is likely to generate an increased *supply* of goods and services. This in turn could create more jobs, further increasing incomes, spending power and production through the 'multiplier effect'.

Boosting spending power has become a concern throughout the industrialized world because incomes for the majority are no longer keeping pace with production capacity. It used to be the case that as productivity rose, real (inflation-adjusted) wages rose, increasing aggregate demand (consumption). This no longer applies. Rising productivity is not being matched by rising average wages, slowing growth.[1]

Governments could try old-style incomes policies, through productivity bargaining. But this would be far harder in an open economy than it was in the 1960s, when it was tried extensively, with mixed results. Instead, households struggling with stagnant or falling wages will have greater resort to credit and debt, increasing the vulnerability of the economy to the bursting of debt bubbles. That is what triggered the 2007–8 crash and threatens to happen again. A basic income system would be a way of maintaining high aggregate demand while making the economy less fragile.

In considering economic growth, relatively little attention has been given to the impact of basic income on small-scale business and entrepreneurship.[2] It would surely be helpful; having economic security would make people more willing to take entrepreneurial risks, knowing that they would have something to fall back on if the venture failed. In developing country contexts, basic income and cash transfers have been shown to have positive effects on entrepreneurship;[3] in Madhya Pradesh, basic income was strongly associated with new entrepreneurial activities.[4] In industrialized countries, basic income would provide essential security for the growing numbers of unwillingly self-employed and independent contractors, as well as for those with entrepreneurial ambitions. More generally, it would encourage people to seek training and job opportunities in line with their skills and motivations rather than those most likely to 'put food on the table'. This would make the economy more productive by facilitating the efficient reallocation of talent and increasing the level of job engagement. In the US, lack of employee commitment has been estimated to cost some $500 billion in lost productivity.[5]

A basic income system would also encourage a shift from paid 'labour' to 'work' – caring for children and the elderly, doing more voluntary work, community work and spending more time on personal development. And it would reduce the pressure to create jobs solely for the sake of boosting employment, including jobs in resource-depleting or polluting industries. In both these ways, a basic income would tilt activity towards ecologically and socially more sustainable growth.

Basic Income as Automatic Stabilizer

A traditional Keynesian argument in favour of welfare states, and social insurance systems in particular, used to be their stabilizing role over the economic cycle. When the economy was booming and inflationary pressure was building up, public spending on welfare benefits tended to decline because there were fewer unemployed requiring assistance. In recessions, expenditure on unemployment and other benefits tended to rise, helping to boost demand and employment.

The capacity of existing welfare systems to act as automatic macroeconomic stabilizers is now much reduced. The extent of social insurance has been eroded by the relentless trend towards means testing and conditional assistance schemes. And the neo-liberal thinking behind austerity programmes, aimed at balanced budgets and public debt reduction, has led governments deliberately to cut public spending in recessions.

A simple basic income would be a form of automatic economic stabilizer, since it would ensure more spending power in recessions. However, elsewhere I have proposed building a multi-tiered system, which would add a 'stabilization' component on top of a modest fixed basic income.[6] The value of the stabilization grant, which would fluctuate according to the state of the economy, could be set by an independent basic income policy committee, along the lines of the Bank of England's Monetary Policy Committee.

A stabilization grant component would be intrinsically fair. When jobs are plentiful people have more opportunity to earn higher incomes, so lower amounts paid as basic income would be reasonable. A higher stabilization grant in recessions would compensate for an overall drop in 'opportunity incomes'.

The existing social assistance system, by contrast, demands that the unemployed chase job opportunities that in a recession are by definition in short supply. Benefit schemes that require recipients to prove they are diligently and continuously looking for jobs effectively reduce their income. Job seeking costs time, money and morale, and in a jobless environment forces people into an activity with a very low potential pay-off.

A stabilization grant system that was not conditioned on proof of job seeking would have the treble virtue of being an automatic stabilizer for the economy, of being less intrusive and arbitrary for recipients, and of saving public expenditure on a bureaucratic apparatus for checking and penalizing vulnerable people.

Interestingly, the Australian government responded to the 2007–8 financial crisis by making one-off grants of A\$1,000 or more to pensioners, carers and children in low-income families, part of a strategy designed to boost household consumption. It worked: Australia was one of the few industrialized countries to escape recession. Though the grants were not a basic income, since they went only to certain groups, they nevertheless showed the effectiveness of stimulating the economy by giving millions of people extra cash to spend.[7]

From QE for Bankers to QE for People

The anti-deflationary monetary policies introduced first in Japan and then more generally in the aftermath of the financial crash of 2007–8 were a missed opportunity to phase in at least a short-term basic income plan. Through so-called 'quantitative easing' (QE), the US Federal Reserve, the Bank of Japan, the Bank of England and the European Central Bank, among others, have injected billions of dollars, yen, pounds and euros into financial markets in a largely unsuccessful bid to stimulate growth.

The allocation of even a modest part of that money to fund a basic income would have been more efficient at boosting growth, less regressive in its impact and clearly affordable. It was an option proposed by various economists at the time.[8] The $4.5 trillion in QE by the US Federal Reserve was enough to have given $56,000 to every household in the country. Similarly, had the UK's £375 billion of QE been diverted to pay a basic income, everyone legally resident in Britain could have received £50 a week for two years. Instead, QE has enriched the financiers, worsened income inequality and hastened the alarming oncoming crisis of underfunded pension schemes.[9]

The idea of giving money directly to people to boost growth was put forward in a famous 1969 article by Milton Friedman, who used the parable of scattering dollar bills from a helicopter for the public to pick up.[10] 'Helicopter money' – printing money to distribute to the public – has been proposed by American bond investor Bill Gross and by the economics journalist Martin Wolf, among others.

The term 'helicopter money' has the drawback of conveying an image of people scrambling to pick up the money fluttering down, with the lion's share going to the swift and the strong. A libertarian might regard that quasi-Darwinian prospect with equanimity; the rest of us might not. A systemic basic income paid in modest regular amounts as an equal right would be more equitable and efficient.

Euro-Dividends

In an innovative proposal linked to basic income that has attracted interest across the European Union, Philippe van Parijs has suggested that every EU resident (presumably, legal resident) would receive a Euro-Dividend averaging €200 per month, paid for by a 20 per cent value added tax.[11] This would amount to about 10 per cent of EU GDP.

A Euro-Dividend would help to provide two buffering mechanisms that the European Union currently lacks, but which exist, to some extent at least, in the United States. The first is easy interstate migration of workers in response to unequal economic developments. Cross-border migration has risen in the EU as membership has increased. But, contrary to exaggerated claims by certain politicians and media pundits, such migration remains hampered by linguistic and other barriers. The second is semi-automatic interstate transfers; when there is a recession in one state, federal transfers go up and tax contributions to the federal government go down, acting as a stabilization policy.

A Euro-Dividend would provide a stabilization mechanism and help deter out-migration from low-income areas. It would also be an expression of a benefit of European integration, conveying the important message that the European Union stands for more than the single market and bureaucratic regulation.

Preparing for the Robots

Rightly or wrongly (or somewhere in between), a major reason for the recent topicality of basic income is the view that before long the silicon revolution, automation and robotics will displace human labour to such an extent that there will be mass 'technological unemployment'. Martin Ford, Nick Srnicek and Alex Williams, and Paul Mason are among those who have argued in influential books that a jobless future makes a basic income essential.[12] The same concerns have added a roll-call of Silicon Valley and other technology titans to the basic income supporters list.

Star bond investor Bill Gross has also come out in support of a basic income as a response to what he perceives as the coming robot-driven 'end of work'.[13] In July 2016, there was even a Facebook Live roundtable held in the White House on automation and basic income, though in a report issued the following December the US President's Council of Economic Advisers rejected the idea, seemingly based on its chairman's critical remarks six months earlier that were dissected in Chapter 4.[14]

A significant convert to the technological unemployment perspective is Andy Stern, former head of the US Service

Employees International Union (SEIU) and the first leading trade unionist to come out in favour of a basic income.[15] In a 2016 book widely publicized in the US, Stern claimed that 58 per cent of all jobs would be automated eventually, driven by the ethos of shareholder value. He told the American media group Bloomberg, 'It's not like the fall of the auto and steel industries. That hit just a sector of the country. This will be widespread. People will realize that we don't have a storm anymore; we have a tsunami.'[16]

Nevertheless, there are reasons to be sceptical about the prospect of a jobless or even workless future. It is the latest version of the 'lump of labour fallacy', the idea that there is only a certain amount of labour and work to be done, so that if more of it can be automated or done by intelligent robots, human workers will be rendered redundant. In any case, very few jobs can be automated in their entirety. The suggestion in a much-cited study[17] that nearly half of all US jobs are vulnerable to automation has been challenged by, among others, the OECD, which puts the figure of jobs 'at risk' at 9 per cent for industrialized countries.[18]

That said, the *nature* of jobs will undoubtedly change, perhaps rapidly. And while this writer does not believe that a jobless (still less 'workless') future is likely, the technological revolution is seriously increasing inequality, with profoundly regressive effects on the *distribution* of income, as powerful companies and their owners capture the lion's share of the gains. That is a further reason why a new income distribution system must be constructed, with a basic income as an anchor, an argument to which Chapter 12 will return.

The disruptive character of what has been dubbed the

'fourth technological revolution' also appears to be more generalized than in preceding seismic changes, which predominantly hit low-skill manual jobs.[19] All levels of job and occupation are being affected. The resultant economic *uncertainty* is creating widespread insecurity; this supports calls for a basic income as the only feasible way of restoring economic security, to keep that uncertainty under some form of social control.

The Economist has argued that, while a basic income might be the answer if there were mass technological unemployment, there was no need for it yet. 'The basic income is an answer to a problem that has not yet materialised.'[20] However, this presumes that the primary rationale for a basic income is the advent of technological unemployment whereas, as the first chapters of this book have tried to explain, most advocates of basic income justify it on quite other grounds, as a response, albeit partial, to economic insecurity, social injustice and freedom denied.

A consensus view could probably be created around the idea that, while it cannot be predicted with certainty that technological change will result in mass displacement of human labour, such an eventuality cannot be ruled out. And we can be reasonably sure that these changes will continue to worsen inequalities and be seriously disruptive, in often unpredictable ways that will hit many people through absolutely no fault of their own. In these circumstances, introducing a basic income system now would be sensibly precautionary and an equitable way to respond to the already visible disruption and inequality.

Sam Altman, president of the American start-up incubator

Y Combinator, has justified his allocation of funds to a basic income pilot (discussed in Chapter 11) on the grounds that we need to know how people would respond if the jobless future were to be realized and a basic income introduced. He told Bloomberg, 'I'm fairly confident that at some point in the future, as technology continues to eliminate traditional jobs and massive new wealth gets created, we're going to see some version of this [basic income] at a national scale.'[21] In another interview, he put that point at 'no fewer than 10 years' and 'no more than 100'.[22]

However, the immediate problem is one of income distribution rather than a sudden disappearance of work for humans to do. Indeed, this could be the first technological revolution that is generating *more* work, even though it is disrupting and replacing paid labour.[23] But it is contributing to the growing inequality of income. Tim Berners-Lee, inventor of the World Wide Web, says he supports basic income as a tool for correcting massive inequality brought about by technology.[24] So does Stephen Hawking, the acclaimed physicist and cosmologist.[25] Even senior economists in the International Monetary Fund have concluded that rising technology-induced inequality means that 'the advantages of a basic income financed out of capital taxation become obvious'.[26] Basic income would be a way in which all would benefit from economic gains resulting from technological advance.

Economic Feedback

The economic feedback effects of a basic income system could be substantial, reducing its net cost. For instance, evidence from cash transfer schemes and basic income pilots shows that cash payments improve nutrition and health, particularly for babies and children, but also for the frail and disabled, who often receive low priority in family budgets. In Canada, a seven-year study of the impact of a guaranteed annual income for the elderly found sharp declines in food insecurity and thus improved health.[27] A study that tracked the children of applicants to the Mothers' Pension programme – the first US government-sponsored welfare programme (1911–35) – found that children of successful applicants lived longer, had more schooling, were less likely to be underweight, and had higher income in adulthood than children of rejected mothers.[28]

There is also strong evidence for improvement in mental health. The well-known Canadian experiment with something close to a basic income, discussed in more detail in Chapter 11, led to fewer hospital admissions for mental illness as well as for accidents and injury.[29] As mentioned in Chapter 4, children in Cherokee tribal families receiving the basic income had fewer emotional problems and behavioural disorders, while parents reported lower drug and alcohol use by their partners.[30] All these benefits tend to reduce other public expenditures, including spending on public healthcare, the criminal justice system and social support services.

One of the under-emphasized aspects of inequality and economic insecurity is the adverse impact on mental and physical health, which is costly for the public as well as the individual. A basic income system would not radically reduce that, but it certainly would help.

The Standard Objections

'It is a system that is barking mad.'

JOHN KEY, NEW ZEALAND PRIME MINISTER, FEBRUARY 2015

'It is one of the most completely ridiculous ideas I have heard in a long time.'

BJARNI BENEDIKTSSON, ICELAND FINANCE MINISTER,
SEPTEMBER 2016

Over the years, the idea of basic income has been met by a remarkably constant set of objections that are raised time and again despite the counter-arguments and evidence. The issue of affordability is discussed in the next chapter, and the issue of labour supply and work in Chapter 8. This chapter will deal with other objections, in no order of implied significance.

Hirschmann's Three Rules

In his book *The Rhetoric of Reaction*, the great political economist Albert Hirschmann pointed out that any big new social policy idea – or one perceived as new at the time – is initially attacked on grounds of futility (it would not work), perversity (it would have unintended negative consequences) and jeopardy (it would endanger other goals).[1]

These arguments were used against proposals for unemployment benefits in the early twentieth century, against family benefits in the 1930s and against what became Social Security (old age pensions) in the US at that time. Yet within a few years of these policies being introduced, the three criticisms melted away, to be displaced by a rhetoric of inevitability and common sense. We should at least ask if the following objections to basic income are similar.

A BASIC INCOME IS UTOPIAN; IT HAS NEVER BEEN DONE BEFORE

Critics maintain that because basic income has not been introduced anywhere thus far, it must be 'basically flawed', as an article in *The Economist* put it. This could be said to apply to any new policy throughout history. For that reason alone, it does not make sense.

In the case of basic income, the criticism can be countered in two ways: in the twenty-first century, we have reached the stage when all other policies for providing people with economic security have been tried and found wanting; and, for the first time, today's society has the institutional and technical means for putting a basic income into effect.

A BASIC INCOME WOULD BE UNAFFORDABLE

This is the most common assertion and it raises sufficiently complex issues to deserve a separate discussion in the next chapter. If a basic income were unaffordable, that would be the end of the subject. But too many critics have rushed to judgement, by implication suggesting that basic income proponents are stupid or unable to do simple maths.

The question to pose to sceptics is this: Would you support a basic income if it were shown to be reasonably affordable? In other words, are those claiming it is unaffordable really opposing it for some other, less defensible reason?

A BASIC INCOME WOULD LEAD TO
DISMANTLING OF THE WELFARE STATE

This standard complaint is typically made by critics on the political left and defenders of paternalistic social democratic welfare states. Once again, it needs to be stated that, whatever some libertarian supporters of basic income may advocate, basic income does not imply the dismantling of public services, nor the replacement of all other welfare benefits. Rather, it should be the floor of a new income distribution system, alongside other needed public services and benefits.

As this chapter was being drafted, a Labour Party candidate for mayor of a London borough was asked by a member of the Citizen's Income Trust what he thought of basic income. His answer was dismissive:

> UBI – interesting idea, but fundamentally a Conservative one designed to remove the apparatus of the welfare state, by cutting some of the public sector jobs that fuel demand in the economy. I'm also concerned that it would be inflationary, leaving the poor where they were to begin with, while those in secure employment get to supplement their income.[2]

The inflation claim will be discussed below. But what are these 'public sector jobs' that so worried the aspirant mayor? They must be those filled by low-paid bureaucrats prying into the lives of claimants to determine whether they 'deserve' to receive means-tested benefits, or who sanction them for being five minutes late for demeaning appointments set up to prove they are behaving in ways stipulated by the conditional system. Could these bureaucrats not find (or be found) something better to do with their time, energy and 'skill'? In effect, that politician and many like him oppose providing ordinary folk with basic security because they want to preserve jobs for those trying to deny them benefits!

Ironically, opponents of basic income on the grounds that it would lead to a dismantling of the welfare state tend to support some variant of social insurance. They should be reminded that social insurance was first introduced by someone vehemently opposed to the political ideology they purport to represent. Otto von Bismarck prohibited socialists and exiled their leaders from Prussian cities. So those criticizing basic income because, in their albeit incorrect view, it is advocated by enemies of socialism should logically be opposed to the fundamental base of old welfare states.

In any event, as noted in Chapter 4, the Beveridge and Bismarck models of social insurance simply do not work in open, flexible economies with a large and growing precariat. The point being made here, however, is that support for or opposition to a policy should not be based on whether someone one does not like supports or opposes it.

A BASIC INCOME WOULD DISTRACT FROM PROGRESSIVE POLICIES, SUCH AS 'FULL EMPLOYMENT'

There are several ways of rebutting this version of Hirschmann's 'jeopardy' point. First, in the second decade of the twenty-first century, where is the pressure to achieve other progressive policies? The growth and level of inequality are almost unprecedented; economic insecurity is pervasive; full employment has been redefined to be about 5 per cent unemployment with much 'underemployment', concealed by labour statistics that are unfit for purpose; and, above all, the growing precariat has been neglected by mainstream politics.

Second, why should 'full employment' be regarded as a progressive policy? What is so desirable about putting as many people as possible in 'jobs', in positions of subordination to 'bosses'? In reality, many if not most jobs are boring, stultifying, demeaning, isolating or even dangerous. If anything, a basic income would help to improve the nature of jobs by enabling more people to refuse jobs they dislike or demand more pay for doing them.

Third, why should basic income be a distraction from other progressive policies, rather than giving them necessary substance? In strengthening people's resolve to act, the reverse is far more likely. Moreover, like 'full employment', some policies long regarded as progressive turn out to be, on closer inspection, anything but. Popular alternatives to basic income are considered in Chapter 9, but there is no reason to suppose it would hinder pursuit of other objectives.

BASIC INCOME ADVOCATES PRESUME THE POOR JUST LACK CASH

Critics commonly assert that basic income advocates have an overly simplistic view to the effect that giving the poor more money would solve all their problems. One such critic claimed,

> Progressives and libertarians alike are loath to admit that many of the poor and jobless are lacking more than just cash. They may be addicted to drugs or alcohol, suffer from mental health issues, have criminal records, or have

difficulty functioning in a complex society. Money may be needed but money by itself does not cure such ills.[3]

Of course, it does not. However, no sensible advocate of basic income believes that cash solves everything. Basic income is not a panacea for all the ills of society, and it is unfair to judge it on that basis, any more than other social policies. As mentioned in Chapter 4, basic income may help to improve mental health, especially in children, in circumstances where anxiety about money is a proximate cause. But social illnesses and vulnerabilities should be tackled by tailored public social services rather than social protection policies, recognizing that all of us, not just 'the poor', may need support at some stage in our lives.

IT IS STUPID TO GIVE MONEY TO THE RICH AS WELL AS TO THE POOR

A standard knee-jerk objection to basic income is: Why give money to people who do not need it? As one critic has written, 'If you want to reduce inequalities, then you can do this much better by giving more money to those who have less (rather than the same amount).'[4] Based on this sort of claim, critics usually add that paying a basic income to everyone automatically makes it too expensive to contemplate. There are three retorts.

First, if basic income is viewed as a 'social dividend', a share of society's inherited commons and wealth should go to everyone, or to every citizen, as a right. A right is universal, or it is not a right at all. And an equal payment to all is worth proportionately more to those on low incomes.

Second, in administrative terms, it is easier and less costly to pay a basic income to everybody and tax back that income from the better-off (see 'A Professor's Teaser' in the next chapter). A universal basic income can easily be designed and implemented with a claw-back from the more affluent (as was done with family allowances in Britain in the 1960s). This would do away with the arbitrary and complex rules for entitlement to benefits that cost so much and that cause so much misery.

Means testing is invariably complex, costly to administer and prone to extensive 'Type 1' errors (not reaching those intended) and 'Type 2' errors (reaching some of those who, under the rules, should not qualify). Every means-tested scheme suffers from low take-up rates, due to stigma, ignorance or fear, and inevitably imposes poverty and precarity traps.

Third, a targeted system does not automatically result in less poverty and inequality. That depends on take-up rates, on degree of progressiveness and on administrative efficiency. Indeed, it has been well argued that targeted systems are *more* likely, not less, to increase inequality.[5] Given the weight of international evidence on the failure of targeted schemes, it must be assumed that the true objective of those who continue to advocate them is to reduce the number who receive benefits.

A BASIC INCOME WOULD GIVE PEOPLE SOMETHING FOR NOTHING

This objection has been raised by moralists of most political persuasions, but was especially prominent among 'Third Way'

CHAPTER 6

politicians and academics in the early years of the twenty-first century. It is coupled with the notion of 'reciprocity', that there should be no rights without contributions and no rights without proven 'responsibility'. Thus recipients of state benefits should be required to show 'reciprocity' by complying with conditions requiring incessant job seeking or even 'workfare'.

The most obvious retort to the 'something for nothing' criticism is that society gives many people a lot of something for which they have not done anything. Anyone opposing basic income on this ground should also oppose all wealth inheritance and all other forms of income that are not derived from productive activity.

They should oppose the international copyright system, which gives descendants of copyright holders an income for up to seventy years after the original author or creator has died. They should oppose all selective tax breaks and subsidy schemes, which mostly benefit the affluent who have done nothing to 'earn' them. They should oppose tax avoidance devices that enable the rich to use public services without contributing to the cost. And they should oppose the many other forms of 'rentier' income derived solely from possession of assets.[6] Unless critics also advocate (and practise) no tax avoidance, no subsidies and no inheritance, the something-for-nothing objection is hypocritical and unsustainable as a logical rationale.

A BASIC INCOME WOULD LEAD TO MORE SPENDING ON 'BADS'

It is often claimed that giving cash to those in need is misguided because people will spend it on alcohol, cigarettes and other 'bads' rather than on their children and essentials such as food, clothes and heating. Instead, help for the poor should take the form of vouchers (such as food stamps) or cards that can be used only for approved spending.

Obviously, this is a thoroughly paternalistic line of attack. Where to draw a line between a 'good' and a 'bad'? Why should a rich person have the freedom to buy and consume whatever the state bureaucracy deems a 'bad', but not a poor person? And does the state really know what is good or bad for us? What is deemed good at one time may be declared bad later, and vice versa. As a principle, the law and regulations should be equal for all.

More generally, there is a moralistic presumption that poor people, especially those receiving benefits, should not be spending money on anything but the bare essentials, denying themselves even the smallest 'luxury' that might make their lives less miserable. As Marx pointed out in 1844, 'every luxury of the worker seems to be reprehensible, and everything that goes beyond the most abstract need seems a luxury'.[7]

Selective paternalism, for those on low incomes or for other groups needing state assistance, is perhaps even worse than general paternalism, since the minority are denied the opportunity to overturn the rule democratically. The unaffected majority will probably not care about or will support the denial of freedom for the minority if they expect to benefit through lower taxes.

It is sometimes claimed that taxpayers have the 'right' to determine how 'their' tax contributions are spent. But this is nowhere the normal practice. In Britain, many people dislike paying for nuclear armaments and there is a vociferous motoring lobby that campaigns, so far unsuccessfully, for taxes on vehicle fuel to be spent exclusively on roads. Why should taxpayers be considered to have special rights in relation to social protection policies, even supposing they were consulted?

In any case, the evidence does not support those opposing basic income on this ground. Basic income pilots and cash transfer programmes have shown that, overwhelmingly, people spend the money on private 'goods'. In the basic income pilots in India and Namibia, those receiving a basic income were more likely to spend *less* on so-called 'bads'. Similar results have been found for cash transfer programmes in Africa, notably in Kenya.[8] Although the reasons for this are speculative, one explanation given in the Madhya Pradesh pilots was that more men were working in the fields and around the home rather than seeking wage labour in the local town, where they had greater opportunity to buy and drink alcohol.[9]

A BASIC INCOME WOULD REDUCE WORK

This often stated objection to basic income will be considered in detail in Chapter 8. Suffice it to state at this stage that the evidence does not support it, and that the impact is much more complex than commonly presumed. Again, the question to pose to anybody inclined to reject basic income on this ground is: if there were convincing reasons and empirical evidence showing that a basic income would not reduce work, would you then support it?

A BASIC INCOME WOULD LOWER WAGES

What is the impact, if any, of a basic income on wages? Some critics, particularly in the trade unions, have claimed that a basic income would lead to lower wages because employers would argue that they did not need to pay as much. However, basic income advocates assert the opposite: a basic income would give people a greater ability to refuse exploitative wage offers and more confidence to bargain for higher wages. A basic income would enable more vulnerable people to say 'No!' *in extremis*.

Those arguing that a basic income would act as a subsidy to wages, pushing them down, should by the same token oppose tax credits linked to jobs, for that is precisely what they are intended to do. The key difference is that tax credits, epitomized by the US Earned Income Tax Credit (EITC) and the British, Canadian and other equivalents, *depend* on the recipient being in low-wage labour. This deters workers from pushing for higher wages, because the increase will be largely negated by lower tax credits.

By contrast, a basic income would go to everybody, whether or not employed or on low wages, and would not be withdrawn as wages rise. This would give workers greater bargaining strength in deciding to accept or reject the wages on offer. Employers needing to fill unattractive jobs would be obliged to offer better pay and conditions to attract applicants (or, where feasible, invest in more automation). But people would also have greater freedom to take on low-paid or unpaid work if they wished.

A BASIC INCOME WOULD BE INFLATIONARY

The argument here is that if everybody were given a basic income, a lot more money would be pushed into the economy; this would send prices soaring, boosting inflation to the extent that people would be no better off than before. The supposed inflationary impact was a central criticism made by Hal Minsky against Milton Friedman's proposal for a negative income tax set out in his 1962 book *Capitalism and Freedom*.[10]

As mentioned in Chapter 5, this is 'one-handed' economics because it ignores the likely impact of extra spending power on the *supply* of goods and services. In developing countries, and in low-income communities in richer countries, supply effects could actually *lower* prices for basic goods and services. In the Indian basic income pilots (see Chapter 10), villagers' increased purchasing power led local farmers to plant more rice and wheat, use more fertilizer and cultivate more of their land.[11] Their earnings went up, while the unit price of the food they supplied went down. The same happened with clothes, since several women found it newly worthwhile to buy sewing machines and material. A market was created where there was none before. A similar response could be expected in any community where there are people who want to earn more and do more, alongside people wanting to acquire more goods and services to improve their living standard.

By benefiting those on low incomes most, a basic income system could also twist the structure of aggregate demand towards more basic goods and services that have a high 'elasticity of supply' – they respond to rising demand by increasing in quantity rather than price. This would also mean more demand for local goods and services, boosting growth and jobs. By extension, funding a basic income through higher taxes on high incomes would accentuate the twist in demand, perhaps even inducing price reductions while generating more sustainable economic growth.

If the basic income was funded by switching public expenditure rather than by additional spending, the inflationary effect would be minimal. As Geoff Crocker has shown, only if aggregate spending power were higher than economic production (GDP) could there be an inflationary impact.[12] The inflation claim would only be valid in relation to an economy that was at or close to 'full employment'. No modern economy is close to 'full employment'. And labour markets are much more open than they used to be, so any increase in the demand for labour could be expected to lead either to more labour force entrants or, more likely, to a relative shift of jobs abroad, dampening the impact on wages.

It is worth pointing out that, in recent years, central banks and governments around the world have been desperately trying to overcome price deflation (falling prices) and to *increase* inflation. Their efforts have been expensive, inefficient, regressive and ultimately a failure. To the extent that the increased demand kept prices stable or gave them a modest upward nudge, a basic income would be beneficial.

A BASIC INCOME WOULD INDUCE IN-MIGRATION

An upsurge in migration, and the recent refugee crisis in Europe, have bolstered claims that a basic income for all would induce mass migration from lower-income countries. These claims have been further strengthened by prejudiced political rhetoric about 'welfare tourism'.

Opponents, including the Swiss government, used this argument to whip up fear during the referendum campaign to introduce a basic income in Switzerland (discussed in Chapter 11), which some observers believed led to its defeat in June 2016.

Again, there are several ways of rebutting this criticism. Most importantly, it is the existing system of social assistance that has generated social friction. Benefits and social housing have come to be based on need rather than rights. So long-time citizens see relative newcomers 'jumping the queue' because they tend to be among the poorest. We should understand the resentment among those who feel they have paid their dues to their community over many years or even generations. A telling study showed the resultant social friction and anti-migrant sentiment in east London.[13]

Far from making this situation worse, a basic income could make things better. Pragmatic rules could be devised that most people would regard as fair. For example, entitlements could be prioritized by duration of legal residence in the community. Or potential migrants could be informed that they would have to qualify as permanent residents or wait a certain length of time, say a minimum of two years, before becoming eligible to receive the basic income. (Residual social assistance should be available for non-qualifying migrants if needed.) In fact, a basic income could be a fair way of discouraging migration while providing an incentive for migrants to enter legally and integrate into society. A basic income system would thus tend to *reduce* anti-migration sentiments compared with existing means-tested systems.

Ironically, one commentator has come out against basic income because he thinks it would 'choke off immigration to the US'.[14] This seems unlikely. However, by making a basic income scheme compatible with rules on acquisition of long-term or permanent residence or citizenship, it would be fairer than almost all existing social protection systems. And giving people greater economic security would make them less likely to see the economy as a zero-sum competition with immigrants for resources, as well as promoting more tolerant and altruistic attitudes.

A BASIC INCOME WOULD BE MANIPULATED BY GOVERNMENTS PRIOR TO GENERAL ELECTIONS

This is an interesting objection. The claim is that if there was a basic income for everybody set by government, then the party in power could raise the level shortly before a general election, effectively bribing the electorate, at least to the extent of giving voters good feelings about the state of the economy. It does seem a real possibility. But it is not an insurmountable obstacle to commonsense policy.

One response would be to make automatic adjustments to the level based on changes in national income, as suggested by Andy Stern.[15] A proposal by this writer, mentioned earlier, would be to create an Independent Basic Income Committee (IBIC), analogous to the 'independent' Monetary Policy Committee of the Bank of England, with members appointed by Parliament for one five-year term.[16]

The IBIC could have terms of reference giving it authority to adjust the level of the basic income according to changes in national income and perhaps the state of the economy. The idea of having a tiered basic income system will be revisited in the final chapter. The point here is that it should be relatively easy to overcome the objection that the basic income would be subject to populist manipulation.

No doubt there are other objections that people have made from time to time. But the above thirteen are certainly the most common. Readers must judge which of them, if any, are credible and then decide whether they are sufficient to reject basic income per se. Every policy should be judged on a ledger of positives and negatives. Advocates of basic income argue that advancing social justice and freedom while reducing inequality and insecurity outweigh the criticisms, most of which do not stand up to closer examination. It remains, however, to confront in more detail the two most contentious issues – affordability and the impact on labour and work.

The Affordability Issue

The most common objection to a basic income is that a country could not afford it. This chapter will try to show that this is not the case. It is a complex issue that needs to be considered as dispassionately as possible, bearing in mind that the desired or target level of a basic income is not pre-determined, that it could be introduced in stages, and that there are various possible ways in which it could be funded.

Back-of-the-envelope Calculations

The usual way of arguing that a basic income is unaffordable is to set a level of, say, 50–60 per cent of median income, multiply this by the size of the population to give the total cost and compare this with current welfare spending. For example, Tim Harford, writing in the *Financial Times*, suggests that the basic income in the UK might be £10 a day. 'Such a payment would cost £234 billion a year across 64 million UK residents, so it could be largely paid for by scrapping all social security spending, which is £217 billion.'[1]

John Kay, in his *Financial Times* column, asserted:

[S]imple arithmetic shows why these schemes cannot work. Decide what proportion of average income per head would be appropriate for basic income. Thirty per cent seems mean; perhaps 50 per cent is more reasonable? The figure you write down is the share of national income that would be absorbed by public expenditure on basic income ... To see the average tax rate implied, add the share of national income taken by other public sector activities – education, health, defence and transport. Either the basic income is impossibly low, or the expenditure on it is impossibly high.[2]

Kay added that most advocates of basic income do not 'engage in the grubby practicalities of numbers', which is rather insulting to the many who have done so. He reached his conclusion without showing any awareness of their research.

These calculations can be criticized on their own terms. For instance, Kay's *Financial Times* colleague Martin Sandbu has pointed out that the appropriate 'average income' for deciding on the level of a basic income should not be based on 'national income' (GDP), which is the total of all goods and services produced in the economy, but 'disposable income', the amount people have to spend after taxes and transfers.[3] Disposable income is less than two-thirds of national income. So, Kay's provocatively high estimate that basic income would absorb 50 per cent of national income would in fact be reduced to 33 per cent.

The Economist has produced a more sophisticated set of 'back-of-the-envelope' estimates in an interactive basic income calculator for all OECD countries.[4] This purports to show how much could be paid as a basic income by switching spending on non-health transfers, leaving tax revenues and other public spending unchanged. Interestingly, even on this very restrictive basis, a cluster of seven west European countries could already pay over $10,000 per person per year.

The United States could pay $6,300 and Britain $5,800. Obviously, for most countries, the level of basic income that could be financed from this tax-neutral welfare-switching exercise would be modest – though, especially for bottom-ranked countries such as South Korea ($2,200) or Mexico (only $900), this largely reflects their current low tax take and welfare spending.

The Economist's interactive calculator also aims to calculate what tax rises would be needed to pay a basic income of a given amount. For the UK, the calculator estimates that the cost of a basic income of one-third average GDP per head would require a 15 percentage point rise in tax take. Its calculations can again be questioned in their own terms. However, all these back-of-the-envelope exercises are flawed in more fundamental ways.

First, they do not allow for clawing the basic income back in tax from higher-income earners, which could be done with no net cost to the affluent or to the Exchequer, simply by tweaking tax rates and allowances so that the extra tax take equals the basic income paid.

Second, they do not take account of administrative savings from removal of means testing and behaviour conditions. Administration accounted for £8 billion of the £172 billion 2013–14 budget of the UK's Department of Work and

Pensions, much of which will have gone to pay staff in local job centres to monitor and sanction benefit recipients. This does not include hundreds of millions of pounds paid to private contractors to carry out so-called 'work assessment' tests on people with disabilities, which have led to denial of benefits to some of society's most vulnerable people.

Third, they compare the cost of a basic income with the existing welfare budget and assume that all other areas of public spending remain intact. Yet governments can always choose to realign spending priorities. The UK government could save billions by scrapping the plan to replace the Trident nuclear missile system, now estimated to cost more than £200 billion over its lifetime. It could save further billions by ending subsidies that go predominantly to corporations and the affluent.

In Britain 'corporate welfare' is estimated to exceed £93 billion a year.[5] In the US, federal subsidies for corporations cost $100 billion a year, according to the right-wing Cato Institute.[6] Farm subsidies go mostly to the biggest landowners, fossil fuel subsidies damage the climate – the list goes on. Most subsidies are regressive, morally unjustifiable and unrelated to economic growth.[7] Though it is not possible to pinpoint a precise amount that could be reallocated, the potential saving from making a bonfire of subsidies should be taken into account. The point is that expenditure switching would provide another source of funds for a basic income, even given fiscal neutrality.

Rather than focus on costly regressive subsidies, a typical tactic of critics is to compare possible spending on a basic income with spending on popular public services. Thus an editorial in the *Guardian* newspaper asked: 'Would this be money better spent on the NHS [National Health Service], schools or childcare?'[8] Framing the issue in this way is prejudicial, deliberately and wrongly implying that basic income would deprive these vital public services of resources.

Fourth, back-of-the-envelope exercises ignore the wide array of tax exemptions and allowances that have come to characterize the modern fiscal system. The UK personal income tax allowance, which in 2016 exempted the first £11,000 of income from tax, costs the Exchequer almost £100 billion a year in foregone revenue. Non-imposition of national insurance on some earners costs another £50 billion. These two exemptions alone amount to nearly 10 per cent of GDP and are strongly regressive.[9]

While raising the personal tax allowance has been presented as a measure to help low earners, high earners gain most of the benefit because more of their income escapes tax and there are knock-on increases in the level of earnings at which higher rates of tax kick in. Meanwhile, low earners already below the tax threshold gain nothing.

It is also worth noting that another effect of raising tax allowances is a reduction in the number of people who pay income tax. Nearly half of all British adults pay no income tax; nearly half of US households pay no federal income tax. Studies have shown that non-taxpayers are less likely to be politically engaged and are thus less likely to vote.[10] That is an additional reason to roll back tax allowances and use the money saved to help fund the basic income.

The cost of other, selective tax reliefs that the UK government has identified has risen to over £117 billion a year, more than the cost of the National Health Service.[11] A further 218 tax reliefs have not been costed, nor has the government analysed their effect on the behaviour they ostensibly exist to promote. In the US, which also has over 200 selective tax reliefs, the ten biggest cost federal coffers more than $900 billion in 2013, nearly 6 per cent of GDP. The three largest reliefs, on state and local taxes, mortgage interest and charitable donations, cost a combined $185 billion a year.[12] All or part of these huge sums could go a long way towards paying for a modest basic income.

Affordability in the UK

Leaving aside for the moment the reallocation of other spending programmes and other sources of finance, the following focuses on several recent UK studies that have looked in detail at the affordability of various basic income systems and levels. Almost all these studies assume what Malcolm Torry has called 'strict revenue neutrality', that is, the basic income is funded solely by adjusting personal income tax rates and allowances coupled with savings on current welfare spending. This has been the standard approach in a long line of basic income costings over the years that include the much earlier efforts of Mimi Parker, among others.[13] Parker, a Conservative, worked closely with her patron, Brandon Rhys-Williams MP, who carried the baton of basic income handed down by his mother, Juliet, into the 1980s.

In addition to looking at how much a basic income would cost, the studies mentioned here try to calculate the impact on households of different types and incomes. One common criticism derived from back-of-the-envelope estimates is that spreading the existing welfare budget across the total population would leave many low-income households worse off, because they would get less from a basic income than they do under the existing system of contributory and means-tested benefits, including tax credits.

This issue can theoretically be tackled in two ways, by designing a basic income system that minimizes losses for those on low incomes, or by introducing, as a transitional measure, a hybrid scheme that pays a basic income alongside existing benefits. In interpreting the results of these studies, it is important to bear in mind that all the models assume that people are now receiving all the benefits to which they are entitled, which is far from the case for means-tested and behaviour-tested benefits.

A simulation prepared for the political think-tank Compass costs a hybrid transitional scheme that would pay a fairly generous basic income (£61 a week for adults over twenty-five, lesser amounts for younger adults, children and pensioners) *in addition* to almost all existing benefits, including the state pension and housing benefit but excepting child benefit, which would be abolished.[14] The basic income would be taken into account in assessing means-tested benefits, so reducing their cost and the number of households dependent on them. The simulation suggests that such a scheme could be fully funded, at a negligible net cost to the Exchequer of £700 million annually, by abolishing income tax personal allowances, ending the lower national insurance contribution rate for high earners and raising income tax rates by 3 percentage points for each band. This would give a combined income tax and national insurance rate of 35 per cent for the basic band (against 32 per cent as of 2016), 55 per cent for the higher band (against 42 per cent) and 60 per cent for the top band (against 47 per cent).

As Martin Sandbu notes, although such a system would involve steep tax increases for the top fifth of taxpayers, they would be partially compensated by the basic income.[15] And under the existing system, low earners face a marginal 'tax' rate of up to 80 per cent or more due to withdrawal of tax credits and other means-tested benefits, while higher earners also face marginal tax rates of over 60 per cent when they pass the point at which they lose, first, child benefit, and then their personal allowance.

Compass has also costed a more generous hybrid scheme, paying an extra £10 a week to all groups. This would increase the tax rates in each band by a further 2 percentage points and cost an additional £8 billion. Both transitional schemes would reduce inequality and have a significant impact on poverty, reducing child poverty by an estimated 38 per cent in the first case and 45 per cent in the second. Sixty per cent of those in the bottom fifth of the income distribution would gain more than 20 per cent from the more generous scheme, with the redistribution paid for by the top fifth. Fewer than 3 per cent of households in the two lowest income deciles would lose more than 5 per cent.

Using a slightly different model of household taxes and transfers, based on 2015–16 values, Malcolm Torry, director of Citizen's Income Trust, has estimated the cost of a more modest hybrid scheme that would pay a 'citizen's income' of £60 a week for those aged 25 to 64, a Young

Adult's citizen's income of £50 a week for those aged 16 to 24, and a Citizen's Pension of £30 a week for those aged 65 and above.[16]

Again, this would be in addition to most existing benefits, though the citizen's income would be taken into account for any means testing. Torry finds that, with the same combined income and national insurance structure as the Compass simulation described above, his scheme could *save* the Exchequer nearly £3 billion a year. (He also costs the novel idea of introducing a basic income solely for one age cohort, all those aged 16, with the intention of gradually extending it to all age cohorts.)

Torry's scheme too would leave 3 per cent of households in the lowest two-fifths of the income spectrum more than 5 per cent worse off, and 1.5 per cent more than 10 per cent worse off, at the point of implementation. However, the £2.8 billion saving to the Exchequer would give plenty of scope to compensate them on an ad hoc basis, bearing in mind that this would be a transitional system. There would be more losers at higher income levels – inevitable for a scheme that aims to redistribute resources and reduce inequality – but for them the losses would be manageable (see Figure 7.1).

Meanwhile, child poverty would be cut by a third while, according to Torry, the scheme 'would achieve manageable and useful redistribution from rich to poor, with those households often described as the "squeezed middle" particularly benefiting from the transition'.

Using Torry's model, the Royal Society of Arts (RSA) did its own calculations for a full basic income scheme based on

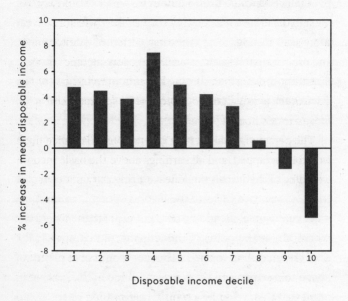

Figure 7.1

The redistributional effect of Torry's hybrid basic income scheme

Source: M. Torry (2016), 'An evaluation of a strictly revenue neutral Citizen's Income scheme.' *Euromod Working Paper Series* EM 5/16

payments equivalent to £71 a week for adults aged 25–64, £143 for adults aged 65+, £82.50 for the first child and £65 for subsequent children aged 0–5, and £56 for children and young people aged 5–24.[17] These amounts, which would *replace* most existing benefits, roughly correspond to existing levels of Jobseeker's Allowance, the state pension, and child benefit and other help for children available to low-income families. Disability support and housing benefits were left out of the calculation, although the RSA proposed a separate reform for means-tested housing benefit.

The personal tax allowance and national insurance floor would be scrapped, and all earnings above the basic income would be taxed at marginal rates starting at 32 per cent (20 per cent basic rate plus 12 per cent national insurance, as now) and rising to a top rate of 52 per cent for earnings over £150,000. Figure 7.2 shows how this would compare with what the RSA terms the 'Himalayas'-style tax curve for 2012–13. In a departure from 'strict revenue neutrality', tax relief on pension contributions would be confined to the basic rate, releasing £10 billion for the basic income pot. The net additional cost of this basic income scheme was put at somewhere between £9.8 billion and £16.4 billion.

According to Anthony Painter, the lead author of the RSA report,

> We estimate that the changes we have made would cost up to 1 percent of GDP over and above the current model (including the abolition of personal allowances). This sounds like a considerable sum. However, it is no greater than the change that Gordon Brown [as Labour Chancellor

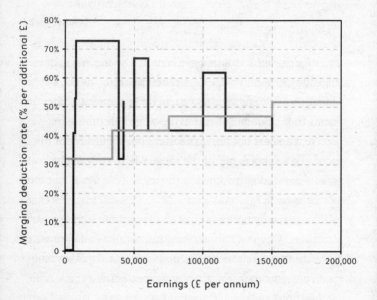

Figure 7.2

Marginal tax rates in the RSA's basic income model compared
with actual rates in 2012–13

— 2012–13 tax system

— RSA

Source: Royal Society of Arts

of the Exchequer] made to tax credits and well below cumulative changes that George Osborne [Chancellor of the Exchequer between 2010 and 2016] has made to personal allowances, VAT, inheritance tax and corporation tax despite austerity.[18]

The RSA also looked at how the National Living Wage, introduced in 2016, and the new Universal Credit might affect operation of a basic income system for specimen families. It found that payment of the living wage (assuming people receive it and are not put on shorter hours) quickly put low-income households out of the range where they might lose from a basic income, making the move to a basic income system even more attractive.

The RSA scheme would give a universal basic income for all resident citizens. EU nationals and nationals of European Economic Area countries living and working in the UK would receive it once they qualified for permanent residence after five years – this was before the Brexit vote – while other migrants would not be eligible. To be entitled to the basic income, all citizens aged 18 and over might be required to register to vote, as a means of strengthening engaged citizenship.

In addition to costing the hybrid basic income scheme mentioned above, Compass too has costed a basic income that would replace most means-tested welfare benefits.[19] Depending on the level of the basic income, and the combination of tax increases and cuts in existing benefits, the net cost ranged from an extra £43 billion a year to a saving of £53 billion. Both costings were based on the same adult basic income

CHAPTER 7

of £73.10 a week, £151.20 for those aged 65 and over and £44.30 for children up to age 18; the big saving in the second case resulted from abolition of the personal tax allowance, which was retained in the first case. Compass calculated that the basic rate of income tax would have to rise to 30 per cent, with a (single) higher rate of 50 per cent. Still, these rates are no higher than, or are well below, those levied, including by Conservative governments, prior to successive income tax-cutting budgets by the Thatcher government in the 1980s.

However, there would be a large number of low-income losers under this Compass scheme, mainly because the payment for children would not compensate for loss of other benefits. The authors took the view that introducing a full-blown basic income scheme in the UK that eliminated, or nearly eliminated, losers among the poorest 30–40 per cent would currently be politically impossible, costing £15–20 billion or about 1 per cent of GDP and requiring even bigger increases in tax rates.

The RSA, by contrast, attempts to minimize the number of low-income losers by redistributing resources to families with pre-school children, though it acknowledges that some households, notably lone parents with school-age children, could be worse off. However, the Compass authors did see a hybrid scheme as a realistic step towards a full basic income system at some point in the future.

All these simulations should be treated as illustrative. Nevertheless, they demonstrate that shifting to a basic income system could be made feasible and affordable. Even accepting the 'strict revenue neutrality' constraint, that a basic income should be funded from personal income taxes and offsetting savings in the welfare budget, increases in tax rates could be kept within reasonable bounds and losers at the lower end of the income spectrum minimized or compensated. Meanwhile, the vast majority in the bottom two deciles of the income distribution would gain, and there would be modest reductions in income inequality.

That said, if basic income could be financed in part from reductions in non-welfare spending programmes, including cuts in regressive subsidies and selective tax breaks, tax *rates* might not need to rise by much, if at all. And this does not take account of possible new sources of finance, such as a sovereign wealth fund, a carbon tax or a financial transactions tax.

Housing Costs

Most basic income calculations for the UK envisage needs-based supplements for disability, but have reluctantly concluded that housing costs would have to be treated separately, as the existing social security system does now. In his 1942 blueprint for the welfare state, Sir William Beveridge confessed himself unable to solve 'the problem of rent' in setting contributory benefit levels; paying a flat-rate allowance for housing would leave people in expensive areas unable to pay the rent while people in cheap areas would have money left over. Paying individual housing costs would give people an incentive to move to expensive accommodation on retirement, when they qualified for the state pension. In the end, the post-war government decided to meet actual housing costs but to means-test claimants needing supplements above national insurance benefits based on contribution records.

The 'problem of rent' is much worse today. In the early years of the welfare state, 60 per cent of the population lived in privately rented accommodation subject to strict rent controls, and an ambitious council house building programme was underway. Now, area differences in rents and house prices are much greater, rents in the private sector have soared, and the sale at a discount of council and social housing has resulted in a massive shortage of affordable homes. The cost of means-tested housing benefit has ballooned to some £25 billion a year.

While Britain's housing crisis needs to be tackled through urgent measures to boost affordable supply, it poses a difficulty here and now for the design of social protection systems. The basic income costings summarized above all assume continuation of the current means-tested housing benefit in broadly its present form, at least for the time being. The one saving grace is that, if the basic income is taken into account in the means test, fewer people will be dependent on this complex, administratively expensive and steeply tapered scheme.

The RSA has proposed (but not costed) three possible solutions to 'the problem of rent' that would be more compatible with basic income principles. One would be to limit the taper so that housing benefit recipients would 'pay' (in lost benefit and higher taxes) no more than the top marginal rate of tax if they earned extra income. A second would be to hand over all housing-related spending to local authorities, which could adapt policy on building, rents and benefits to local circumstances. The third would be to pay a 'basic rental income' to everyone who rents rather than owns a property, financed by a land value tax.

Of course, the UK housing situation is not unique. Other countries too face similar problems, especially the lack of affordable housing in the big cities and wide regional and urban/rural variations in housing costs. However, a number of northern European countries such as Germany, Sweden and France opted for more generous earnings-related social insurance benefits that enable most people to cover their rent. One comparative study showed that Britain ranked ninth out of ten countries when calculating housing benefit plus unemployment benefit and income support as a percentage of average income.[20] The 'problem of rent' may thus be less of a problem for the design of basic income schemes in other countries.

Affordability in Other Countries

As early as 1985, the Dutch Scientific Council for Government Policy proposed a partial basic income scheme, which it found to be eminently affordable. There have also been estimates of the fiscal cost of introducing a basic income in Belgium, Canada, France, Germany, Ireland, Spain and South Africa. In New Zealand, Gareth Morgan and Susan Guthrie concluded that a flat tax of 30 per cent was sufficient to pay a basic income for adults of NZ$11,000 per year, and a lower one of NZ$8,500 for youths aged 18–20.[21]

In the United States, Andy Stern has proposed that every American adult (234 million people) should receive a basic income of $1,000 a month, which is roughly the federal poverty line. He estimates the gross cost at $2.7 trillion a year, about 15 per cent of GDP. To pay for it, he would save $1 trillion a year by ending most existing anti-poverty programmes, including food stamps ($76 billion), housing assistance ($49 billion) and the Earned Income Tax Credit ($82 billion).[22] He would cut military spending and phase out most tax breaks, which cost $1.2 trillion a year. He also favours a federal sales tax, a financial transactions tax (which ten European Union member countries have in the works) and perhaps a wealth tax.

The affordability issue essentially comes down to two sets of choices – how high should the basic income or social dividend be, and what are society's fiscal priorities? There is nothing sacrosanct about existing tax systems, most of which are excessively complex and highly regressive. And this is without counting the enormous sums that are lost to government coffers through tax avoidance and evasion.

As one commentator pointed out, the Panama Papers showed that the US could afford a basic income because they revealed the extent to which the rich were avoiding tax.[23] The Tax Justice Network has estimated that the global elite has between $21 trillion and $32 trillion stashed in zero- or low-tax jurisdictions, depriving countries of $190 billion to $280 billion in revenues.[24] Meanwhile, they are receiving a lot of 'something for nothing', since they gain from public infrastructure and services, property rights conferred on them by government and international regulations, and so on. Separately, the International Monetary Fund (IMF) reckons that the shifting of profits to tax havens by multinationals has led to lost government revenues of $600 billion a year.

A PROFESSOR'S TEASER

Here is an interesting teaser from Harvard economics professor Greg Mankiw, in a blog post entitled 'A quick note on a universal basic income'.[25]

Consider an economy in which average income is $50,000 but with much income inequality. To provide a social safety net, two possible policies are proposed. Which would you prefer?

— A universal transfer of $10,000 to every person, financed by a 20-percent flat tax on income.
— A means-tested transfer of $10,000. The full amount goes to someone without any income. The transfer is then phased out: You lose 20 cents of it for every dollar of income you earn. These transfers are financed by a tax of 20 percent on income above $50,000.

I have seen smart people argue as follows: Policy A is crazy. Why should Bill Gates get a government transfer? He doesn't need it, and we would need to raise more taxes to pay for it. Policy B is more progressive. It targets the transfer to those who really need it, and the transfer is financed by a smaller tax increase levied only on those with above-average incomes.

But here is the rub. The two policies are equivalent. If you look at the net payment (taxes less transfers), everyone is exactly the same under the two plans. The difference is only a matter of framing.

The professor's argument is logically sound, although in practice the two policies are not equivalent. Means testing necessarily involves administrative costs for the state, and personal costs for the claimants, that reduce the value of any payment below its nominal value. Means-tested benefits are also uncertain and unstable, because the earned income on which they are based is uncertain and unstable. So, while the exchequer cost of the two policies may be equivalent, the value to recipients is not. All the more reason to go for the non-means-tested universal payment and claw it back from higher earners through the tax system.

Dynamic and Feedback Effects

A fundamental drawback of both back-of-the-envelope exercises and simulation models is their essentially static approach, ignoring the potential *dynamic* effects of basic income on economic activity. For instance, as noted earlier, a basic income would remove the disincentive posed by poverty and precarity traps to take low-wage jobs, increase hours of paid labour or push for higher pay. This 'moral hazard' (discouraging people from doing what they would otherwise wish to do) has a treble cost: the continuation of dependence on low state benefits, the economic output foregone, and the loss of tax and national (social) insurance contributions that would flow into national coffers.

The current means-tested system also creates a huge immoral hazard, tempting people in and around the precariat to enter the black economy, thereby avoiding tax and national insurance contributions altogether. Since a basic income would not be lost when people took jobs, there would be less incentive to conceal extra earnings, again producing additional tax revenues. The economic benefits from increased activity, and higher tax revenues generated by a dramatic reduction in the implicit marginal tax rate for low-income earners, could be expected to more than outweigh any adverse impact (if indeed there was one, which is doubtful) from moderate increases in tax for higher-income earners. A study by the London School of Economics Centre for Economic Performance concluded: 'Theory and evidence both show that the level of work of high-paid employees hardly responds to changes in tax rates.'[26]

Then there are other feedback effects, as noted in Chapter 5. A basic income leads to better mental and physical health, lowering demands on health and social services. This should produce cost savings, releasing more funds for basic income or improved services.

Other Sources of Finance

A widely held and appealing idea is to help fund a basic income through the proceeds of a carbon tax to discourage emissions of greenhouse gases that cause climate change.[27] Calculations for the US by the Citizens' Climate Lobby suggest that a $15 per ton carbon tax could raise $117 billion a year, which, after various adjustments, could finance a yearly dividend of $811 per household ($323 per person).[28] A majority of households would gain (the dividend would outweigh price increases due to the carbon tax) and the impact would be highly progressive, with low-income households gaining proportionately more. High-income households would lose on average but relative to income the losses would be negligible.

A more traditional proposal is a land value tax. Thomas Paine envisaged funding for his scheme coming from a 'ground rent' charged to property owners. Henry George campaigned for a land rent levy to finance a basic income. Land taxes would be progressive, since land ownership is broadly in line with income and wealth. And in principle they could raise large sums. According to estimates cited by *The Economist*, a land value tax of 5 per cent charged on all US land would raise over $1 trillion, enough to pay every American $3,500 a year.[29] This is an attractive idea, especially since property taxes in most countries are a mess, often regressive and in need of reform. But the political difficulties of introducing such a tax would be considerable.

Wealth taxes, inheritance taxes, a tax on financial transactions and a tax on robots have all been mentioned as possible sources of finance for a basic income. Another suggestion is for Google, Facebook and other corporations to pay for the data users now provide for free, from which they make the bulk of their profits, which could then be shared out as a basic income.[30]

In Denmark, an ingenious funding mechanism has been proposed by the SamfundsTanken (The Society Thought Think-Tank) run by Soren Ekelund, a venture capitalist.[31] This could be called a 'social venture fund' approach. The local council would offer to pay part of employee wages as a basic income (which would also be paid to those without jobs) if firms agree to a profit-sharing deal with the council. This would boost profits (because the firm would pay out less in wages), which (through the profit-sharing arrangement) would generate funds for the council to finance the basic income. It is a complex scheme, but is illustrative of the ingenuity that could shape a new system.

Sovereign Wealth Funds and Social Dividends

The financing option favoured by this writer would be to fund a basic income from the construction of sovereign wealth funds, along the lines of the Alaska Permanent Fund or the Norwegian Pension Fund. This option, which draws on the work of Nobel Prize winner James Meade in his book *Agathatopia*, would allow a country to build up the fund over the years and raise the amount paid out as basic income, or social dividend, as the fund developed.[32] Viewed as a rightful share of income flowing from our collective wealth, the social dividend approach is politically attractive since it would not require either dismantling existing welfare systems or raising taxes on earned income.

The Alaska Permanent Fund was pioneered by Jay Hammond after he was elected Republican governor of the US state of Alaska in 1974. Set up in 1976, it receives one-eighth of state revenues from oil production. The payment of universal 'dividends' from the fund to all legal residents of Alaska finally started in 1982. This model has long appealed to advocates of basic income within the BIEN community and can be regarded as a nascent fund for payment of either basic capital grants or basic incomes.[33]

Others favouring a sovereign wealth fund approach

include Peter Barnes, who has suggested a 'Sky Trust' modelled on the Alaska Fund that would be financed by charging fees to companies for using 'universal assets'. These would include both natural assets (air, water, minerals and other resources) and socially built assets, such as the intellectual property regime and the legal and financial infrastructure. Barnes estimates that charges on universal assets, including pollution taxes, taxes on extraction of natural resources, fees for use of electromagnetic spectrum, a tax on financial transactions and a levy on royalties and licence fees from intellectual property, could finance a dividend of $5,000 per person per year across the United States.[34]

In the UK, Stewart Lansley has suggested paying a basic income from a 'social wealth fund' financed by a charge on share ownership.[35] He calculates that a 0.5 per cent annual levy on ownership of shares in the top 100 companies quoted on the UK stock market would raise over £8 billion, while a 1 per cent levy would raise twice that. More than half these sums would be a charge on overseas owners.[36] This writer has proposed a levy on rental income from private ownership and exploitation of all types of property – physical, financial and intellectual – that would be used to build the fund.[37]

The governance structure would need to be democratic and run on ethical principles, ensuring inter-generational equity by making the fund sustainable long after revenue sources have been depleted. The importance of ethical governance, exemplified by the Norwegian Pension Fund, is highlighted by a deplorable UK government proposal in 2016 to set up a Shale Wealth Fund.[38] The fund would receive up to 10 per cent of the revenue generated by fracking (hydraulic fracturing) for shale gas, which could amount to as much as £1 billion over twenty-five years. This would be paid out to communities hosting fracking sites, which could decide to use the money for local projects or distribute it to households in cash.

It is hard to avoid the conclusion that this is a bribe to secure local approval of environmentally threatening fracking operations, to which there has been considerable public opposition. Beyond that, there are many equity questions. Why should only people who happen to live in areas with shale gas be beneficiaries? How would the recipient community be defined? Would the payments go only to those living in the designated community at the time the fracking started? Would they be paid as lump sums or on a regular basis, and how long would they last? What about future generations? Can cash payments compensate for the risk of harm to the air, water, landscape and livelihoods?

All these questions cast doubt on the equity and ethics of any selective scheme. They underline the need for the principles of wealth funds and dividends from them to be established before they are implemented, and for a governance structure that is independent from government and business. But provided these conditions are fulfilled, this route constitutes a proven and viable way to help finance basic income or social dividends. Not to develop sovereign wealth funds, or to use them for opportunistic and regressive political purposes, would be another road not taken.

Affordability Is Political

The affordability criticism is superficially appealing to those who wish to oppose a basic income. But ultimately, the issue is a political one. Tax rates in industrialized countries are historically very low, and there is no reason to think they are at an optimal level. In addition, selective tax breaks and the very extensive range of regressive subsidies given out by governments and supra-national bodies are vast and mostly unjustifiable, morally or economically.

At the same time, the existing welfare system is complex, inefficient, morally dubious and very expensive. In many countries poverty is increasing. And inequality is rising rapidly, with an extraordinary growth in the rental income going to elites, plutocrats and plutocratic corporations.[39] A large part, or even all, of the funds for a basic income could come from obtaining for society enough of this huge rental income that comes simply from ownership of income-yielding property of all kinds. Those who claim that a basic income could only be afforded by slashing social services or sharply raising income tax rates are misleading, deliberately or naively.

In the end, the issue of affordability comes down to the priority society gives to social justice, republican freedom and economic security. In those terms, not only is a basic income affordable; we cannot afford *not* to afford it.

The Implications for Work and Labour

'Obviously any program that provides income without linking it to work will discourage work to some extent.'

MICHAEL TANNER, CATO INSTITUTE, 2015[1]

Is it so obvious? A remarkable number of commentators and social scientists lose their common sense when it comes to talking or writing about work. While every age throughout history has drawn arbitrary distinctions between what counts as work and what does not, ours may be the most perverse.

Only in the twentieth century did most work that was not paid labour become non-work. Labour statistics persist in this travesty. 'Work' is counted only if it is for pay, in the marketplace. A century ago, Pigou famously pointed out that if he hired a housekeeper, national income went up, economic growth increased, employment rose and unemployment fell. If he subsequently married her, and she continued to do precisely the same activities, national income and growth went down, employment fell and unemployment rose. This is absurd (and sexist).

The absurdity continues today. A parent who looks after their own child is doing just as much 'work' as someone who is paid to look after the child of another (and is probably more 'productive' as well). And the growing 'gig' economy offers many more examples of activities that are treated differently depending on whether they are paid. For instance, dog-owners can use an app, BorrowMyDoggy, to hire some-one to walk their dog or to 'dog-sit'. For statistical purposes, a recreational pursuit, dog walking, becomes 'work', walking someone else's dog. This increases national income and employment, to the delight of governments. By walking your own dog (or looking after your own child), you are doing a disservice to the economy!

Meanwhile, the amount of other, very real but unpaid work is extensive and rising. In the UK – and it is similar in other countries – the unremunerated economy (caring for children and the elderly, housework, voluntary work in the community and so on) is estimated to be worth well over half the size of the money economy.[2]

Even these estimates do not count the 'work' we all do in our dealings with government (filing tax returns scarcely counts as 'leisure'), as consumers (self-service checkouts) and in what I have called 'work-for-labour', unpaid work around jobs or job seeking, which has expanded with 'always on' connectivity. The precariat in particular must do a lot of work (in their eyes) that is not counted or remuner-ated – hunting for jobs, enduring complex time-consuming recruitment processes, waiting for on-call labour, queuing and form-filling for meagre benefits of some kind.

This is relevant to assessing the actual and potential impact of basic income on work and labour. A common claim is that paying people a basic income would lead to 'laziness' and – which is not the same – a lower supply of labour. In that context, there has been a seemingly interminable philo-sophical debate about whether 'lazy' people should receive a basic income. The classic image is a young man surfing the waves off Malibu. Yet it is doubtful whether this young man could rely on what would be a modest basic income to develop a good life that would allow him to continue surfing for very long.

Most people would want to earn more if they could. And if a few individuals chose to surf all day and live on the basic income alone, it would cost the state vastly more to chase them up and force them to do 'work' of some kind. Moreover, many of the greatest minds and greatest artists were 'idle' in their youth, sometimes enabled to be 'idle' by the 'basic income' provided by or inherited from well-to-do parents. Had they been forced into workfare or some tedious job, their creative genius might have been lost to us.

My contention is that a basic income would *increase* both the amount and the productivity of 'work', and could also increase the quality of 'leisure', in the ancient Greek sense of *schole*. This term, from which the English word 'school' is derived, meant being free from the necessity to labour, which Aristotle argued was a necessary condition for full participation in cultural and political life. That aside, would it be so bad – socially, economically and ecologically – if some people took advantage of a basic income to reduce the amount of labour and/or work?

Long hours of labour are not necessarily conducive to productivity, quality of output or service, or decision making; indeed, there is plenty of evidence that long hours are counterproductive, as well as damaging to health.[3] I would like my dentist or surgeon to be fresh and rested. This applies to more mundane activities as well.

In addition, if a basic income did reduce the amount of

labour supplied, the group most likely to do so would be those with relatively low potential productivity and earning power. The loss to the economy, if any, would thus be small. The debate should also be put in the context of concerns about a 'workless' future, discussed in Chapter 5. Exaggerated or not, the predictions of the technological pessimists would relegate to the margins any likely change in labour supply due to basic income.

Tertiary Time

We have been moving away from societies and production systems based on 'agrarian time', where patterns of labour and work are dictated by the seasons, weather and light, or on 'industrial time', where labour is dictated by the clock and measured in blocks of time. Under 'industrial time', it made sense to think that labour involved clocking in and out for eight or nine hours a day for five or six days a week, for forty or more years, followed by a block of retirement, if lucky.

The twenty-first century will be dominated by what should be called 'tertiary time', in which activities labelled 'work' and 'labour' blur into each other, being done on and off formal workplaces and in and outside designated working time. This blurring makes the measurement of labour increasingly arbitrary and misleading – which makes the measurement of wage rates increasingly arbitrary as well.

People will be paid by firms, employment agencies or labour brokers for only part of the work they do. For most of us, the ratio of work (unpaid) to labour (paid) will probably rise. Those benefiting from this unpaid work are in effect gaining rental income from a much enlarged form of exploitation.

This provides another justification for a basic income, paid to everybody to compensate for the work they do that is fundamentally social in character, and financed from the rental income of the individuals and firms that derive the benefit. They may have no intention to exploit in this way; it is just impossible to measure and properly remunerate all the work-for-labour that tertiary time entails.

Would a Basic Income Reduce or Increase Work?

Before coming to the empirical evidence, the first thing to say is that today's means testing and behaviour testing for entitlement to state benefits create very strong disincentives to taking low-wage jobs. Critics who claim that a basic income would reduce 'work' (by which they mean paid labour) rarely acknowledge the extent to which current schemes do so.

Yet it is intuitively obvious that someone is more likely to take a job if assured of keeping, say, 68p of every pound earned, as would be the case with a basic income, than if they received only 20p, the current situation in Britain (especially since that 20p could easily be eaten up by the extra costs of having a job – transport, childcare, suitable clothes and so on). And someone obliged to work for a gain of just 20p in the pound might be more inclined to do the job shoddily or resentfully.

If incentives matter, the basic income route is surely to be preferred. A basic income would overcome the poverty trap that results from withdrawal of means-tested benefits, as well as the associated precarity trap that in part reflects fears of being unable to recover access to benefits if needed. It would thus encourage people with low skills to enter the labour market, and to enter the legal part of the labour market rather than the black economy. It would also enable people to take part-time jobs without fear of losing benefits, which would be especially helpful for people with care responsibilities or those with disabilities unable to commit to full-time jobs.

Turning to the empirical evidence, many critics base their claim that a basic income would reduce 'work' on a series of local US experiments in six states conducted between 1968 and 1980, plus the well-known Mincome experiment in Canada in the 1970s. In fact, these were negative income tax experiments that gave people on low incomes something close to a basic income. Standard labour force data were gathered, which led economists such as Gary Burtless to conclude that the basic income led to a modest reduction in work.[4]

However, these data, which have been the subject of an extraordinary volume of econometric analysis, referred only to paid employment or to job seeking, not to the many other forms of work. Someone working fewer hours in a job to spend that time looking after a child or elderly relative was automatically adjudged to have reduced their 'work'. Moreover, as Burtless admitted, a negative income tax rewards the under-reporting of labour and earnings because the lower the declared earnings the higher the income supplement. This 'immoral hazard' means the perceived reduction in labour supply may have been spurious.

The conceptual defect of these analyses aside, it is noteworthy that the measured effects were small. One excellent review of as many of the studies as he could locate, several hundred of them, led Karl Widerquist to conclude that the impact on labour supply was mostly statistically insignificant or so small as to be of no serious concern to policymakers.[5] Yet the studies have been extensively cited as showing a reduction in work.[6]

At best, they showed small cuts in paid labour for some groups, notably mothers with young children and teenagers still at school. In the Canadian Mincome experiment, 'mothers with newborns stopped working because they wanted to stay home longer with their babies, and teenagers worked less because they weren't under as much pressure to support their families, which resulted in more teenagers graduating'.[7]

Similarly, the US experiments found that people took the opportunity to better their lives, including studying for a degree and setting themselves up in business. There were double-digit increases in high-school graduation rates in New Jersey, Seattle and Denver.[8] As Michael Howard, a long-standing basic income advocate, has pointed out, 'People withdrew from the labour market, but the kind of labour market withdrawal you got was the kind you would welcome.'[9] One could say they switched from labour to work. Does this sound like reducing work, let alone being a bad outcome?

In two experiments the main apparent change was a slight increase in the length of time some people spent unemployed.

However, this should not be interpreted as 'laziness'; it might have had a beneficial longer-term effect in enabling them to find a job better suited to their needs and capabilities.

Others who assert that a basic income would reduce work have relied on intuition and/or have taken a moralistic view – the 'something for nothing' argument. As one commentator put it, 'Giving someone a material compensation without something of value produced in exchange is questionable from economic, social and ethical standpoints.'[10] Yet this is to assume that only labour in the marketplace has value, which is clearly nonsense. All forms of 'work' have value, even if it is hard or impossible to put a figure on it.

Some critics go further than simply arguing that a basic income would reduce labour and work. The French Catholic neo-conservative Pascal-Emmanuel Gobry has conjured a vision of a future dystopia in which basic income leads to millions of people 'listing away in socially destructive idleness' with 'the consequences of this lost productivity reverberating throughout the society in lower growth and, probably, lower employment.'[11] There is no evidence to support any such assertion. It is an insult to the human condition. We want to improve our lives if we can, rather than live on a bare minimum.

Barbara Bergmann is another who has claimed that a basic income, at a 'comfortable' level, would 'dis-incentivise work'. Then, she argues, a reduction in the labour supply would reduce tax revenues, leading governments to raise tax rates, so discouraging paid work further.[12] Again, there is no evidence to support this view.

Opinion polls in a number of countries have found that

when people are asked if they would reduce work and labour if they had a basic income, the overwhelming majority say they would not. However, when asked if other people would reduce work and labour, they tend to say others would. Other people are lazy, but not me! There is also a presumption on the part of critics that people on low incomes will reduce labour and work in response to a basic income, whereas they presume no such thing for richer people. After all, billionaires such as Bill Gates, Warren Buffett and Mark Zuckerberg still work, though they certainly do not need the income!

Billionaires aside, a 1999 study of lottery winners showed that all had continued (or wished to continue) work of some kind. However, only a small minority were still in the jobs they had before. Instead, most were doing work, both paid and unpaid, that they enjoyed. And in a series of studies that asked people what they would do if they won the lottery, a clear majority said they would go on working but not necessarily in their present jobs.[13] Whether they preferred to continue what they were doing depended, not surprisingly, on how much they liked their jobs independently of the money they were earning. People in the professions and the 'salariat' were far more likely to say they would continue in the same job or occupation than those lower down the social scale, who could be presumed to have more boring or unpleasant jobs and expressed lower job satisfaction.

A poll ahead of the June 2016 referendum on basic income in Switzerland asked people if they would cease their economic activity if a basic income were in place.[14] Only 2 per cent said they would, in the context of a suggested basic income of 2,500 Swiss francs per person – which most people would regard as 'comfortable'. However, a third thought others would! Over half said that if they had a basic income they would take the opportunity to obtain training, and over a fifth said they would try to go independent. Forty per cent said they would do some or more voluntary work, and 53 per cent said they would spend more time with family. Basic income is not about giving people money to do nothing, but giving them an opportunity to do what they wish and are able to do.

It should also not be forgotten that even if some people reduced their labour supply in response to a basic income, others could be expected to increase it. There has been a tendency to focus exclusively on the alleged negative effects.

This leads to the less-considered claim by advocates that basic income would tend to increase the amount and *quality* of work. There is cross-national psychological evidence to support this view.[15] In a series of experiments, it was found that people with basic security tended to work more, not less. They were also more cooperative, which suggested that the work group would be more productive. Having basic security gives people greater confidence, energy and trust in others to work more and better.

Such effects are likely to be particularly strong in low-income communities. Thus, in the Namibian basic income pilot discussed later, overall economic activity rose after the basic incomes started.[16] In the larger pilots in Madhya Pradesh, work and labour among adults increased, particularly in the case of women; this was largely because many recipients started secondary economic activities, mostly on an own-account basis.[17] School-age children were the only group where labour declined. Some shifted to full-time schooling and some to schooling combined with helping in a family farm or business, two types of work that disrupted their studies less than the old pattern of casual wage labour.

These findings may be dismissed by those only concerned with what would happen in rich industrialized countries. But the behavioural responses are likely to be similar. People usually want to improve their lives from the position they are now in. If you can say that about yourself, would you not expect that to apply to others?

Work and Labour in the Precariat

An important theme in the debate on basic income is the breakdown of the twentieth-century income distribution system linking incomes and state benefits to the performance of labour, with roughly stable shares of national income going to labour and capital. Today, increasing numbers of people cannot obtain an adequate income from the work and labour they are required or expected to do, however hard and long they work.[18] Globalization, technological change and 'flexible' labour markets mean that real wages in industrialized countries, on average, will stagnate for the foreseeable future, leaving many in the precariat permanently trapped in the low pay/benefit nexus.

Some critics of basic income contend that labour's share of national income has fallen only in countries where unions are weak and that, if they were strengthened, wages and worker living standards would rise.[19] The trouble with that argument is that the labour share of national income has fallen even where unions and collective bargaining systems have remained relatively strong, as in Austria.

A basic income would underpin the total income gained by the precariat. It would also enable those on low incomes to do odd jobs for other low-income people for a modest amount. At present, potential suppliers of labour cannot afford to work for a small sum, especially if they risk losing means-tested benefits, while potential clients cannot afford to pay the worker the going rate. A basic income would facilitate low-income trades and help take them out of the black economy.

The Sexual Division of Labour and Work

One controversial aspect of basic income has been the effect on the work patterns of men and women. Some critics such as Ingrid Robeyns have claimed that it would strengthen the traditional dualism by which women are 'relegated' to domestic work.[20] But there is no reason to think this would be the case. If women had their own basic income, they would have greater economic security and be in a better position to decide their own mix of work and labour. Thus Carole Pateman has argued that a basic income would reduce the sexual division of labour, as have Ailsa McKay, Anne Alstott, Kathi Weeks and others.[21]

It cannot be presumed that an individual basic income paid separately to women and to men would overcome the many gender inequalities within households or families. But it would surely help. All countries at present assess social protection needs with reference to households rather than individuals. This ignores gender inequality within households that can restrict women's access to money, even if the household is 'well-off' on paper.

Women's need for independent access to money as a basic protection, no matter how wealthy their partners might be, has been pointed out time and again over the past forty years by the movement against domestic violence and rape. One of the strongest findings from the negative income tax experiments in the United States was that the payments gave some women the means to end abusive relationships and become independent. (Ironically, a steep apparent increase in marital break-ups in two of the experiments – later shown to be a statistical error – was a major factor in killing political support for guaranteed income in the US.)

The assessment of household-based benefits also involves a high level of state intrusion into people's personal lives. In Britain, women members of claimants unions active in the 1970s demanded that welfare be paid on an individual basis (and also called for a basic income) to stop the state 'rifling through their drawers'.[22]

A basic income paid to everybody would enable caregivers, mostly women, to replace their own work with paid labour if they wished, and would enable 'care-recipients' relying on the gift work of relatives to purchase care labour services. In Brazil, the *bolsa família* cash transfer scheme has boosted women's economic activity outside the home by helping to pay for childcare and fares for public transport. In many developing countries, a basic income would also increase women's ability to claim equal priority for healthcare, counteracting the tendency to give priority to 'the breadwinner'. Better healthcare would enable women to do more work and, if they chose, more paid labour, simply because they would have less ill-health. This is another instance of a basic income not 'obviously' diminishing the incentive to work.

One form of labour that basic income would likely reduce is prostitution or sex service work. Of course, trafficking and forced prostitution should be punished. But outlawing or penalizing sex service work per se is illiberal and counter-productive. Criminalizing either side of the arrangement is a recipe for worse forms of exploitation and for driving such activity underground. However, a basic income would strengthen sex workers' bargaining situation and be an emancipatory way of helping those wanting to escape such work to do so.

Finally, in response to the claim that a basic income would involve no 'reciprocity', giving income for nothing in return, a legitimate feminist retort would be that, traditionally, men have been free-riders on unpaid domestic work done mostly by women. A basic income would be justified to compensate for this work.[23] Once again, the structured unfairness reflects the arbitrary prioritization of paid labour over unpaid work. A basic income would help to rectify this lack of reciprocity, even more so if it involved a slight 'tax' on wage income to compensate for work that is not paid.

The 'Right' to Work

It has long been contended that there is a 'right to work'. Is there such a right? And if so, how would a basic income affect it? The first step in answering these questions is to clarify what a 'right to work' means. Rights are about advancing and defending human freedom, and by definition are universal and inalienable. And if something is a right there is a corresponding duty (normally of governments) to ensure that the right is upheld or to work towards that goal. It follows that a 'right' has to be something that can, at least in principle, be delivered.

What is it that proponents of a 'right to work' think should be delivered? By 'work' they usually mean paid jobs in subordinated employment. Yet a 'right' to labour for an employer is scarcely freedom-enhancing. It is more like an obligation. A right to work only makes sense if interpreted to mean a right to a freedom to develop one's creative, productive and 'reproductive' capacities. And a right to work in this sense can be honoured only if an individual has a prior right to a basic income, because only a basic income can give to everybody the freedom and security to develop their talents and do the mix of work, paid and unpaid, that they wish.

The evolution of the notion of the right to work is instructive. Asserted by the utopian socialist Charles Fourier in the early nineteenth century, the 'right to work' was subsequently dismissed by Karl Marx, who commented that under capitalism it was 'an absurdity, a miserable pious wish'. Later, Pope Leo XIII enshrined the right to work in his famous encyclical *Rerum Novarum* (On the Conditions of Labour) of 1891. Issued at a time of growing worker discontent all over Europe, and the associated rise of international socialism, it was a paternalistic response to the ills of unbridled capitalism that counter-balanced the 'right to work' with a series of duties workers owed to their employers.

In the twentieth century, the idea of a 'right to work' soon became entangled with an alleged 'duty to labour'. This reached its apotheosis in the Soviet Union but was echoed in the West by Pope Pius XII's nonsensical statement in 1941 that labour was both a right and a duty of everybody. The elision of 'right' and 'duty' continues today with arguments for 'no rights without responsibilities' and 'reciprocity', by which is meant the duty of people receiving benefits to do or seek labour in return. This negates the very idea of a right since a right cannot be conditioned on reciprocity.

After the Second World War, the 'right' was formalized in Article 23 of the *Universal Declaration of Human Rights* of 1948, as follows: 'Everyone has the right to work, to free choice of employment, to just and favourable conditions of work and to protection against unemployment.' This commitment coincided with a sudden faith in the ability, and thus duty, of governments to create 'full employment' (which really meant 'full employment' of men).

The International Labour Organization went a step further in its *Employment Policy Convention No.122* of 1964. Although the Convention did not include an obligation on governments to commit to a 'right to work' in those words, it was subsequently interpreted that way. In 1983, the ILO's Employment Committee said: 'The promotion of full, productive and freely chosen employment provided for in the Employment Policy Convention and Recommendation, 1964, should be regarded as the means of achieving in practice the realization of the right to work.'

At the highest international level, therefore, employment and work were treated as synonymous. Nor was the distinction recognized by the Soviet Union, with its rigid doctrine about everybody's obligation to labour, or by social democratic or labour parties, with their adherence to labour values, or by the Catholic Church, with its paternalistic approach to poverty.

Once faith in Keynesian macroeconomic tools and social democratic social policies began to crumble, from the second half of the 1960s onwards, the 'right to work' tended to be treated with more circumspection. The United Nations' 1966 *International Covenant on Economic, Social and Cultural Rights* was more detailed and nuanced than the 1948 Declaration, stating: 'The States Parties to the Covenant recognize the right to work, which includes the right of everyone to the opportunity to gain his living by work, which he freely chooses or accepts, and will take appropriate steps to safeguard his rights.'

The Catholic Church too modified its pronouncements. In 1981 Pope John Paul II had issued the encyclical *Laborem Exercens* (Performing Work), which reiterated the confusing claim by Pope John XXIII in 1963 that there was a 'natural right' of employment. However, the muddle arising from equating employment with work was recognized in *Centesimus Annus* (Hundredth Year), produced in 1991 to celebrate the centenary of *Rerum Novarum*.

While *Centesimus Annus* supported the use of labour market policies to curb unemployment, it held back from advocating a right to employment, concluding that 'the state could not directly ensure the right to work of all its citizens unless it controlled every aspect of economic life and restricted the free initiative of individuals'. And if the state could not guarantee the right to work, then who or what could? The encyclical rightly baulked at the absurd idea that private employers themselves should have a duty to provide jobs.

In 2004, an international group including representatives of relevant United Nations bodies (and including the present writer) drew up a *Charter of Emerging Human Rights*,[24] which embraced the idea of work in all its forms and rejected the notion of a duty to labour. The Charter declared support for a right to existence, under conditions of dignity, comprising rights to security of life, to personal integrity, to a basic income, to healthcare, to education, to a worthy death and to *work*, defined as:

> The right to work, in any of its forms, remunerated or not, which covers the right to exercise a worthy activity guaranteeing quality of life. All persons have the right to the fruits of their activity and to intellectual property, under the conditions of respect for the general interests of the community.

It is surely only in this sense that the 'right to work' has meaning. Everyone, irrespective of gender, ethnicity, caste, religion or sexual orientation, should have the right to exercise a 'worthy activity' of their choosing and should not be prevented by arbitrary barriers (such as onerous and unnecessary licensing requirements) from practising what they are qualified to do and wish to do.[25] Far from being in conflict with the right to work, as some have argued, a basic income is a necessary underpinning. Apart from giving people the means to develop their capacities, a basic income would enable them to refuse jobs they do not wish to do. Ultimately, the right to work must include a right not to work. A desperately insecure person can have no such right.

Participation Income

Ever since debates on poverty and basic income began, some have argued that income support should be conditional on 'making a contribution to society'. The late Tony Atkinson was a longstanding proponent of a 'participation income',[26] while something similar was proposed earlier by André Gorz.[27] In his recent writings, Atkinson proposed that everybody should receive a basic income, but that in return they should do at least thirty-five hours of 'recognized' work activity per week.

The obligation might look fair, but in practice would not be. The condition would not affect those already in full-time jobs and earning a good income, whereas for others who could only do or obtain jobs involving hard manual labour or paying very low wages, the obligation would be arduous, costly and difficult to maintain. The condition would also distort the labour market, pushing wages down at the lower end by increasing the supply of labour, and so impoverishing others who would have done nothing to 'deserve' it. That too would be unfair.

The administrative costs of monitoring such a scheme would be enormous, unless it were treated as merely a gesture to gain popular approval and not enforced. And it would leave awkward questions about what activities would count and how they would be counted. Would caring for a frail grandmother count as recognized work? If so, how would the bureaucratic official determine whether someone was caring for her or watching a football match on TV? Would a report from the person receiving the care be required to vouch for it?

The scope for gaming the system would be considerable, as would the scope for discretionary judgements by bureaucrats. Even if recognized work activity were limited to voluntary social work, subjective judgements would proliferate. Would a supervisor want to alienate those doing voluntary work by reporting a person for doing only twenty-five hours rather than thirty-five? In practice, a participation income scheme would be a recipe for multiplying petty unfairness. And, as noted earlier, a right is not a right if it is conditioned on 'reciprocity', in whatever form.

The Royal Society of Arts, in its suggested basic income scheme, also proposed a 'contribution contract' for recipients aged eighteen to twenty-five.[28] Under the non-binding contract, made with friends, family and community, they would agree to contribute in some way in return for the basic income. There would be no monitoring by government, and no sanctions would be threatened if the contracts were not honoured. Such contracts would probably do no harm and might help in the political legitimation of a basic income. But a few people might complain that their nephew or neighbour was not honouring the contract, blotting their character without due process. The idea is best forgotten.

In Praise of More Idleness

'I meant to do my work today –
But a brown bird sang in the apple tree,
And a butterfly flitted across the field,
And all the leaves were calling me.'

'I MEANT TO DO MY WORK TODAY',
RICHARD LE GALLIENNE (1866–1947)

Contrary to the preaching of dour labourists, there is nothing intrinsically wrong with a bit of laziness. Great philosophers through the ages have argued in its favour. Aristotle explicitly recognized the necessity of *aergia*, laziness, for contemplative thought. Bertrand Russell wrote a celebrated essay, *In Praise of Idleness*. Paul Lafargue, Karl Marx's son-in-law, authored a subversive book entitled *The Right to be Lazy* that communists detested because it made the case against forcing everybody to labour more intensively. Today, however, the words 'idleness' and 'lazy' are used pejoratively to convey indolence, time wasting and drift.

What is wrong with idleness? In modern society, more than ever, we need to slow down and recall the wisdom of Cato when he said, 'Never is a man more active than when he does nothing.' We are in danger of losing the capacity to reflect, to deliberate, to ponder, even to communicate and to learn in the true sense of that term.

Many great historical figures, from Galileo to Adam Smith, made their contribution to civilization precisely because they were 'idle' in the conventional economic sense.[29] Charles

Darwin admitted that he was able to embark on his epic voyage on HMS *Beagle* because he came from a wealthy family whereby he had 'ample leisure from not having to earn my own bread'. René Descartes said that his breakthroughs that helped revolutionize western philosophy and mathematics were possible only because he 'had no feeling, thank God, that my circumstances obliged me to make science my profession so as to ease my financial condition'. Of course, what they did should be called 'work', but our labour statistics would have treated their unremunerated endeavours as idleness.

In most cases, the later achievements of these 'gentlemen of leisure' could not have been predicted. This argues for everybody to have freedom to be idle if they wish. If they have the energy and the talent, their subsequent contribution will be greater. If they do not, there will be little loss to society and the economy.

For example, many people do sport for fun and recreation. Some people are paid handsomely for the same activities, because they are 'good' at them. There is a demand for their skills and a market for them. However, it would seem unfair to give public money to selected individuals to do something that they *might* become 'good' at, ignoring the many others whose potential is unknown. Yet this is what the British government does when it uses National Lottery money to fund potential Olympic champions. In effect, it gives them a basic income enabling them to spend as much time as possible on their chosen sport.[30]

Why not give to others as well (potential winners or not)? Why should other people not have the financial security to develop their capabilities, whatever they might be? The

Olympic funding policy recognizes that people need basic security to develop their talents, potential and vocation. But the policy should apply to everybody equally, which is precisely what a basic income would do.

This brief reflection on laziness ends with a caveat. Advocates of a basic income would be making a political and intellectual mistake if they said it would give everybody a 'right to be lazy', implying a life of indolence. It is more attractive to see a basic income as facilitating a slowing down – a slow-time movement – and a greater control over time, in which some periods of idleness figure without embarrassment, condemnation or punitive sanctions.

Creative and Reproductive Work

A basic income would allow more people, and not only the well-to-do, to pursue their passions. This would not only be personally satisfying but could yield big dividends for society, through the encouragement of entrepreneurship, through creative endeavour and through socially valuable pursuits at all levels. As John O'Farrell has written,

> Anyone who ever created anything did so with a modicum of financial security behind them. That's why Virginia Woolf needed 'a room of her own and £500 a year'. For centuries we have tapped the potential of only a small proportion of the British people; the rest have been powerless to initiate or discover where their true talents lay.[31]

Our societies need people to have more leisure, not only for personal downtime, but for strengthening ties with family and friends and taking part in civic and political life. Unpaid work, from running parent-teacher associations to visiting the elderly, is essential for communities to function and flourish. Yet involvement in voluntary organizations of all kinds has declined almost everywhere, in the US largely (though not wholly) reflecting the increased labour force participation of women who formerly were the main drivers of volunteer bodies.[32] A basic income would also enable people to take time for political involvement and debate, helping to restore 'deliberative democracy' now sorely lacking in most countries.

Shifting to 'reproductive' work such as caring for relatives or work in the community could be expected to have beneficial environmental effects, because it would mean a shift to resource-conserving activities away from resource-depleting ones. Shorter working hours in jobs are correlated with smaller ecological footprints.[33] And basic income would allow people to reject or spend less time on what David Graeber calls 'bullshit' jobs that they find hateful or meaningless.[34]

As mentioned in Chapter 2, basic income would also make it easier for governments to impose carbon taxes and other environmental measures designed to curb pollution and mitigate climate change, by compensating people for the extra costs of the goods and services affected or for livelihoods lost or disrupted. Some supporters of the 'degrowth' movement see basic income as an integral part of an economic reordering alongside other policies to promote 'prosperity without growth', at least in the way it is conventionally measured.[35] By making income less dependent on employment, basic income would encourage people to question the drive for jobs at any cost and encourage a rethink on the relationship between jobs, production and consumption.

Disability and Capacity-to-work Tests

Left to last because of their inherent folly are behavioural 'work' tests that are increasingly part of conventional social security systems. Governments are faced with the reality that many people have 'disabilities' or 'impairments' that prevent them from doing work or labour, or make it difficult and costly for them to do so. Yet targeting state benefits on the 'deserving poor' leads politicians to try to reduce the number of people eligible for disability benefits by applying 'ability to work' tests. These are inevitably arbitrary and discriminatory. They have also sparked public suspicion and hostility towards those with disabilities, as was demonstrated by some very unpleasant physical attacks on disabled people in the UK after the rules were tightened. [36]

Stricter and more exclusionary rules have been introduced in many other countries in Europe and North America. The US Supreme Court has made it harder for people with disabilities to prove they are unable to work, and has thus contributed to the reduction in entitlement to benefits. Everywhere, work tests have hit those with episodic disabilities such as back pain or depression particularly hard. On a 'good' day, they might be judged capable of employment, even though a 'good' day may be followed by 'bad' ones.

Ability-to-work tests also create a ridiculous moral hazard. If a person tries hard to overcome a disability constraint and is judged 'able to work', they may lose benefit and still be unable to obtain a job. If they do not make that effort, they are less likely to lose benefits. So trying to overcome a disability is penalized.

This policy stigmatizes and punishes already disadvantaged people. It would be far better, morally and administratively, to delink income security from behaviour of any kind, and to provide specific disability benefits based on estimated extra costs of living and the lower probability of earnings from employment. This would properly reward a person with any given disability for making an effort to obtain an income from labour. Abandoning 'ability to work' tests and instituting an unconditional basic income would *increase* the incentive to develop the ability to work.

Medical assessments should determine what extra costs of living are associated with specific forms of disability, and what effect these are likely to have on earnings. Then supplements to the basic income could be calculated, based on those extra costs and lower prospective earnings. That would be less stigmatizing and would help those with disabilities to receive a socially just compensation.

Prioritizing Work and Leisure

A basic income set at a modest level is most unlikely to deter work and labour. On the contrary, it is more likely to enhance the quantity and quality of work. It would also give meaning to the 'right to work'. We must differentiate between work and labour, and between recreation and leisure. All must be recognized and all are needed, not just labour and recreation. That is why the demand to reconceptualize work is Article 1 of the twenty-nine articles of my suggested precariat charter.[37]

Existing social security systems impose a treble penalty on the valuable work we all do that is not labour: first, we do not get paid for doing it; second, we deprive ourselves of the time that could be used in doing labour that would be paid; and third, we do not build entitlement to contributory social benefits that come from labour but not from most other forms of work. If a basic income helped shift our focus from jobs and labour to other forms of work that we value more, and to forms of leisure that are cultivating, invigorating and/or political, that would be a significant achievement.

Unfortunately, prejudiced perspectives on work have dogged mainstream political discourse. In a House of Commons debate on basic income in September 2016, employment minister Damian Hinds said: 'Even the most modest of universal basic income systems would necessitate higher taxes . . . At the same time it would cause a significant decrease in the motivation to work amongst citizens with unforeseen consequences for the national economy.'

He added that a basic income would 'disincentivise work' in contrast to the government's scheduled Universal Credit scheme. That statement was wrong in every respect: the marginal 'tax' rate on earnings under the Universal Credit scheme can be over 80 per cent compared with 32 per cent (at current tax and national insurance rates) with a basic income. The minister also failed to recognize that there are other forms of work that are not labour in jobs.

A basic income would increase the incentive and opportunity to do work perceived as most important for the individual. Better still, it might stimulate a desire and ability to enjoy more productive leisure, with more reflective laziness in the spirit of *schole*. In an economic system based on incessant labour and consumerism, we need to slow down. A basic income would encourage us to do so.

The Alternatives

What are the main alternative policies to basic income that have been proposed or implemented to address today's crises of economic insecurity, inequality and poverty? This chapter discusses a national minimum wage and its 'living wage' variant; contributory social insurance (national insurance in Britain); means-tested social assistance; subsidized food and other basic goods, including vouchers and food stamps; workfare and welfare-to-work schemes; and tax credits, including the UK's misnamed 'Universal Credit' now being rolled out. Each has been touted as a better option than basic income and all are currently in practice in developed economies across the globe.

A fair comparison requires that they be judged on the same criteria. In each case, the following questions should be posed: Does the policy improve social justice, as discussed in Chapter 2? Does it offer a way to enhance freedom, in the republican sense defined in Chapter 3, or does it offend it? Does it reduce inequality, again in the broad sense outlined in Chapter 4, or increase it? Does it extend socio-economic security or deepen the insecurity? Does it substantially reduce poverty? All these questions must be considered in the context of globalization, the technological revolution and the neo-liberal economic policy framework that has been shaping the global market economy.

The social justice principles outlined in previous chapters provide a useful checklist for evaluating any policy. To recall, these are:

The Security Difference Principle – a policy is socially just only if it improves the security of the least secure groups in society.

The Paternalism Test Principle – a policy is socially just only if it does not impose controls on some groups that are not also imposed on the most free groups in society.

The Rights-not-Charity Principle – a policy is socially just if it enhances the rights of the recipients of benefits or services and limits the discretionary power of the providers.

To these can be added two more:[1]

The Ecological Constraint Principle – a policy is socially just only if it does not impose an ecological cost borne by the community or by those directly affected.

The Dignified Work Principle – a policy is socially just only if it does not impede people from pursuing work in a dignified way and if it does not disadvantage the most insecure groups in that respect.

Each policy should be evaluated with these principles in mind. Of course, there are trade-offs in some cases, but we should be wary of any policy that demonstrably runs counter to them.

STATUTORY MINIMUM AND 'LIVING' WAGES

Almost all governments in the globalization era have cur-
tailed collective bargaining and constrained trade unions, as
part of their agenda to make labour markets more flexible.
Most have combined that with a wage floor, introducing
national statutory minimum wages as in Britain and, more
recently, Germany, or putting more emphasis on existing
minimum-wage legislation, as the US has done, even while
allowing the wage's real value to decline.

Paradoxically, a statutory minimum wage is most likely to
work well in an industrial labour market in which stable full-
time jobs predominate. They are least likely to function as
intended in a highly flexible, tertiary labour system in which
measuring work and labour is often hard if not impossible.
Minimum wages are usually set as an hourly rate. But how,
for example, do you measure an 'hour's work' in a tertiary
economy when people are no longer clocking in and out of
fixed workplaces but increasingly working at odd times in
different places? And, unlike a basic income, a minimum
wage does not alter the bargaining position of workers. If you
know you have something to fall back on, you can more
easily say 'no' to an exploitative wage offer, whether above or
below the minimum wage. If you do not have a basic income,
and you do not like a wage on offer, the employer can just say
'lump it'.

A minimum wage is also complex and costly to monitor
and enforce. Since the UK National Minimum Wage Act was
introduced in 1998, only nine employers have been pros-
ecuted for not paying it, out of hundreds of firms found to be
breaking the law. Those who do not respond to 'naming and

shaming' must be pursued in lengthy proceedings through the courts. In addition, minimum wages only cover employees, ignoring those without jobs as well as the growing numbers of self-employed and so-called independent contractors that are now a feature of all industrialized countries. And they are an inefficient way of tackling poverty because, in Britain at least, most people on the minimum wage do not live in the poorest households.

Opponents of a minimum wage, or who consider its level 'too high', usually claim that it will result in companies employing fewer workers in order to save on payroll costs. In fact, the evidence suggests that the impact on unemployment is small. But employers save costs in other ways that can leave workers little better off or even worse off than before.

For example, suppose at a minimum wage of £10 an hour, a firm providing cleaning services hires 100 workers for thirty hours a week. If the minimum wage were raised to £12, the firm could cut the remunerated hours to twenty-five, leaving payroll costs unchanged and the workers no better off. (Probably they would be worse off because they would have to do the same amount of cleaning work in fewer hours, or work extra hours unpaid.)

This is precisely what happened after the British government introduced a National Living Wage in 2015.[2] In one case a firm providing cleaning services to the government's own tax office (HMRC) cut cleaners' weekly hours below thirty, pushing its workers into a cruel poverty trap; in addition to fewer paid hours that negated the rise in the hourly rate, they lost entitlement to working tax credits, which go only to people putting in at least thirty paid hours a week. The cleaners were left worse off, so much so that some were told they would receive more money if they had no job and instead claimed full benefits.

However, in an example of the harm done by complex social assistance schemes, one woman who had lost her tax credits was obliged to stay in the job because, by claiming social assistance benefits instead, she would almost certainly have lost her family home. As she was still living in the same three-bedroomed house her children grew up in, the so-called 'bedroom tax', which reduces the amount of housing benefit awarded to people who are deemed to have more than the legal minimum number of bedrooms for their immediate family, would have left her unable to pay the rent and obliged to move to smaller accommodation. Unsurprisingly, she was shortly thereafter admitted to hospital with high blood pressure from the stress.

In terms of the social justice principles, minimum wages do not satisfy the Security Difference Principle, since they do not offer much security to the most insecure groups in society, particularly in modern 'flexible' labour markets. While they score reasonably well on the Paternalism Test Principle and the Rights-not-Charity Principle, they do nothing to advance freedom; they merely make some labour more financially viable. At best, they are neutral with regard to the Ecological Constraint Principle, although they favour resource-using labour over resource-conserving and 'reproductive' work. The time of a minimum wage as a useful, major instrument of social and labour market policy has surely passed.

SOCIAL OR NATIONAL INSURANCE

For much of the twentieth century, welfare systems were grounded in principles of social insurance based on the Beveridge or Bismarck models. The essence of the system was solidarity; people with a low probability of an insured risk cross-subsidized those with a higher probability. These insured risks were called 'contingency risks', such as unemployment, sickness, accident, disability and pregnancy. In each case, actuarial calculations of premiums and benefits could be made, derived from statistical probabilities of these events occurring.

In reality, social insurance systems were never as solidaristic as their defenders claimed, nor as universal as they pretended, particularly disadvantaging women. But they worked reasonably well, with wide democratic support, as long as the contributory base was assured and broad, as long as enough people paid contributions or had contributions paid for them, and as long as the risks covered were those that worried or affected people most.

In the twenty-first century, these conditions no longer apply as they did. With more people in and out of unstable labour, the contributory base is being eroded, obliging governments to dip into general revenue to top up social insurance funds. By the same token, people are increasingly unable to build up adequate contribution records entitling them to insurance benefits, leaving them dependent on means-tested assistance in hard times. And more people are exposed to risks for which there is little or no insurance cover to be had.

Meanwhile, higher-income earners, facing low contingency risks, have become more reluctant to cross-subsidize the growing numbers facing high risks. This has undermined the political legitimacy of and support for social insurance benefits, fuelling calls for cuts in benefits and contribution rates.

Above all, as described in Chapter 4, there has been a change in the nature of economic insecurity. Those in the precariat in particular have increasingly volatile earnings, and their insecurity is one of uncertainty, for which social insurance is ill-equipped. Social insurance worked adequately in an economy based largely on stable industrial full-time employment. That is a long way back from what we have today and from what beckons in the future.

Social insurance in a flexible tertiary economy does not pass the Security Difference Principle, though it does well on the Paternalism Test Principle and the Rights-not-Charity Principle. For the same reason that the minimum wage fails, it does nothing for the Ecological Constraint Principle, since it rewards 'labour' over 'work'. In sum, it offers little to the most deprived and insecure, while failing to promote social justice or republican freedom.

MEANS-TESTED SOCIAL ASSISTANCE

The loss of faith in social insurance leaves the main core alternative to a basic income as means-tested social assistance 'targeted' on those identified as 'poor'. It is a 'core' alternative because, once adopted, the introduction of other policies becomes almost inevitable in order to back it up.

In the construction of welfare states in the twentieth century, there was broad recognition of Richard Titmuss' well-known adage that state benefits that are only for the poor are invariably poor benefits. This is largely because the rest of society therefore has no interest in defending them. However, when welfare states came under strain in the 1980s and 1990s, governments of all complexions changed tack, constructing an edifice of means-tested social assistance schemes often justified as necessary to 'defend' the welfare state in straitened times.

The idea of means testing is deceptively simple: spend limited money on those who need it most. Less spending allows for lower taxes. Meanwhile, means testing legitimizes welfare spending in the eyes of the public, since politicians can claim that the money is going to the most needy. However, study after study has demonstrated the egregious flaws in the system, suggesting that the real motive for means testing is not that of helping the poor. Here are ten of those flaws.

First, measuring income is complicated and involves arbitrary cut-off rules. Taking savings and 'wealth' into account encourages dis-saving, which reduces resilience at times of financial stress.

Second, applying means tests entails high costs, both for the administration and for claimants who must travel to benefit offices, wait, queue, fill in lengthy forms, produce supporting documents and so on, all of which take time and often hard cash.

Third, means testing involves intrusive questions, including about claimants' intimate personal relationships, that may be followed up by home visits, for example, to check that there is no live-in partner earning an income. It is a regime of prying, invasion of privacy, and presumption of guilt rather than innocence, which demeans the staff running it as well as claimants.

Fourth, as a result, the process and the prospect of it are stigmatizing. This is often deliberate, to reduce the cost of welfare by deterring claimants. As one adviser to recent British and American governments put it, claimants should be treated meanly and encouraged to blame themselves for their hardships.[3] You do not have to be a Christian to appreciate Malcolm Torry's riposte that 'means-tested benefits that stigmatise their recipients grant no recognition to our status as made in God's image and as possessing a dignity bettered only by God's.'[4]

This leads to the *fifth* failing, low take-up. Evidence from almost every means-tested scheme in every country where they are applied shows time and again that many people entitled to the benefits do not receive them. This is due to a reluctance to claim, from fear, shame or ignorance; to failure to claim successfully, perhaps by misunderstanding a question or giving a 'wrong' answer; and to denial of benefits for trivial reasons (such as lateness for an appointment) by street-level bureaucrats doing what they perceive as their job and what they think will advance their own careers.

In Britain, take-up of means-tested unemployment benefit, renamed Jobseeker's Allowance (JSA), has been falling and is now claimed successfully by only half of those estimated to be entitled to it.[5] In the 2014–15 financial year, £2.4 billion in JSA went unclaimed, worth £3,000 to every entitled family that was not receiving it. Another benefit with poor take-up is Pension Credit, which is supposed to help low-income people, especially women, who have not paid enough national insurance contributions to qualify for the full state pension or who have no other income to top up the state pension. In 2014–15, four in ten eligible pensioners failed to claim credits worth up to £3 billion – £2,000 for each eligible family not receiving it.

In the US, only a quarter of those entitled to means-tested housing assistance receive it, often after years on a waiting list for vouchers, only a limited number of which are issued each year.[6] The TANF (Temporary Assistance for Needy Families) programme reaches fewer than a quarter of families in poverty, even as the number of those families has risen.[7]

Sixth, means testing undermines social solidarity, separating 'us' from 'them'. We, who support ourselves, pay taxes to support them, the scroungers. This utilitarian perspective is a sad reality today, reinforced by declining social mobility and the ability of the more affluent to protect themselves, through private insurance and accumulated assets, against practically every risk they face. It is a factor encouraging politicians to allow state benefits to fall in real terms and to seek ways of reducing the number of people able to claim them.

The *seventh* and most well-known failing is the notorious poverty trap, which is accompanied by the precarity trap outlined in Chapter 4 and elaborated elsewhere.[8] In the US, the poverty trap resulting from means testing means that in thirty-five states people on benefits who take a minimum-wage job would *lose* money (a 'tax' rate of more than 100 per cent).[9] Some commentators have proposed that benefits should be withdrawn more slowly once an unemployed person obtains a job, to reduce the deterrent to taking low-wage employment. But this would be unfair on others in such jobs receiving the same or perhaps lower wages, who did not previously qualify for benefits.

This leads to the *eighth* failing, the inevitable drift to workfare, which is discussed in more detail below. By confronting people with marginal tax rates of 80 per cent or more in going from meagre benefits to low-wage jobs, means testing creates a strong disincentive to do so. In those circumstances, the state is left with little choice but to force people to take low-paid labour.

A *ninth* failing is that means-tested social assistance deters stable household formation. Benefits are typically determined on a household, not individual, basis, and on a per-person basis are lower for couples than for single-person households. Why form a household, which might be experimental, if you are going to lose money? By contrast, being paid individually and equally, a basic income system would encourage family living if desired. It would be strictly neutral as to relationships and household setups, which is what equity considerations should require.

A *tenth* failing relates to income-tested Jobseeker's Allowance, which is determined on the basis of family income. If one of a couple is unemployed, the couple loses financially if the other is doing a small amount of paid labour. So it pays for him or her (and it usually is the wife or female partner) to stop doing that labour. This is one reason why, in the UK in recent years, households have become increasingly divided into labour-rich (two earners) and labour-poor (no earners).[10]

Social assistance via means tests and the inevitable behaviour tests fails all social justice and republican freedom principles. To reiterate, policies that are only for the poor are indeed invariably poor policies.

SUBSIDIZED FOOD AND VOUCHERS

One widely adopted policy, especially in developing countries, is the provision of subsidized food and other items targeted at 'the poor'. India's PDS (Public Distribution System) is the largest such scheme, but there are many others. Voucher schemes, such as the US food stamp programme SNAP (Supplemental Nutrition Assistance Program), have similar objectives. In both cases the rationale is that, since the poor lack essentials, the state should provide them or the means to obtain them, and those items alone. Another justification, used in developing countries, is that subsidized food protects the poor against food price fluctuations.[11]

The objections to this type of policy are multiple. *First* and foremost, such schemes are paternalistic; they presume to know better than people themselves what 'the poor' need. Worse, they aim to dictate what 'the poor' can have. In the US, for example, food stamps not only confine people to buying food, but often can only be used for certain types of food and drink deemed 'healthy'.

Voucher schemes and aid in kind implicitly if not explicitly presume that people given cash will tend to spend it on non-essentials, especially 'bads' such as alcohol, drugs or gambling. In fact, numerous studies have shown that people given cash benefits do not increase spending on 'bads'.[12] But, even if the presumption were correct, these schemes are not freedom-enhancing. Why should the poor, but not others, be forbidden to spend a bit of extra income on something they enjoy? And, in any case, if someone wishes to spend on 'private bads' (or what we good people decree are 'bads'), they can do so with money that is freed up by the voucher or subsidized food. Or they can sell on the vouchers (at a discount) for cash.[13] The sale of food stamps continues in the US, despite being illegal, because people need cash for other essentials such as nappies (diapers) that food stamps do not cover.

Second, vouchers or subsidized items are costly to provide, administer and monitor, necessarily involving a large bureaucracy. To provide one rupee's worth of food under India's Public Distribution System costs the government 3.65 rupees.[14] While India may be an extreme case, the cost of providing food aid is one reason why United Nations humanitarian organizations are increasingly turning to cash assistance. One study that compared food, voucher and cash aid found that providing food aid in kind cost nearly four times as much as the equivalent in cash.[15]

Third, vouchers are worth less to the beneficiaries than the cash equivalent; cash can be used everywhere, whereas vouchers are only accepted in certain places or are accepted only if the shopkeeper chooses to do so. This results in less competition for the custom of voucher holders, enabling those shops that do accept vouchers to raise their prices. Vouchers thus buy less than cash would do; one study found that Lebanese shopkeepers accepting vouchers issued to Syrian refugees pocketed an estimated $1 million a month in 2014 through higher prices.[16] And vouchers or food aid in kind impose higher costs on their recipients, in travelling to the designated shops, waiting time and so on.[17]

Fourth, they involve means testing, with all the failings

that go with this approach. In the US, which should have a relatively efficient administrative apparatus, a quarter of those living officially in income poverty do not receive the targeted food stamps. Moreover, a third of those who do receive them need to go to food banks as well, while others skip meals and do without, because the stamps are estimated to finance food needs for only about three weeks in the month.[18]

Fifth, vouchers or aid-in-kind stigmatize recipients, whether deliberately or not, and induce a visible supplicant status and mentality. *Sixth*, they encourage the provision of low-quality goods and services and disdain on the part of those delegated to administer or provide them. In the US, housing vouchers have been associated with increased concentration of impoverished people in poor neighbourhoods where the vouchers are more widely accepted by landlords.[19]

Seventh, they are prone to corruption and/or rent seeking by special interests. In the US, food stamps have been vigorously promoted by farm-state Republicans. In India, less than 10 per cent of the food the government buys for its Public Distribution System reaches the poor; almost half mysteriously disappears between warehouse and ration shop, and most of the rest is left to rot in government storage.[20] Moving to a basic income scheme, based on direct provision of cash to the intended beneficiaries, would remove layers of intermediaries and their lobbying potential at a stroke.

Although food and other subsidies may seem to satisfy the Security Difference Principle by reaching out to the most insecure groups in society, some of the most vulnerable are locked out of such schemes. They surely fail the Paternalism

Test Principle and the Rights-not-Charity Principle. They are also costly to administer, inefficient and prone to corruption and rent seeking. An experiment in Ecuador that ran simultaneous trials of cash assistance, food vouchers and in-kind food aid found that less than 10 per cent of those receiving cash would have preferred another form of assistance, whereas a quarter to a third of the others wanted to change.[21] Those who received cash valued being able to use some of the money for other essentials, including savings. It was one of many studies that have found a preference for cash over what bureaucrats think people want and need.

GUARANTEED JOBS

It is sometimes claimed that a 'job guarantee' would be preferable to a basic income because jobs are believed to have some sort of intrinsic value beyond the income they bring in (a sense of identity and contribution to the community, structured time, interaction with fellow workers, and so on) that makes people happier. Proponents of a 'job guarantee' include Lord (Richard) Layard, who was Tony Blair's 'happiness czar', in the UK[22] and Harvey and Quigley in the US, following the earlier advocacy by Minsky.[23]

The objections to this policy include some that apply with even more force to the next policy option, namely workfare. A job guarantee would be a deception. What sort of jobs would be guaranteed? At what rate of pay would they be provided? What would be the consequence for declining the specific job being 'guaranteed'? Since it is completely unrealistic to guarantee everyone a job that suits them, makes use of their skills and pays well, in practice the job would be low-level, low-paid, short-term and 'make-work', or at best low-productivity, labour. Cleaning the streets, filling shelves in supermarkets and similar menial activities are an unlikely road to happiness. Those arguing for a job guarantee would certainly not want those jobs for themselves or their children.

One reason given for supporting guaranteed jobs is that surveys suggest unemployed people are less happy than people with jobs. This is hardly surprising. Being involuntarily unemployed, especially when benefits are meagre, hard to obtain and maintain, stigmatizing and uncertain, is not a happy situation. That is surely quite different from being outside a job voluntarily, with income security and without stigma. Retired people, for example, are not disproportionately unhappy. As Kate McFarland has written, 'It's not that our culture values jobs because jobs intrinsically make us happy; it's that being employed tends to make us happier because we are stuck in a culture that values jobs.'[24] Even so, Gallup polls have consistently found that less than a third of US employees feel 'engaged' (enthusiastic and committed) in their jobs, especially millennials and those in low-status or routine jobs. Worldwide, less than a fifth of those with jobs feel engaged.

Proposals for spreading employment, for instance, by shortening working hours, shade into those for a job guarantee. Emran Mian, director of the Social Market Foundation, argues for a redistribution of labour, 'even if that might reduce economic efficiency, rather than hand out money'.[25] The New Economics Foundation says a shorter working week would lower unemployment.[26] Yet it is hard to see how this would be achieved by regulatory devices, as the French have found with their thirty-five-hour week legislation. Without the underpinning of a basic income, statutorily reducing working hours would impoverish many people on low wages while doing little to create additional jobs.

Most 'job guarantee' advocates also ignore the fact that market economies need some unemployment to function. A seminal article by A. W. Phillips in 1958 posited an inverse relationship between the level of unemployment and the rate of inflation. And although the exact nature of the relationship has been a matter of controversy ever since, most economists accept that there is a 'natural' rate of unemployment at which inflation is broadly stable. (This is often referred to as the NAIRU or non-accelerating inflation rate of unemployment). In a market economy, therefore, no government can guarantee a job to everybody who wants one.

A job guarantee, to the extent that it could be operationalized, might satisfy the Security Difference Principle, if suitable jobs could be provided for those with disabilities or other impairments as a matter of priority. That is unlikely. Jobs will tend to be allocated to young people, supposedly to prevent their 'marginalization'. The policy would certainly fail in republican freedom and social justice terms, since it imposes duties on some groups that are not imposed on the most free, and enshrines a Charity-not-Rights rule. Would everybody really be guaranteed a job they would like, or even one matching their competences? It is hard to imagine.

WORKFARE

Workfare is a natural progression of reforms to the welfare state that have been going on since the 1980s. As this writer predicted long ago,[27] once governments opted to revive means testing as the mainstream part of the welfare system, it was inevitable that workfare would be introduced.

If social assistance is based on targeting the 'poor', a distinction is soon made between those who are poor through no fault of their own and those who 'choose' to be poor or who become poor through mistakes and personal failings. This tired dichotomy has played throughout the history of social policy and 'charity'. But once policymakers go down that road, they must make the next arbitrary distinction. Only those who accept the job offered by the state in return for their benefit 'deserve' that benefit. Otherwise they must be 'sanctioned'.

Workfare in its modern form began in the 1980s in the US state of Wisconsin, where Republicans introduced a requirement for welfare claimants to take a job, inevitably low-paid, if they wished to receive benefits. Unsurprisingly, this lowered the number of claimants, which was seized on as showing that many were fraudulent or not really in need of state benefits.

Republicans in Congress soon backed this measure, drafting President Bill Clinton's epoch-defining welfare reform in 1996 that fulfilled his campaign pledge to 'end welfare as we have come to know it'. The *Personal Responsibility and Work Opportunity Reconciliation Act* set limits on the length of time people could claim welfare, imposed stricter conditions for eligibility, and mandated job and job-related requirements. 'Welfare-to-work' subsequently became the mantra of Third Way politicians and parties everywhere, and workfare arrangements proliferated in all industrialized countries.

While this is not the place to go into a detailed analysis of the experience, there is plenty of evidence to show that in the US workfare has reduced welfare rolls at the cost of plunging many families into deeper poverty.[28] The same is true for workfare programmes elsewhere that push people into low-paid jobs or withdraw benefits for those refusing or unable to take such jobs. But irrespective of this evidence, workfare is a pernicious policy.

It involves coercion and imposition of a 'duty to labour' on benefit claimants that is not imposed on others. It is also paternalistic, implying that the state knows what is best for the individual and for society. The claim that workfare promotes the development of skills and 'work habits' is contradicted by the nature of the jobs lined up for the unemployed, as is the claim that workfare promotes social integration because people not in jobs are socially marginalized or 'excluded'.

Pushing people into dead-end short-term jobs disrupts their own job searching, studying or training, potentially *reducing* their ability to escape from poverty and economic insecurity. There is even evidence that participation in workfare leads to lower lifetime earnings by giving people a history of low-level temporary jobs that do not match their qualifications or experience.[29]

Workfare also has dysfunctional and distortive labour market effects. It puts downward pressure on wages by supplying cheap labour in competition with those doing similar jobs in the open labour market. These people, already among the most vulnerable and insecure, may even lose their jobs because they can be substituted by workfare participants.

The main political reasons for workfare have nothing to

do with making people 'happy'. They are, in reality, a desire to reduce the state's obligations to the disadvantaged, and the fact that governments have little alternative to coercion if they operate means-tested social assistance programmes that create strong financial disincentives for people to take low-wage jobs. It is a chain of reasoning that begins with a faulty design. Workfare offends the Security Difference Principle, hurting the least secure. It offends the Paternalism Test Principle, wilfully. And it is a policy that is contrary to any vision of freedom and social justice.

TAX CREDITS

Tax credits became the go-to option of social democratic governments in industrialized countries in the wake of the strong downward pressure on wages linked to globalization and 'flexible' labour markets. Tax credits top up low wages, stopping at a threshold level of earned income. Necessarily, the schemes are complex and operate somewhat arbitrary rules of entitlement.

Tax credits in the US started modestly in the 1970s with the Earned Income Tax Credit (EITC). They were considerably expanded under President Bill Clinton in the 1990s and have grown to become the most expensive welfare scheme in the world, costing nearly $80 billion a year. A quarter of all Americans are eligible for tax credits and over 26 million received them in the 2015 tax year, averaging about $3,200 for a family with children. Childless adults are largely excluded from the scheme.

In the UK, tax credits also had modest beginnings in 1999. Working Tax Credits and Child Tax Credits for low-income parents were introduced in 2003 and became central to New Labour's social and labour market policy reforms. By 2013–14 the cost had ballooned to £30 billion a year, 14 per cent of all welfare spending, as the number dependent on tax credits rose to over 3.3 million from just over 2 million ten years earlier. Including housing and council tax benefits for those in jobs, government spending to compensate for low wages rose to £76 billion a year, representing a third of all expenditure on welfare and easily the biggest welfare payment after pensions.[30]

UK tax credits are being merged into a new Universal Credit scheme, which unifies some benefits but suffers from the same drawbacks as Working Tax Credits and other means-tested assistance. Foremost among these is the wretched poverty trap, with a marginal 'tax' rate on earnings of up to 80 per cent or more. In the US, similar or even higher marginal 'tax' rates also act as a disincentive to boost earnings once the credit starts to be withdrawn. Sure enough, in both the US and the UK, the system has led to secondary earners in tax credit households, mostly married women, reducing hours in paid labour or dropping out of the labour market.[31]

Tax credits also breed errors and petty fraud. According to the US Internal Revenue Service, about a quarter of all tax credits are issued improperly, costing the public over $14 billion a year.[32] While welfare detractors point to fraud, some if not most of this may be due to the complexity of the schemes that result in mistakes or misunderstandings. In the UK, tax credit recipients have to give Her Majesty's Revenue and Customs (HMRC) an estimate of their earnings – but this can be difficult if not impossible when earnings and hours fluctuate. If earnings turn out to be higher than the estimate, recipients, by definition on low incomes, have to refund the overpayment, leading to further impoverishment and indebtedness.[33]

Tax credits are a subsidy to capital, whatever impact they have on poverty and the incomes of wage workers. One US estimate suggests that for every dollar spent on the EITC the low-wage worker gains 73 cents while the employer gains 27 cents by paying lower wages.[34] In a similar finding for the UK, researchers have concluded that about three-quarters of the value of tax credits goes to workers, the rest to employers.[35]

An obvious failing of tax credits is that, with few exceptions, they only help people in jobs. Those who cannot obtain a job, or are not in a job for whatever reason, are excluded. And tax credits act as a deterrent to technological advance. By cheapening labour costs, they reduce cost pressure on employers to make productivity-enhancing innovations. Tax credits fail social justice and freedom principles and have perverse labour market and economic effects.

UNIVERSAL CREDIT

At the time of writing in early 2017, the British government was still in the extraordinarily prolonged and expensive process of phasing in the so-called 'Universal Credit'. Announced in 2010, it has operated on a very limited scale since 2013 and, after a host of delays and setbacks, is set to roll out fully by 2022. Though unique to Britain, it embodies many of the elements that have figured in social policy reforms globally.

The Universal Credit is neither 'universal' nor a 'credit'.

Intended to integrate six separate means-tested benefits and tax credits, it cannot sensibly be called 'universal', since it is designed only for those on low incomes. It also involves extensive behavioural conditionality, which makes a further mockery of the word 'universal'.

Individuals or households will receive an income transfer paid monthly to top up what they received in the past month, calculated on a particular day. This fails to recognize that the incomes of many low-income households vary from month to month and week to week, for example, with changes in the numbers of hours worked.[36] A US study found that three-quarters of people in the lowest 20 per cent of earnings experienced month-to-month changes in income of 30 per cent or more.[37] Being paid in arrears, it is therefore in that sense not a 'credit', let alone an amount known in advance. And, being based on the previous month, it will not reflect current circumstances.

There will still be a severe poverty trap, with the Universal Credit subject to a 'taper' of 63 per cent. After adding in payment of tax and national insurance, and the loss of means-tested Council Tax Support not included in the Universal Credit, recipients could face a marginal tax rate of more than 80 per cent on all earned income. And the precarity trap is worsened by a regulation forty-two-day wait for a first payment (up to sixty days including processing delays), inevitably pushing many claimants into debt, rent arrears and recourse to food banks.

The Universal Credit is also even more conditional and punitive than the benefits it will replace, since it imposes a 'claimant commitment' not only by the unemployed to seek and take jobs but also by those who have part-time employ-ment to look actively for extra hours and pay. If recipients are judged not to be looking hard enough for full-time jobs, they can have their benefits removed for up to three years. And the scheme extends conditionality to more people than before, including partners of those with jobs.

Claimants will be monitored, in jobs and out of them, by 'work coaches' and 'advancement support advisers' to make sure they are complying with the conditions. The cost of an army of work coaches will surely be huge, and if it is not, it will fail on its own terms. Policymakers may delude them-selves into thinking this Orwellian notion is meant to be helpful, but it is paternalistic, intrusive, stigmatizing and a daily humiliation, which may well induce some claimants to slink out of the scheme in shame. Sadly, there are indications that this withdrawal is actually desired.

While the 'claimant commitment' is likened by officials to an employment contract, it is nothing of the kind, since it is imposed on claimants and impoverishing sanctions can be inflicted by bureaucrats without any due process.

Moreover, because the means testing for Universal Credit is based on household income, it tends to encourage the estab-lishment or persistence of single-earner households. Perversely, because the second person in a couple receives less than the first, it also encourages couples to break up. And from 2016, no payment is made for a third or subsequent child, only for the first two. Universal Credit is thus moralistic and puni-tive towards large families who may have greater needs.

The worst feature of Universal Credit is its reliance on threats and sanctions rather than labour incentives. It thus will tend to put downward pressure on wages in general and worsen labour market inequalities. It is hard to take seriously the government's claim that 'Universal Credit delivers the government's pledge to move from a low-wage, high-welfare society to a higher-wage, lower-welfare one.'[38] There is no way in which it encourages a rise in wages. And, unlike a basic income, it also discriminates explicitly in favour of labour against other, potentially more valuable forms of work.

The many egregious failings of Universal Credit make it all the more surprising, and shameful, that politicians and social scientists have shown such passivity during the roll-out. Anybody who cares for freedom and justice should be critical of a regime that threatens to impoverish people without due process, installs a system of snoopers to chase up vulnerable people, and uses means testing and behaviour testing shown to lead to exclusion, low take-up and stigmatization. Universal Credit may push more people into low-level jobs, but in doing so it will surely lower wage rates for the precariat in general.

As Frank Field MP and his colleague Andrew Forsey concluded, 'The political historians may be interested in how a programme, so full of risk and potentially at such great cost, came to be the Coalition's flagship welfare reform policy with so little public and maybe cabinet debate.'[39]

NEGATIVE INCOME TAX

The proposal for a negative income tax (NIT), associated most with Milton Friedman, is often seen as a form of basic income, and Friedman himself tended to represent it that way, notably in a message sent to BIEN. It is therefore important to stress two crucial differences. The negative income tax would be linked to *family* income or earnings, and (like tax credits in the US) it would be paid to low-income earners retrospectively, *after* the end of the tax year. It would really be a selective means-tested scheme, with all the associated drawbacks.

That second aspect means the payment amount would not be known in advance and almost certainly it would not be available at a time of immediate need. It would be more akin to a windfall gain (or an annual capital grant) than a steady source of basic income security.

Although an NIT would be a useful anti-poverty device, it would do little to advance republican freedom or provide assured economic security, nor would it be a vehicle for social justice. It would not apply to people without jobs or with incomes too low to pay tax. About 20 million US households do not file federal tax returns, presumably because their income is too low. They would not be covered by a negative income tax system, contrary to the primary objective.

In addition, US experiments with an NIT in the 1970s found that people had an incentive to under-report their labour and earnings to obtain the NIT supplements. A basic income would not entail this kind of immoral hazard. All in all, a negative income tax would not score as well as a basic income on the social justice principles.

PRIVATE CHARITY

Finally, there are those who argue that the state should withdraw from all forms of welfare and leave it to individuals and 'charities' to look after people in need. The right-wing libertarians would ideally like to rely on charity completely, but dare not suggest this, as mass generosity on the required scale would be too great an expectation. But there are more fundamental reasons for opposing the growing reliance on charity and philanthropy.

Charity is based on the sentiment of 'pity' and, as the philosopher David Hume noted, pity is akin to contempt. Private charity as a central feature of social policy may satisfy libertarians, but it profoundly offends the central idea of republican freedom, that of non-domination. Being dependent on the good will of others is not consistent with full freedom. On the contrary, it compromises the freedom of the giver as well as the supplicant.

The spread of charity has largely reflected the manifold failings of means-tested social assistance, the unfairness of conditionality, the deliberate sanctions taken against vulnerable people and the spread of economic insecurity. In the UK, for instance, over 40 per cent of referrals to food banks run by a major charity, the Trussell Trust, are due to benefit delays and sanctions.[40]

The fact that so many people in modern society are going to food banks and shelters demonstrates social policy failure. Private philanthropy should be marginalized again; it is an undemocratic way of shaping society and the selective well-being of individuals, groups and communities.

The Failure of Alternatives

Most of the alternatives to a basic income fail badly on most of the social justice principles, shown in summary form in Table 9.1. Some might quibble with certain aspects, particularly

	SECURITY DIFFERENCE PRINCIPLE	PATERNALISM TEST PRINCIPLE	RIGHTS-NOT-CHARITY PRINCIPLE	ECOLOGICAL CONSTRAINT PRINCIPLE	DIGNIFIED WORK PRINCIPLE
Minimum wage	✗	✓	✓	—	—
Social insurance	✗	✓	✓	—	—
Means testing	✗	✗	✗	—	✗
Subsidies, vouchers	✗	✗	✗	—	—
Job guarantee	✗	✗	✗	—	✗
Workfare	✗	✗	✗	—	✗
Tax credits	✗	✓	✓	—	✗
Negative income tax	✗	✓	✓	—	✗
Charity	✗	✗	✗	—	✗
Basic income	✓	✓	✓	✓	✓

Table 9.1

How different welfare schemes satisfy social justice principles with the presumed neutrality of alternatives to basic income with regard to their ecological implications. Job-oriented schemes, for instance, have tended to give precedence to short-term job creation over environmental concerns. However, the key point is that all the alternatives score less well than a basic income.

Defenders of existing welfare schemes should explain why, despite ever increasing expenditure, poverty rates remain stubbornly high and social mobility seems to be declining. In the United States, after falling sharply from the 1960s up to about 1979, the poverty rate has scarcely budged. Greater outlays on means testing, tax credits, workfare, food stamps and all the other 126 anti-poverty schemes that experts have counted have produced little improvement.[41] Surely, that in itself is a signal that a new road is needed.

CHAPTER 10

Basic Income and Development

'The answer to whether or not we could have a universal basic income could well be "a yes, but under certain conditions".'

ARVIND SUBRAMANIAN, CHIEF ECONOMIC ADVISER, GOVERNMENT OF INDIA, SEPTEMBER 2016

Up until the beginning of this century, international development aid consisted primarily of money transfers or technical advice from rich country governments to governments of developing countries, or flows from development agencies or non-governmental organizations (NGOs) to governments. Few seemed to think it was a good idea to give the poor money. There were no significant direct cash transfers to people.

However, subsequent years have seen a spate of 'conditional cash transfer' schemes (CCTs) in developing countries, many funded by multilateral aid, as well as nominally 'unconditional cash transfer' schemes (UCTs), the latter chiefly aimed at the elderly and/or children in poor households. Foreign governments and donors have also supported pilot (experimental) 'basic income' schemes, while others have been funded by United Nations or other international agencies, or by NGOs or philanthropic donors.

The World Bank has estimated that in 2014 cash transfer schemes of various types reached 720 million people in 130 developing countries.[1] Of the forty-eight countries surveyed in Africa, forty were operating UCTs, double the number in 2010. The world seems to have woken up to the

remarkable idea that the best way of dealing with income
poverty is to give people more income. And the evidence has
dispelled the long-held prejudice that money given to the
poor would be wasted and would not contribute to growth
and development.

Cash transfer schemes that at present are overwhelmingly
targeted at 'the poor' have the potential to prepare the way
for basic income.[2] But four factors have so far impeded the
transition – a belief in 'targeting' (only the poor should
receive the cash), 'selectivity' (some groups should have priority), 'conditionality' (recipients should be required to
undertake certain actions or behave in certain ways), and
'randomization' (policy should only be introduced when it
has been tested, or evaluated, by randomized control trials,
and thus be 'evidence-based').

This chapter briefly surveys findings from cash transfer
schemes of most relevance for basic income and then con-
siders the outcomes of genuine basic income pilots. But the
fourth factor needs to be dealt with first, since a fetish with
a particular method of evaluation risks distracting attention
from what is most important and delaying progress in policy
implementation.

In randomized control trials (RCTs) of cash transfers,
some people are given cash, others are not, and the results
for the two groups are compared over time. This methodology is derived from medical trials, where some patients are
given a treatment, some are not given a treatment and some
are given a placebo. However, by definition, allocating transfers randomly cannot test the community-wide effects
of a universal benefit. And, while RCTs can test simple

hypotheses such as improved school attendance, they are less robust and 'scientific' for more abstract hypotheses such as enhanced freedom or social justice. Nor can they deal with the ethical issues surrounding selectivity, targeting and conditionality.

That rather strong caveat aside, the vast literature generated by evaluations of cash transfers, many involving RCTs, shows convincingly that cash transfers result in lower poverty and achieve many of the outcomes desired by policymakers, such as improved school enrolment and attendance, better nutrition, better health and more income-generating activity. And while there is a tendency of 'randomistas' to claim that only RCTs provide 'scientific' methodology for 'evidence-based' policy, other forms of evaluation have reached similar and equally valid conclusions.

Targeting and Selectivity

There are several forms of targeting – household means testing, proxy means testing, geographical targeting, community-based targeting and so-called 'self-targeting' – but all of them aim to focus cash transfers on 'the poor', using a notional poverty line. Yet a 'poverty line' is both arbitrary and subjective. Many people who are in or near poverty experience fluctuating incomes and may be just above the poverty line one week, just below it in another. In India, procedures are so cumbersome that determining whether a household is poor is often done years before entitlement to a benefit is put into effect.[3]

In all countries, targeting is riddled with errors, both

conceptual and practical, due to ignorance, fear, mistakes, bureaucratic indifference and discretionary decision making. Means testing always involves large errors of exclusion (eligible people do not benefit) and inclusion (ineligible people do benefit). Proxy means tests that try to determine eligibility by some indicator correlated with income poverty, such as thatched roofs rather than tin, are no better.[4]

In India, about half of all poor households do not have a BPL (below-poverty-line) card and about one-third of the non-poor (under the rules) have one.[5] A study in the Indian state of Karnataka found that more than two-thirds of those questioned who were ineligible for BPL cards (for example, owning a water pump) in fact had them, while a sixth of those eligible for the cards did not.[6] Research in Gujarat, Delhi and Madhya Pradesh showed that a large proportion of those in dire need did not have BPL cards or were denied them for some spurious reason.[7] Often the poorest were least likely to have them.

Targeting also creates poverty traps, with accompanying moral and immoral hazards. If a household obtains a benefit only if it is classified as poor, then it pays to stay poor. Increasing income to just above the poverty level means losing more than the extra earnings. So, there is a disincentive to earn extra. This moral hazard prompts the immoral hazard. Someone gaining a little more income will have an incentive to conceal it, so as not to lose entitlement to the benefit.

In addition, high administrative costs are inherent to means testing.[8] When evaluations measure the cost of a scheme, they should take account of the fact that funds spent on administration could have been used to give benefit recipients more money. Targeting also addresses yesterday's, not tomorrow's, poverty; it aims to help those who have fallen into poverty rather than those in danger of doing so. Yet the most effective way to reduce poverty is to prevent it, as preventing poverty costs less than helping people out of it.

Several studies have considered whether targeted or universal schemes have more effect in reducing poverty. Due to exclusion errors, targeting performs worse. In the four largest Latin American countries, targeted schemes, on average, reached less than half the poorest fifth of the population. Similar failings emerged in Brazil's *Bolsa Família* and Mexico's *Oportunidades*.[9] In China, cities that used more targeting were less likely to reduce poverty.[10] Universal schemes are more effective in reducing poverty and inequality than schemes ostensibly targeted on the poor.

Conditional Versus Unconditional Cash Transfers

Conditional cash transfer schemes are now operating in more than sixty developing countries, up from two in 1997.[11] Most are targeted on the poor, and many have a multiplicity of conditions, though the most common schemes pay mothers on condition they ensure their children's regular attendance at school and take them for health checks and immunizations. Unconditional cash transfer schemes are used in twice as many countries, but are usually selective in covering just one group – pensions for the elderly or allowances for children, for example – and again are mostly targeted on the poor.

A much contested issue is whether behavioural conditions are justifiable or even needed. They aim to promote certain actions and are thus paternalistic, assuming policymakers know best what poor people need. Even if they succeed in their own terms, and the desired behaviour is promoted, conditions compromise freedom and can rarely be justified on moral grounds. In practice, applying conditions will usually be arbitrary and, if they are taken seriously, will involve sanctions of some sort if they are not met.

Conditions may seem reasonable at first glance. But requiring mothers to make sure that children are in school 85 per cent of the time, say, puts an additional burden on women and creates stress, since by implication the benefit will be withdrawn if the condition is not met. The conditionality is not only paternalistic but potentially very unfair, since the most vulnerable, the least educated, and those living furthest from schools and clinics, are likely to suffer most.

One review of eight studies directly comparing a CCT to a UCT found that CCTs had a greater impact on education, health and nutrition outcomes than UCTs.[12] However, it noted that this was not necessarily the result of the conditionality as such; just as important may have been 'clear communication about the importance of using services and related support'. A study in Morocco found that simply labelling an *unconditional* transfer as an education grant increases the likelihood that behaviour would be directed towards that goal.[13]

Another review of thirty-five programmes found, unsurprisingly, that explicitly conditional and enforced CCTs had a bigger effect on school enrolment and attendance than unconditional schemes in those specific respects.[14] But UCTs also boosted school enrolment and attendance, showing that, even without prompting, families wished to send children to school. And other benefits of unconditional transfers may be significant.

For example, in Malawi both conditional and unconditional cash transfers to adolescent girls resulted in higher school attendance rates, though the conditional transfers did better on this measure.[15] However, teenage pregnancy and marriage rates dropped far more sharply among girls receiving the unconditional transfer, almost entirely due to the impact among girls who dropped out of school. Who can say which will have the more positive impact in the long term?

Relevant Findings from Cash Transfers

Cash transfer schemes differ from basic income in several ways: they are typically targeted at 'the poor', so are not universal; many apply behavioural conditions; many pay to households or to one person in a household, not to all individuals; and many, though not all, have been short-term experiments. Nevertheless, the results of cash transfer programmes point to what could be achieved by introducing a universal basic income.

First and foremost, the evidence is now overwhelming that direct cash transfers result in sharp declines in poverty.[16] That may seem obvious, but for many years giving money to people in developing countries was seen as wasteful because it would be spent on 'private bads' or drive up prices of basic goods and services, leaving the poor no better off.

All the studies show that, with very few exceptions, people who receive cash transfers do not spend them on alcohol, tobacco or drugs, but rather use them to improve household welfare.[17] Cash transfers have also led to a decline in crime and domestic abuse.[18]

The evidence on inflation is encouraging too. For instance, a study of direct food aid versus direct cash transfers in rural Mexico found that providing free food tended to lower food prices, which in turn discouraged local farmers from growing more food and depressed their income. However, the direct cash transfers had no effect on prices, presumably because the additional demand gave producers an incentive to supply more food and other items to the local market.[19]

In some cases, cash transfers may produce short-term price inflation, where markets are undeveloped or if the transfer amount is large relative to local living standards. In those circumstances, complementary policies may be required, including informing potential suppliers of goods and services to expect greater demand. But these are surmountable challenges.

Many studies of the effects of cash transfers have shown welfare improvements. For example, most have led to better child nutrition. In Colombia, a CCT boosted children's average height-for-age.[20] In Mexico, the CCT reduced stunting among babies by 39 per cent for girls and 19 per cent for boys. Sri Lanka's *Samruddhi* cash scheme also led to improved child nutrition.[21] More generally, in rural Malawi, cash transfers had a sizeable impact on food security and food diversity.[22]

In many places, including India, CCTs have been associated with a reduction in neonatal and perinatal deaths. There is also evidence, mainly from Latin America, that CCTs boost the use of preventive health services, being associated with more frequent health check-ups.[23] The same effect has been found in India.[24] Apart from any conditions, cash transfers help people afford the user fees for health services (and/or the costs of travelling to clinics) that are a reality in most developing countries.[25] And when people have money to pay for medical services, public and private providers are put under pressure to improve quality and performance.

With CCTs, it is often unclear how much of the effect is due to the conditionality and how much to the cash. Fortunately, unconditional transfers appear to have similar positive effects.[26] For example, unconditional transfers have been shown to lead to dietary diversity, a development associated with better child nutrition.[27] And in the Namibian basic income experiment described later in this chapter, people made more use of health services, without prompting, because the extra money made a visit to the local clinic more affordable.

The evidence for the positive effects of cash transfers on children's schooling, in terms of school enrolment and attendance, is voluminous.[28] Both conditional and unconditional schemes have been associated with a rise in school enrolment, in Latin America and in African countries. In Mexico, secondary school enrolment rose by a third and school drop-out rates fell by 20 per cent after the national cash transfer scheme *Oportunidades* was introduced (initially as *Progresa*). Similarly, in Malawi, cash transfers raised enrolment and reduced the school drop-out rate for adolescent girls.[29] In South Africa, the effect was particularly large for young children,[30] while the international evidence points to a strong impact on enrolment for girls, in Bangladesh and Cambodia as well as in Latin America.[31]

Again, it is difficult to separate the effect of the cash from the effect of the conditionality. However, the Malawi study on adolescent girls suggested that cash alone had a positive effect on education and was much more cost-effective. The finding was accidental; due to an oversight, recipients in one area were not told about the conditions, which were then not enforced. The evaluation concluded that 'a $5/month transfer to a household made unconditionally had roughly the same impact on schooling outcomes as a $15/month transfer made conditional on school attendance'.[32]

More regular school attendance does not necessarily improve educational performance measured by test scores, which may reflect poor quality schools in many areas where cash transfer programmes have been implemented.[33] But there do seem to be significant positive effects on cognitive development.

Meanwhile, the evidence has definitively repudiated claims by critics of cash transfers that they would discourage 'work' and encourage women to have more children to claim additional benefits (claims also directed at cash transfers in rich countries). Instead, by empowering women to make their own choices, cash transfers have resulted in later marriage, lower fertility and less unwanted sexual activity.[34]

Studies have also shown an increase, not a decrease, in work, particularly when secondary activities are included.[35]

Cash transfers have been used to set up small income-generating businesses, enabling investment in equipment such as sewing machines and tools. Sometimes people have reduced casual wage labour to spend more time on their own farms, because the cash transfers can be spent on fertilizers, seeds or livestock that make their farms more productive.

A cash transfer scheme in rural Mexico found that each US dollar provided generated US$2 in additional income on average; small-scale farmers generated US$3 per US dollar provided, reducing income inequality.[36] Another cash transfer scheme in Mexico found that over a quarter of transfers were invested in income-generating activities.[37] In Zambia, households receiving cash transfers increased spending by 60 per cent more than the transfer amount as a result of increased earnings from farm and non-farm production.[38]

Putting more purchasing power in people's hands is bound to boost the local economy through 'multiplier' effects, even allowing for some inflation. While the impact can be hard to measure when cash transfer programmes are small or involve scattered individuals over a wide area, one evaluation of seven transfer schemes found that for every dollar transferred, the income of the local economy rose by between $1.10 and $1.85, after adjusting for inflation. And those ineligible for transfers may gain directly as well, from gifts and loans from recipients.[39] Again, this shows that the community effects of basic income are likely to be greater than the sum of effects on individual recipients.

The findings from the many studies of conditional and unconditional cash transfer schemes in developing countries can be summarized as showing statistically significant declines in income poverty, increases in food expenditure and nutrition, less school absenteeism, improved cognitive development, more use of health services, more use of savings for investment, particularly in livestock and agricultural assets, and modest increases in local economic growth.

Basic Income Pilots

Apart from targeted, selective and conditional cash transfer schemes, there have been two pilots designed to test out a true basic income in the sense defined in Chapter 1, with one obvious limitation, that they are temporary or short-term, rather than long-term or 'permanent'.

NAMIBIA

The first basic income pilot in a developing country was implemented in the small Namibian village of Otjivero-Omitara in 2008–9, covering about 1,000 people.[40] The study was carried out by the Namibian Basic Income Grant Coalition, with money raised from foundations and individual donations. Everyone in the village, including children but excluding over-sixties already receiving a social pension, was given a very small basic income of N$100 a month (worth US$12 at the time or about a third of the poverty line), and the outcomes compared with the previous situation. The results included better nutrition, particularly among children, improved health and greater use of the local primary healthcare centre, higher school attendance, increased economic activity and enhanced women's status.[41]

The methodology would not have satisfied those favouring randomized control trials that were coming into vogue at the time. No control village was chosen to allow for the effects of external factors, in the country or economy, because those directing the pilot felt it was immoral to impose demands, in the form of lengthy surveys, on people who were being denied the benefit of the basic income grants. However, there were no reported changes in policy or outside interventions during the period covered by the pilot, and confidence in the results is justified both by the observed behaviour, and by recipients' opinions in successive surveys.

School attendance went up sharply, though there was no pressure on parents to send their children to school. The dynamics were revealing. Although the primary school was a state school, parents were required to pay a small fee for each child. Before the pilot, registration and attendance were low, and the school had too little income from fees to pay for basics, which made the school unattractive and lowered teachers' morale. Once the cash transfers started, parents had enough money to pay school fees, and teachers had money to buy paper, pens, books, posters, paints and brushes, making the school more attractive to parents and children and raising the morale and, probably, the capacity of its teachers.

There was also a substantial fall in petty economic crime such as stealing vegetables and killing small livestock for food. This encouraged villagers to plant more vegetables, buy more fertilizer and rear more livestock. These dynamic community-wide economic effects are usually overlooked in conventional evaluations, and would not be spotted if cash was given only to a random selection of individuals or house-holds and evaluated as a randomized control trial.

Another outcome, unplanned and unanticipated, was that villagers voluntarily set up a Basic Income Advisory Committee, led by the local primary school teacher and the village nurse, to advise people on how to spend or save their basic income money. The universal basic income thus induced collective action, and there was no doubt that this community activism increased the effectiveness of the basic incomes.

Smaller grants continued after the pilot ended, with similar results, and the experiment has proved politically influential inside the country, despite consistent opposition from the local representatives of the IMF. The sustained support is partly due to the status of Bishop Zephania Kameeta, former chair of Namibia's Basic Income Grant (BIG) Coalition, who had backed the pilot enthusiastically and was appointed in 2015 as minister for poverty eradication and social welfare.

In December 2015, Namibian President Hage Geingob declared basic income grants to be part of his anti-poverty strategy. But in June 2016, the government initiated a food bank programme, while basic income seemed to have been put on the back burner. Was this yet another instance of a road not taken?

INDIA

Three basic income pilots were conducted in India in 2009–13, coordinated by SEWA, the Self-Employed Women's Association, a union of women workers.[42] Funds were mobilized, first from the United Nations Development Programme and then, more substantially, from the United Nations children's fund UNICEF.

The first and smallest pilot gave several hundred families holding BPL (Below-Poverty-Line) cards in an area of West Delhi a choice between continuing with the subsidized rice, wheat, sugar and kerosene provided under the official Public Distribution System (PDS) or receiving a monthly basic income of equivalent value, to last for one year. About half chose the cash option; not surprisingly, many people were reluctant to shift from a familiar to an unfamiliar system.

After a few months, however, many of those who had continued with the rations asked the research team if they could switch to the basic income. Since this would have confused the experiment, a switch was not permitted. Nevertheless, it indicated that people had learned from talking to others in their community about the advantages of the cash payment. By contrast, none of those who had opted for the basic income expressed a desire to switch back to rations. After one year, the outstanding result was that nutrition and eating habits had improved among the basic income recipients, but not among those who had continued with the subsidized rations.

In the second, much bigger pilot, in Madhya Pradesh, about 6,000 men, women and children in eight villages were given a monthly basic income for eighteen months that would give a low-income family of five roughly 30 per cent extra. What happened was evaluated both by comparison with prior conditions and by comparison with a slightly larger number of people in twelve otherwise similar villages.

A third pilot gave a basic income to all residents in one tribal village, and their experience over the next twelve months was compared with that of all residents in an otherwise similar tribal village.

A unique feature of the second pilot was the testing of Voice, the hypothesis being that the positive effects of a basic income would be greater if vulnerable people had access to an organization that could defend and promote their interests. Accordingly, in four of the 'basic income' villages there was a 'Voice' institution (SEWA) already operating on behalf of individuals or families, and in the other four 'basic income' villages there was no such body. Similarly, in six of the control villages SEWA was operating, and in the other six it was not.

What emerged was strong evidence that villagers benefited most from having advice and assistance in setting up bank accounts and handling money. However, the positive effects of the basic income were felt in both SEWA and non-SEWA villages.

For the first three months, the basic income was paid by handing over cash in person. Subsequently, it was deposited in bank accounts opened for the purpose if recipients did not already have one. (In the third pilot in the tribal village, the basic income was paid in person throughout.) Each man and each woman received their own basic income, and half the adult amount was paid to each child through the mother's or surrogate mother's account. Unlike the cash transfer schemes mentioned earlier, the payment was both unconditional and universal – everybody living in the community at the outset received the basic income.

The main results of the Madhya Pradesh pilots can be summarized in four dimensions.[43] First, the welfare effects were overwhelmingly positive, in terms of improved sanitation, improved child and adult nutrition, better health, better healthcare, and improved school attendance and educational performance. In general, people spent the extra money sensibly; contrary to a prediction made by Sonia Gandhi, leader of the then-ruling Congress Party, among others, spending on alcohol and tobacco actually fell.

When, later, villagers were asked why that was so, the most common response was that the men had more work to do. Moreover, a cash transfer paid to individual family members may have been regarded as intrinsically for welfare and productive uses (an implicit 'labelling effect') rather than for 'temptation goods'.

Second, social equity improved. The benefits were more marked for people with disabilities, for women compared with men, and for scheduled caste and scheduled tribe families compared with upper castes. All those structurally disadvantaged groups had access to their own income, many for the first time, and mothers were able to look after the needs of girl children. School registration and attendance records for girls showed big improvements, more so than for boys, although theirs improved as well. And whereas previously young girls were more likely than boys to be underweight for their age, by the end of the pilot they had gained more than the boys had done. Gender equity undoubtedly improved.

Third, and contrary to what critics had predicted, the basic incomes were associated with *increased* work and labour, not less, except among children who went to school instead. By the end of the pilot women in particular were doing more secondary economic activities (such as making clothes or, in one case, bangles), a phenomenon easily overlooked by conventional studies that focus on changes in 'main activity'. Overall, there was considerably more economic activity in the basic income villages, in ways that reduced income inequality and in several respects fostered community development, such as the creation of a cooperative fishpond and a collective initiative to improve village drainage.

The fourth, unanticipated outcome was most encouraging of all. The basic income had emancipatory effects, giving individuals more control over their lives. Some were able to reduce indebtedness; some escaped from inter-generational bonded labour; others were able to put money aside or borrow from family or neighbours, reducing their dependence on exorbitant moneylenders; and many of those who, for the first time, had money of their own were empowered to take their own decisions and challenge social norms. As mentioned in Chapter 3, for example, young women in one village felt able to defy their elders and go unveiled in public.

Thus the emancipatory value of the basic income, even though it was very modest, exceeded its monetary value.[44] As with any commodity, the scarcity of money in those villages made it expensive to acquire, enabling moneylenders to charge interest at 50 per cent and impose arduous conditions, such as requiring borrowers to labour on their land as and when needed. The basic income provided vital liquidity, which drove down the price of money and gave villagers some control of their finances, particularly at moments of personal crisis.

Because of the combination of the four effects – welfare, equity, economic growth and emancipation – the authors of the study concluded, surely reasonably enough, that the basic income was in those villages, and could be nationally, a *transformative* policy.

The Affordability Question

It is often assumed that low-income countries cannot afford basic income. However, the level of the basic income would obviously be set in relation to resources available and could be gradually increased over time. As the basic income pilots have shown, even very small amounts, guaranteed and paid regularly, can transform the lives of poor people.

Many developing countries have introduced universal or near-universal pensions for the elderly, including Bolivia, Botswana, Mauritius and South Africa. These often act as a basic income for an entire household, including grandchildren, with associated benefits in terms of better nutrition and school attendance. In Namibia, more than 70 per cent of pension income is shared and spent on food and education for grandchildren. A few countries, such as Argentina and Mongolia, pay universal mother-and-child benefits. Thus resources can be found if there is the political will to do so. There are four possible ways for developing countries to do this.

First, a basic income could be financed by increasing taxes. Most developing countries have notoriously inadequate and undeveloped tax systems and collect a low share of national income, especially from income tax. So the taxation route is probably easier in a developed country with a relatively sophisticated tax system and administrative apparatus. However, Brazil has raised funds for social programmes by taxing financial transactions.

Second, funds could come from switching public expenditure. Apart from spending excessively on the military, or 'white elephant' prestige projects, many developing countries operate expensive and highly regressive subsidy schemes for food and fuel. In 2013, the IMF calculated that fossil fuel subsidies amounted to half government revenues in Iran, 43 per cent in Bangladesh, and 31 per cent in Pakistan.[45] Earlier, the IMF estimated that the wealthiest 20 per cent of households received six times as much benefit from fuel subsidies as the poorest 20 per cent, simply because they used much more fuel – for their cars, air conditioning and so on.[46]

In India, central and state subsidies accruing to the better-off groups in society (not directed at the poor) may account for 9 per cent of national income (GDP), and a further 6 per cent of GDP consists of revenues foregone in the form of tax breaks that are granted mainly to companies.[47] A basic income equivalent to three-quarters of the official poverty line paid to every Indian would cost about 10 per cent of GDP (ignoring any impact on economic growth). Even a level of about half the poverty line would make a substantial difference to living standards for the vast majority.

Switching from regressive subsidies would avoid steep increases in tax rates (though most developing countries could usefully raise more revenue by expanding their currently narrow tax base). The first to be phased out should be subsidies that distort local markets and those that impinge on the freedom of ordinary people. In the Indian case, and probably elsewhere as well, there would be no need to introduce a basic income as an alternative to existing social programmes.

A *third* method of funding is through the sovereign wealth fund, social dividend route mentioned in Chapter 7. This is eminently suited to developing countries rich in oil and other minerals, or valuable commodities such as timber, the revenues from which go mainly to rent-seeking elites. Many have already set up sovereign wealth funds, but these have been used mainly as investment vehicles to help stabilize future government finances. In Goa, India, the Goenchi Mati Movement is pressing for the proceeds of iron ore mining to go into a permanent fund, similar to Alaska's Permanent Fund, which would be used to finance a citizen's dividend. Bolivia, Zambia and Mongolia are already using taxes on natural resources to pay for social benefits.

Sovereign wealth funds do not need to be financed by natural resources, however. In Macao, China, where the main asset is its casinos, all residents receive an annual state bonus, mainly funded by lottery revenues, which has amounted to over US$1,000 equivalent in recent years. This so-called 'Wealth Partaking Scheme', operating since 2008, runs alongside a one-off capital grant equivalent to US$1,250 at age twenty-two, paid into qualifying individual provident fund accounts.[48] An intriguing example from mainland China concerns Huaidi, an 'urban village' in Hebei province, which uses property assets deriving from land compensation and land development rights to fund a basic income for all residents as well as a wide range of in-kind benefits and public services.[49]

The *fourth* method involves funding by donors. There is considerable scope for redirecting more bilateral and multilateral aid towards basic income schemes and, as indicated in Chapter 11, there is already a substantial private philanthropic interest in financing experiments and pilots.

Although reducing poverty, economic insecurity, malnutrition and ill-health should be the primary driving forces, an additional factor is the stress being placed on societies all over the world from distress and other forms of migration. A basic income system in impoverished and low-income communities in developing countries would surely encourage more people to stay in and (re)build their communities.

From Subsidies to Basic Income

Often pressed by the international financial institutions, several countries have begun trying to reduce food and fuel subsidies with compensating targeted cash transfer schemes, with mixed success. They include Egypt, India, Indonesia and Thailand, among others. However, one country, Iran, has come remarkably close to introducing a basic income.

In December 2010, the Iranian government increased food and energy prices by up to twenty times, in a bid to slash its costly subsidy bill estimated at US$50–60 billion and curb wasteful energy use. At the same time, households began to receive a regular cash grant to compensate for the increased cost of living. The grant was universal and unconditional, with the one proviso that those who were subject to income tax had to submit tax returns. For this reason, many of the richer citizens preferred not to apply to receive the 'basic income', which also reduced the gross cost.[50]

For some years, two-thirds of Iranian adults received a government payment, a higher proportion than in any country in the world, with over 90 per cent of the payments going directly into bank accounts.[51] For the poor, who benefited least from subsidized energy prices, the grant more than compensated for any loss and had a significant effect in reducing poverty and inequality, especially in rural areas.[52]

Critics initially attacked the scheme as inflationary; there was an initial inflationary spurt when the scheme was launched, but it was kept in check by temporary government measures. Sadly, however, although the grant scheme cost about half what fuel subsidies were costing, a growing budget deficit led the government to introduce a means-tested system in 2016. As a result, the number of people receiving payments is expected to halve.

Basic Income as Humanitarian Aid

The last ten years or so have seen a big expansion in the use of cash transfers to help refugees and survivors of natural or man-made disasters. In the immediate aftermath of such disasters, food, water, shelter and medicine are obviously priorities. But once that phase has passed, enabling people to recover and re-establish their economic activities and rebuild their communities is best achieved by giving them the means to help themselves.

The world responded with great generosity after the Indian Ocean tsunami in December 2004, which killed over 230,000 people and laid waste to coastal communities in fourteen countries. Large amounts of money were mobilized for aid, and many NGOs sent teams to help. This writer, who was working on projects in Sri Lanka at the time, saw not just the devastation but how NGOs were literally competing to provide assistance. The generosity and goodwill were genuine. But often the assistance was not what the communities wanted or needed. Providing everybody in the tsunami-affected communities with basic income cash transfers would have given them more choice on how to move forward with their lives, instead of being showered with goods that they did not want or had no longer-term use for.[53]

In the aftermath of the Iraq war in 2003, a guaranteed basic income by the 'international community' for, say, three years, might have avoided much of the chaos and bloodshed that followed, giving Iraqis a stake in the reconstruction of their society and helping to build communities more resilient to the sirens of extremism. A basic income might also have helped after the US invasion of Afghanistan in 2001, providing a material reason for the population to support political change.

The UN's World Food Programme (WFP), which compared 'food versus cash' in four countries, found that in three of the four – Ecuador, Uganda and Yemen (before the civil war) – cash transfers led to better nutrition at lower cost, meaning many more people could be helped for the same outlay. (In the fourth, Niger, severe seasonal food shortages meant that in-kind deliveries improved dietary diversity more than cash.)[54] This has led the WFP to put more emphasis on cash transfers; today, just over a quarter of WFP's aid globally is cash-based.

In Lebanon, home to well over a million Syrian refugees, the UN Refugee Agency (UNHCR) decided to use its limited 'winterization' funds to pay cash transfers to vulnerable families living above 500 metres altitude. These were unconditional, although recipients were told they were intended for buying heating supplies. Recipient families were then compared with a control group living just below 500 metres.

The researchers found that cash assistance did lead to increased spending on fuel supplies, but it also boosted school enrolment, reduced child labour and increased food security.[55] One notable finding was that the basic income tended to increase mutual support between beneficiaries and others in the community, reduced tension within recipient families, and improved relationships with the host community. There were significant multiplier effects, with each dollar of cash assistance generating more than $2 for the Lebanese economy, most of which was spent locally.

In October 2016, the UN High Commissioner for Refugees said:

> The use of cash-based assistance has been a real game changer in the way we help refugees and we have now decided to make it a worldwide policy and expand it to all our operations, where feasible . . . Refugees know best what they need. The broader use of cash-based assistance means

that many more will be able to decide how to manage their family's budget. This will help them lead more dignified and normal lives.[56]

A further pragmatic advantage of such a policy is that it would help to reduce the pressure on people to migrate in distress and desperation. And it would reduce the cost and inefficiencies inherent in other forms of foreign aid.

Basic Income for Conflict Avoidance

It is a sad irony that many countries possessing natural resources with high income potential have floundered into civil strife as factions compete for their share of the bounty, often monopolized by despotic leaders. Sharing the resource wealth across the country is one suggested way to defuse the threat of political conflict, usually by transferring part of the earnings to local area governments and, in particular, to the area where the natural resource is exploited, be it oil, diamonds or other minerals. In some cases, this fiscal devolution route has limited the conflict, if the amount transferred is large enough. However, in others it has triggered conflict by giving local dissidents the means to pay for insurrection.[57] It turns out that the optimum way to defuse or prevent potential conflict is to pay direct cash transfers to all individuals, which would make it much more difficult for secessionist movements or local political parties to appropriate the resources.

These 'direct dividend' payments, essentially a basic income, would also help overcome the 'resource curse' or 'Dutch disease', so named because when natural gas was discovered in Dutch waters it drove up the exchange rate, decimating local manufacturing through loss of exports and an influx of cheaper manufactured goods from abroad. As argued by the 'oil-to-cash initiative' of the Center for Global Development, the dividends would boost both private consumption and the provision of public goods by fostering citizens' scrutiny of government expenditures.[58] This would lead to more growth and development, further reducing the risk of conflict.

Developing Basic Income

In late 2016, the government of Mexico City drew up a new city constitution that includes a commitment to introduce a basic income in the sprawling metropolis. This followed a recommendation earlier in the year by the United Nations Economic Commission for Latin America and the Caribbean encouraging member states to investigate adoption of a basic income guarantee. The Mexico City constitution sets a precedent that is likely to be copied across Latin America and more widely. It marks a further stage in the development of an economic right, one that may become a norm in the years ahead.

In India, the finance minister of the state of Jammu and Kashmir announced in his January 2017 budget his intention to phase in a basic income; it may be targeted but his rationale was clear.[59] And the federal government was contemplating basic income at a national level. Its annual *Economic Report*, issued alongside the budget at the end of January 2017, included a special chapter discussing the pros and cons of a basic income.[60] There may be a long way to go, but the very fact that the central government of the most populous country in the world is considering basic income testifies to a new legitimacy. Shortly afterwards, the Indian finance minister said he expected more piloting of basic income to begin within a year.

Paradoxically, it could be easier to introduce a basic income system in developing countries than in rich ones. Transition costs would be much less, simply because it would not be necessary to untangle an enormously complex welfare system with dozens if not hundreds of selective, targeted and quasi-universalistic schemes.

This is not to suggest that dismantling well-entrenched subsidy schemes would be inconsequential. But these are so obviously distortionary and regressive that those defending them would be on weaker moral and social grounds. Iran managed to achieve widespread public acceptance of its decision to reduce food and energy subsidies by coupling the compensatory cash grants with a public relations campaign highlighting the deficiencies and unfairness of the subsidy regime.

There has been a remarkable conversion to cash within the humanitarian aid community across the world, while cash transfers and basic income have been legitimized as mainstream development policy. If more resources can be channelled into such schemes and governments in developing countries, at local as well as at national levels, persuaded to put more faith in basic income, all the signs are that this would lead to rapid declines in economic insecurity and poverty and more sustainable development.

Basic Income Initiatives and Pilots

'I . . . pondered how men fight and lose the battle, and the thing they fought for comes about in spite of their defeat, and when it comes turns out not to be what they meant, and other men have to fight for what they meant under another name.'

WILLIAM MORRIS, 1886

The past few years have seen a surge in basic income initiatives and pilot schemes in countries and communities with widely different levels of income. Initiatives aim primarily to raise public awareness of basic income, to put pressure on politicians and policymakers, and to stimulate people to join the 'movement'. The main objectives of pilots are to test alternative *designs* of basic income schemes and evaluate outcomes in relation to claims by both advocates and critics, for example, on consumption of 'bads' or participation in the labour market.

This chapter will first look at recent citizens' initiatives and then consider the value of pilots, with a brief review of those done in the past and those in the planning stage at the time of writing.

The Basic Income Earth Network (BIEN)

The Basic Income European Network, later the Basic Income Earth Network (BIEN), was formally established in September 1986 at a meeting in Louvain-la-Neuve, Belgium. It was symbolic more by chance than design that Thomas More's *Utopia* was first published in Louvain, in 1516; in 2016, celebration of *Utopia*'s 500 years coincided with those for BIEN's thirtieth birthday, again held at Louvain-la-Neuve.

Members of BIEN, now drawn from all over the world, have produced copious research and writing on the many issues thrown up by the simple idea that everybody in society should have a basic income as a right. Funded by member subscriptions, BIEN holds an international congress every two years; the first took place in Antwerp in 1988 while the 2016 Congress was held in Seoul.

By early 2017, there were thirty-four affiliated networks promoting basic income, in Argentina, Australia, Austria, Belgium, Brazil, Bulgaria, Canada, China, Finland, France, Germany, Iceland, India, Ireland, Italy, Japan, Mexico, the Netherlands, New Zealand, Norway, Poland, Portugal, Quebec (Canada), Scotland (UK), Slovenia, South Korea, 'Southern Africa' (covering several countries), Spain, Sweden, Switzerland, Taiwan, the UK (with two, the Citizen's Income Trust and Basic Income UK) and the United States.

BIEN can claim to have kept the debate going through times of political disdain, trying to refine intellectual arguments, deal with objections, encourage costings and collect evidence from all over the world. Initially, a multilingual newsletter reported on work in various countries, now online as *Basic Income News*. And BIEN has spawned a peer-reviewed journal, *Basic Income Studies*.

However, the key event has been the BIEN congress convened, so far, every two years. After the inaugural event in Louvain in 1986, the venues were a roll-call of some of the great cities of western Europe; Antwerp in 1988 was followed by

Florence, London, Paris, Amsterdam, Vienna, Berlin, Geneva and Barcelona in 2004. The last took place under the aegis of the World Social Forum and brought in hundreds of extra participants who had been attending other events at the time.

At the end of the Barcelona Congress, members voted overwhelmingly to convert BIEN into a global network, and agreed informally to alternate future congresses between a European venue and one outside Europe. Ensuing events were held in Cape Town, Dublin, São Paulo, Munich and Montreal. However, the informal rule was quietly sidelined with the 2016 congress in Seoul, attended by participants from all over the world. Growing interest and the fact that over thirty national networks had been formed prompted a decision in Seoul to hold a congress in Lisbon in September 2017 and another in Tampere, Finland, in mid-2018.

Hundreds of papers on all aspects of basic income have been written, presented and discussed at these congresses. Those of us who have participated from the outset have often remarked how we have learned something new at each and every event. Only a small fraction of the papers have been published, but historically minded scholars should find many gems.[1] BIEN has from the beginning been open to, and encouraged, the expression of a wide range of perspectives on basic income. It is in that spirit that the network has continued to thrive.

The Swiss Referendum of June 2016

The Swiss referendum on basic income of June 2016 attracted intense and widespread international debate and media attention. At one level, the most obvious, it failed. But there is good reason to think it advanced the cause. It was started by a few enthusiasts, without funds or organization, and snowballed into a joyous series of actions whose legacy should stand future movements in good stead.

Switzerland's unique form of 'direct democracy' allows groups of citizens to call for national referendums on specific policies. This requires the validated signatures of 100,000 Swiss citizens in support of the proposal, to be collected within a year of launching the initiative. Despite a lack of funds or support from any of the established political parties, the organizers obtained 141,000 signatures from across Switzerland, of which 129,000 were validated.

With few funds and no party backing, the organizers were unable to buy publicity on TV, radio or in the newspapers. To counter this disadvantage, they resorted to some clever stunts that gained considerable public attention, in Switzerland and around the world. Despite the refusal of Swiss banks to cooperate, the campaign managed to accumulate 8 million gold-coloured five-cent coins – one for every Swiss resident – which were dumped outside the national parliament building across from the Swiss National Bank. The video of the occasion was widely viewed.

A poster that set the Guinness world record for the largest ever printed took up most of Geneva's biggest square, asking rhetorically, 'What would you do if your income were taken care of?' An aerial photograph of the poster became a campaign symbol. And there were colourful street marches with children dressed as robots. The organizers even arranged one morning to use some of their limited funds to hand out ten-franc banknotes to commuters in Zurich station. That certainly made the news.

These gimmicks were a mixed blessing. They achieved their primary objective of gaining publicity. But they unbalanced the campaign, appearing to imply that a basic income would enable people not to work and that campaigners believed robots were about to displace people in jobs. They also focused attention on largely urban issues, and it was to be the rural vote that was overwhelmingly negative.

The crucial error, however, was not of the campaign's doing. The wording of its proposed amendment to the Swiss Constitution gave no figure for the level of the basic income, which was left to Parliament to decide. But early in the campaign, two people wrote a little book advocating a monthly basic income of 2,500 Swiss francs – about £1,700 or US$2,500. Although this figure was not authorized by the campaign, it was seized upon by referendum opponents who said the campaign wanted a basic income that was unrealistically high and unaffordable. Soon the international media were also reporting that the referendum was about 'giving every Swiss 2,500 Swiss francs a month, or over £20,000 a year'. Opponents also used the scare tactic of claiming that basic income would lead to a sharp increase in migration into Switzerland, although under the referendum proposal Parliament would decide on eligibility conditions for migrants.

The wording of the proposed amendment to the Swiss Constitution was:

Article 110(a) Unconditional basic income
The Confederation shall ensure the introduction of an
    unconditional basic income;
The basic income shall enable the whole population to
    live in human dignity and participate in public life;
The law shall particularly regulate the way in which the
    basic income is to be financed and the level at which
    it is set.

In the end, nearly a quarter (23 per cent) of those who voted supported the initiative, on a turnout of 46.4 per cent. Although this was portrayed abroad as a resounding rejection of basic income as a social policy, the leaders of the campaign were justified in regarding it as a success. The campaign had engendered a serious conversation across Switzerland, in the media, in cafés and at home. Many more people had come to understand what basic income was about. And the debate and results were reported all over the world, a rare occurrence for Swiss referendums, which are regular events.

While fewer than one in five who voted in rural areas supported the initiative, the story was very different in the major towns and cities. In Geneva, the proposal gained 35 per cent support and in Zurich over 54 per cent. In an opinion poll the week after the referendum, over two-thirds of those questioned thought the vote was the *beginning* of a longer-term conversation about introducing a basic income, not the end of it. Even many of those who had voted against it said it should be reconsidered later. The medium-term prospects are surely stronger as a result. As one of the leaders of the campaign suggested, anticipating defeat: 'The Swiss debate is like a movie trailer for the main event and trailers always end with the phrase, coming soon . . .'[2]

It is perhaps too early to say whether the Swiss referendum was a defeat that has put back the cause or whether it is a stepping stone for the eventual introduction of a basic income. But there is a saying in Switzerland that no major reform has ever been passed in one referendum; it usually takes two.

The UBIE Initiative

At about the same time as the momentum for the Swiss referendum campaign was starting to build, a group of enthusiasts from across Europe, many of them BIEN members, decided to launch a European Union 'people's initiative'. The Unconditional Basic Income Europe (UBIE) campaign of 2014 aimed to obtain the signatures of one million EU citizens within one year, which would have obliged the European Commission to examine the feasibility of introducing a basic income in the EU.

Again without funding, and initially without an organizational structure, the campaign succeeded in mobilizing thousands of activists in twenty-seven EU countries, resulting among other things in the establishment of new national basic income networks. Ultimately, over 300,000 signatures were obtained, creating a solid base for another such campaign in the near future, possibly in 2018.

Meanwhile, both UBIE and BIEN are promoting an annual International Basic Income Week, the 2016 event being the ninth. This provides a platform for public debates and presentations on basic income, helping to energize supporters and to create and spread awareness.

Pilots Past

Cash transfer schemes and basic income pilots in developing countries were reviewed in Chapter 10. Cash transfers of one kind or another, both targeted (social assistance, pensions) and universal (child allowances in many countries), are of course the norm in industrialized countries, so this section will focus just on two experiments in North America that have been specifically linked to basic income.

THE DAUPHIN, MANITOBA EXPERIMENT

Along with a pilot in Winnipeg at the same time, the Manitoba Basic Annual Income Experiment (Mincome) has achieved legendary status among supporters of basic income, even though it was a negative income tax rather than a full basic income scheme. Jointly funded by the federal and provincial governments, the experiment was conducted between 1975 and 1977 in Dauphin, Manitoba, when the Liberals were in government, only to be suspended after the Conservatives came to power and before the data could be evaluated. Nearly forty years later, researchers unearthed 1,800 dusty cardboard boxes at Canada's National Archives containing the original files, which have been painstakingly collated and partially analysed by Evelyn Forget and others.[3]

Mincome was what some have called 'targeting within universalism'.[4] Since all town residents had the option of collecting the Mincome payments, it was both universal and unconditional. Anybody could enrol in the scheme and would qualify for payments if their household income fell below the designated threshold, whatever the reason. People with no labour income could access the full guarantee, equivalent to just under half the median household income. For every Canadian dollar earned, the Mincome amount was reduced by 50 cents, ending once earnings reached C$39,000, roughly the median household income at the time.

More than 2,000 people – a fifth of Dauphin's population – received benefits at some point during the three-year experiment. While Mincome was intended to test the effects of a 'guaranteed annual income' on employment, the data also enabled researchers to look at the impact on various measures of well-being. Families receiving Mincome had fewer hospitalizations, accidents and injuries, including from domestic violence, and a lower incidence of serious mental disorders than similar non-recipient families. Youths, especially boys, were less likely to drop out of high school. Meanwhile, there was little change in hours worked by people with full-time jobs, but students and mothers with young children did reduce time in paid jobs, enabling them to spend more time on their studies or looking after their children.[5]

Because Dauphin was a 'saturation site' for the Mincome experiment, where all residents were in principle eligible for payments, it was also possible to detect community effects. The increase in boys staying on at school was partly attributed to peer influence. Students from families receiving income top-ups, previously most at risk of dropping out, were under less pressure to leave school and find jobs. But students from non-recipient families were also more likely to stay on at school if their friends from recipient families were doing so, an example of peer influence that arises when benefits are universal.

Furthermore, unlike existing welfare programmes, Mincome was perceived as less stigmatizing and this seemed to carry through into people's social interactions. Mincome recipients socialized more than welfare recipients, used their time in similar ways to non-participants with higher socio-economic status, and were much more likely than welfare recipients to say they never felt embarrassed or uncomfortable with people not on Mincome or welfare.[6]

THE ACCIDENTAL PILOT:
CHEROKEE INDIANS AND THE CASINO

In 1993 researchers at Duke University in North Carolina began 'The Great Smoky Mountains Study of Youth', designed to track the mental health of 1,420 school-age children from low-income families. Four years into the study, in 1997, the Eastern Band of Cherokee Indians opened a casino on their reservation, and tribal leaders decided to distribute half the profits equally and annually to all tribal members. Over the course of the study, the payments amounted to about $4,000 a year per person, boosting household incomes by almost a fifth on average. (This did not include the children's payments, which were banked for them until the age of 18.)

The 'basic income', paid unconditionally, fortuitously provided the basis for a unique longitudinal pilot. About a quarter of the children in the study were tribal members, so for a decade the researchers were able to compare their development with that of the other children in the study. The results were remarkable. Children in families receiving the basic income, controlling for other factors, did better at school, and there was a 'dramatic decrease' in juvenile crime. They had a lower incidence of behavioural and emotional disorders and higher scores for 'conscientiousness' and 'agreeableness', two personality traits shown to have long-term positive life outcomes in terms of holding down a job and maintaining personal relationships.[7] Conscientiousness is the tendency to be organized, responsible and hardworking, while agreeableness is the tendency to act in a cooperative and unselfish manner.

Children appeared to have benefited from better relationships between parents (partly because there was less financial stress and less arguing about money), which also improved the relationship between parents and children. Drug and alcohol use among parents declined. Most encouraging of all, the positive changes were most pronounced in the children who began as the most deprived or disturbed. The basic income helped those who needed it most.

THE NAMIBIAN AND INDIAN PILOTS

As discussed in the last chapter, the basic income pilots in Namibia and India provided compelling narratives. While the research methodologies might not satisfy the purists who treat randomized control trials as the gold standard, they combined qualitative and quantitative data to provide a richer interpretation of the effects of giving a basic income to whole communities. And the design was as close to a true basic income as was feasible for a short-term pilot. The payments were basic, paid in cash, paid monthly, paid individually, paid to everybody and paid unconditionally. Thus they allowed identification of individual, household and community effects.

Pilots Present and Planned

A series of announcements has made 2017 a 'year of the pilots', initially creating something close to euphoria among basic income supporters. Yet the mood has since changed to disappointment as timidity and expediency have taken over, with ulterior motives in play. Pilots should aim to test whether basic income has the effects its advocates claim in terms of reducing inequality and economic insecurity, and promoting personal freedom and community cohesion. This means testing a genuine basic income – universal, unconditional, given to every individual in a community on a regular basis. Regrettably, for a variety of reasons, most of the planned 'basic income' pilots are not designed to do this. Here is the state of play at the start of 2017.

FINLAND'S NATIONAL INSURANCE AGENCY

In 2015, the newly elected Finnish Prime Minister, Juha Sipilä, announced that a basic income pilot would be instituted as part of what was called 'experimental governance'. Some €20 million has been allocated for the project. In March 2016, KELA, the national insurance agency with responsibility for the pilot, summarized its aim as follows:

> The basic income experiment is one of the measures aimed at reforming the Finnish social security system in

accordance with changes in working life, to make social security more participatory and incentive-based, to reduce bureaucracy and simplify the complex benefit system in a manner that would be sustainable from the perspective of general government finances.

In advance of finalizing the pilot design, KELA issued a review paper on the various options and summarizing the legislative and legal challenges to be overcome before its implementation in 2017–18.[8] These included rules, under the Finnish Constitution and EU law, that forbid discrimination between groups in the allocation of welfare.

A full basic income pilot was quickly ruled out as too expensive. Instead, from January 2017, €560 (about $620) a month is being provided, tax free, to a random sample of 2,000 registered unemployed aged between twenty-five and fifty-eight receiving KELA unemployment-related benefits. They will continue to receive any current benefits in excess of €560, such as housing allowances, to ensure they are not worse off than before. Participation for those selected is mandatory and, for the two years of the experiment, this group's decisions and outcomes will be compared with the decisions and outcomes of another randomly selected 2,000 unemployed.

In contrast to unemployment benefit, the payment will not be withdrawn if the unemployed person obtains a job during those two years. But the purpose of the experiment, as now devised, is essentially limited to testing the effect of an unconditional payment on job incentives. Thus the Ministry of Social Affairs and Health stated: 'The primary goal of the basic income experiment is related to promoting employment.'[9] The head of the KELA working group that drew up the plan told the press that 'it would encourage people who are afraid of losing their unemployment or other benefits to take short-term jobs'.

In this form, the payments will simply act as a regressive wage subsidy. Those who receive the money and obtain a job will not only be better off than those who remain unemployed, but they will be better off than others doing the same jobs. There may also be a substitution effect if recipients are prepared to accept lower wages as a result, displacing those already in the jobs or putting downward pressure on their wages.

A more ambitious scheme was politically feasible; opinion polls showed that nearly 70 per cent of Finns supported the idea of basic income, at a higher level than has been set. To highlight the fiscal timidity, if scaled up to the whole population, the amount implied by the pilot is less than existing government expenditure on social benefits. As a simple back-of-the-envelope estimate, paying every Finn €560 a month would cost about €36 billion a year, compared with about €42 billion currently spent on cash benefits.

A basic income is not, or should not be, an instrument of social engineering, a thinly veiled attempt to induce people to behave in ways the state thinks they should behave. If the set objective is to induce the unemployed to take low-paid, short-term jobs, and the payments do not in fact result in more unemployed taking such jobs, will 'basic income' be judged to have 'failed'?

One of the hopes of basic income advocates is that it will

enable people to have more control of their time, and to shift to 'work' that is not 'labour', should they wish to do so. This might include unpaid care work, voluntary work in the community, retraining or education. None of these possible and valuable outcomes can be assessed with the proposed pilot. However, it should be noted that most of the funds allocated by the government for the experiment have been kept in reserve for a more substantial pilot to start in 2018, which may come closer to basic income principles.

DUTCH MUNICIPALITIES

The year 2016 also saw growing interest in doing basic income pilots elsewhere. In the Netherlands, a number of municipalities sought to take advantage of a newly enacted law offering local authorities the chance to experiment with innovative social policies. The 2015 *Participation Act* toughened 'workfare' conditions for receiving welfare support, which require people to apply for (and accept) jobs, enrol in return-to-work programmes and do mandatory 'volunteer' work. The Act also gave local councils, which administer social assistance, the power to specify their own conditions, such as volunteer or care work in return for benefits, but at the same time it left room for experimentation.

By the second half of 2016, numerous Dutch municipalities, led by Utrecht, Groningen, Tilburg and Wageningen, had developed plans for various forms of basic income experiment. However, the biggest challenge was gaining approval from the central government; the right-wing People's Party for Freedom and Democracy (VVD), the senior partner in the coalition government, had consistently opposed the idea of basic income. In September 2016 the government said it would allow no more than twenty-five municipalities, with about 22,000 welfare claimants in total, to start pilots from January 2017. And it set strict conditions on how the two-year pilots were to be carried out. This has deterred previously enthusiastic local authorities from going ahead. As of early 2017 only eight were planning pilots; others were waiting for the outcome of the general election in March 2017.

Initially, pilot proponents wanted to see what would happen if behavioural conditions were scrapped and the poverty trap removed, by paying an unconditional benefit that would allow recipients to earn extra income without penalty. The primary hypothesis was that 'workfare' conditions for entitlement to benefits, and sanctions for not fulfilling them, were unnecessary, infringed personal freedom and generated insecurity and hostility. In general, people want to improve their lives by earning income and do not need to be forced to do so.

However, the pilots due to be launched in 2017 will not test anything close to a basic income. Rather than allow local authorities to operate their own experiments, the government has decided to impose its own design, broadly following a complex proposal originally drawn up for Utrecht known as 'Weten Wat Werkt' (Know What Works).[10] This divides the total sample of intended recipients into six groups, intended to test different levels of conditionality on incentives to take jobs and leave welfare rolls.

The first group will receive the normal benefits (€973 for a single person, €1,390 for a married couple) but will not be subject to formal sanctions if they do not seek employment.

A second group will be subject to additional obligations and checks designed to 'reintegrate them into the labour market'. A third group will be allowed to keep 50 per cent of their earnings beyond their welfare payment, up to €199 a month for a single person and €142 for a married couple. A fourth group will be some sort of hybrid of the first three, and the last two will be control groups, one in the municipality, one outside it, subject to the existing welfare regime. Participation will be voluntary, but once in, people cannot withdraw.

Even in its own terms, this complexity would pose severe challenges for any evaluation. But the government has further undermined the value of the experiments by stipulating that, after six months, the municipality must check whether people in the first group have voluntarily made enough efforts to find employment. If the bureaucrats decide they have not, they will be excluded from the trial and revert to the normal 'workfare' conditions. Thus, far from being lifted, sanctions will remain a threat.

This hodgepodge of a design has predictably drawn a spate of criticism. Social scientists from the four collaborating universities of Groningen, Tilburg, Utrecht and Wageningen wrote to the Dutch Parliament to say no scientific evaluation would be possible. As Professor Ruud Muffels pointed out,

> The effects of sanctions have been extensively studied. I wonder what kind of information you want to find. It will also complicate the interpretation of the results of the pilot. If freedom has consequences – the participant can be

banned from the experiment after one year when he or she is not 'active enough' in seeking a paid job – this line of enquiry cannot be tested.[11]

Another critic lamented:

We wanted a simple pilot based on trust rather than on repression. We wanted to give benefit claimants more freedom, more choice, more purchasing power. Now we have a complicated set of rules. What remains is a puzzle, which makes it difficult to shape the experiments and understand the results.

The Dutch experiments will thus be neither a basic income scheme nor consistent with liberal values, more a paternalistic exercise in social engineering. Moreover, the constraints have led most of the formerly interested local authorities to drop or postpone participation. A major difficulty is the requirement for one experimental group to be subject to even harsher job-related conditionality than the present system; this is bound to deter people from volunteering to take part as they will not know in advance to which group they will be allocated.

THE CANADIAN PROVINCE OF ONTARIO

Canada has long seemed a prime candidate to be the first country to introduce a basic income. A 'guaranteed minimum income' via a negative income tax was recommended by a Senate committee as early as 1971 and by a Royal Commission (the Macdonald Commission) in 1985. In 2015–16, politicians in several Canadian provinces indicated interest in sponsoring basic income experiments, including Alberta, British Columbia, Prince Edward Island and Quebec. The Liberal Party, which won the general election of 2016, passed a motion at its subsequent party conference supporting a 'minimum guaranteed income'.

Things have moved fastest in Ontario, where the provincial government has earmarked about C$25 million to establish a three-year basic income pilot project, which it says will aim 'to test the growing view that a basic income could help deliver income support more efficiently, while improving health, employment and housing outcomes for Ontarians'. Hugh Segal, a former Conservative Senator and long-time advocate of basic income, was invited to prepare a discussion paper on options,[12] which provided the basis for a government consultation document in late 2016.[13] A pilot of some sort was expected to be launched in mid-2017.

As Segal admitted in his report, the pilot is unlikely to meet all the criteria for testing a proper basic income, but the plan looks more promising than the Dutch and Finnish experiments. The primary aim is to test variants of a basic income, and the consultation document has recommended three designs: a basic income that would replace the main existing social benefits under Ontario Works and the Ontario Disability Support Program; a basic income as a negative income tax; and a basic income paid to working-age individuals of eighteen to sixty-four years of age with no rules limiting extra earnings. In addition, the government wants to test two benefit levels and two tax-back rates to be applied to any earned income. Evaluations would be based on a randomized control trial and three 'saturation site' studies that would allow testing of community-level effects.

A pilot on these lines obviously risks over-complication, especially as, like the much earlier Mincome experiment, it will only supplement the incomes of individuals that fall below a certain level. Moreover, confining eligibility to working-age adults excludes two income-vulnerable groups, children and the elderly, an important drawback. One in five Canadian children lives in poverty, one of the highest rates in the OECD. Eligibility will also be restricted to people resident for at least a year, though for a pilot this seems reasonable.

Despite the drawbacks, the Ontario basic income pilot is so far the most promising of those planned to start in 2017. There will be no behavioural conditions and the basic income will be paid to individuals (although it is not clear if the basic income will be paid to each individual or merely calculated on the basis of the number of individuals in the household), with supplements for those with disabilities and designated caregivers. Segal has recommended a monthly income guarantee of C$1,320 per person, about 75 per cent of the provincial poverty line, with an extra $500 for disability, to be paid for a minimum of three years.

Y COMBINATOR, CALIFORNIA

In 2016, the start-up 'accelerator' Y Combinator announced a plan to conduct a small-scale basic income pilot in Oakland, California, for which $20 million has been put aside, probably to be supplemented by other donors. A 'pre-pilot' was launched in September 2016 to test logistics and study design, and a three- or four-year pilot was set to start in mid-2017.[14]

Sam Altman, the young venture capitalist who is president of Y Combinator, has said he wanted to fund a study on basic income because of the potential of artificial intelligence to eliminate traditional jobs and widen inequalities. He is not primarily interested in studying the impact on employment, assuming that there will not be many jobs out there. Rather he wants to find out what people choose to do when basic needs are taken care of. 'Do people sit around and play video games, or do they create new things? . . . Do people, without the fear of not being able to eat, accomplish far more and benefit society far more?'[15]

At the time of writing, the project design and the level of basic income to be paid were still to be refined. The initial idea was to provide 100 randomly selected families in poor districts of Oakland with an unconditional basic income for five years. However, a pilot on this basis would not manifest potential community-level effects. It was subsequently decided to conduct two community-wide pilots, in which every adult would receive a basic income for two or three years, which would come closer to a proper test of something like a basic income.

Setting the level of the basic income for the pilot is another tricky decision. If it is significantly above what might be generalized state-wide or nationally, a basic income may be dismissed as fiscally impractical. A smaller amount might also have significant positive effects and be seen as more realistic. While the project team have decided to renounce publicity for the duration of the pilot, these points should be borne in mind in interpreting the eventual results of what could be a valid and useful experiment.

GIVEDIRECTLY, KENYA

GiveDirectly, a California-based crowd-funded charity, has gained wide publicity for its activities in east Africa, where it has provided low-income men and women with large lump-sum or monthly unconditional cash transfers. Using randomized control trial (RCT) methodology, evaluations have found similar results to other cash transfer studies, with recipients reporting higher living standards, more investment in productive assets, greater food security and improved 'psychological wellbeing'.[16] People were happier, more satisfied with life, less stressed and less depressed.

As of early 2017, GiveDirectly planned to mobilize $30 million for what it claims will be the largest basic income experiment ever. Continuing with the RCT methodology, villages in two Kenyan counties will be divided into three groups: in forty villages all adult residents will receive a monthly basic income for twelve years; in eighty villages all adult residents will receive a basic income for two years; and in another eighty villages all adult residents will receive a lump sum equivalent to the two-year basic income. In all, some 26,000 individuals will receive cash transfers worth about 75 US cents a day. Data will also be collected from a control group of a hundred similar villages.

The stated main objective of GiveDirectly is the eradication of 'extreme poverty', which is a worthy goal but is not the prime rationale for a basic income system. At the time of writing, the hypotheses to be tested had not been finalized, though one aim of the proposed study is to look at the impact of a long-term basic income on risk-taking, such as starting a business, and another is to look at village-level economic effects.

The sheer size of the planned experiments may backfire by distorting the social and economic context. The project has already run into problems of low participation rates in one county, where people have refused the no-strings largesse, believing it to be linked to cults or devil worship. That said, unlike the pilots proposed in Europe, this experiment will test a genuine basic income by providing a universal, unconditional income paid to all individuals in a community. So the hope must be that the researchers, advised by well-known economists from prestigious US universities, will ask the right questions.

Separately, another crowd-funded charity, Belgium-based Eight, is launching a small basic income pilot in Uganda in January 2017. This will give all residents of a village in the Fort Portal region, about fifty households, an unconditional cash transfer of just over $18 a month ($9 for children) for two years. Outcomes will be compared with a baseline survey carried out beforehand. Eight (so-named because €8 a week provides a basic income for an adult and two children in Uganda) says it will be looking at the impact of the basic income on education participation of girls and women, access to healthcare, engagement in democratic institutions, and local economic development. It hopes to scale up to more villages subsequently.

A similar experiment is planned in India by Cashrelief, a non-profit organization, which hopes to provide all residents of a poor village with a basic income for two years. It will monitor outcomes on income, assets and spending on health and education, as well as watch out for community effects.

In Brazil, from 2008–14, a local NGO, ReCivitas Institute,

gave a monthly basic income of about US$9 to 100 residents of Quatinga Velho, a small poor village in São Paulo state, funded by private donors. In January 2016, it launched Basic Income Startup, another donor-funded project, which will give individuals a 'lifetime' basic income, adding another individual for each $1,000 donated. ReCivitas hopes this idea will be replicated elsewhere in Brazil and internationally.[17]

Although Quatinga Velho has clearly benefited from the basic income, the experiment is not, strictly speaking, a pilot as there has been no attempt at evaluation. The organizers say they are already convinced basic income works and the priority is to implement it. A law committing Brazil to introduce a basic income was signed by President Lula in 2004, after a tireless campaign by then Senator Eduardo Suplicy and others.

CROWD-FUNDING BASIC INCOME

Quietly, as a form of demonstration, crowd-funding schemes have been launched to provide selected individuals with a basic income. Mein Grundeinkommen (My Basic Income) in Germany, set up in 2014, has given over fifty people €12,000 for one year, chosen by lottery, no questions asked. In the Netherlands, MIES (Society for Innovations in Economics and Community) awarded its first basic income in 2015 to a man chosen because of his unpaid work in the community, notably a communal agriculture project known as Garden City. He has been receiving the equivalent of $1,000 on top of his income from his copywriting job. When asked what was the first thing he purchased with his basic income, he replied, 'I bought time.'

In the United States, basic income advocate Scott Santens crowd-funded his own basic income through Patreon, a crowd-funding platform aimed at artists, musicians, bloggers, photographers and other creatives, which has attracted 143 funders ranging from venture capitalists and Facebook engineers to women's rights activists. With $1,000 a month as his basic income, Santens is now a full-time activist and worker for basic income for everybody.

Another initiative associated with basic income is the Grantcoin Foundation's digital currency grants. In 2016 hundreds of applicants in seventy countries received these so far tiny grants that can be traded electronically. Such cryptocurrency schemes are in their infancy, and it is far too early to say whether they have a significant role to play as a secondary basic income scheme. But they should be watched with interest.

IN THE AIR ELSEWHERE

By late 2016, political parties and movements in several countries were proposing basic income pilots. In Britain, following Jeremy Corbyn's re-election as leader of the Labour Party, John McDonnell, Shadow Chancellor of the Exchequer, announced at the 2016 party conference that Labour would consider advocating a basic income in its manifesto for the 2020 general election, with the proposal of a pilot as a first step. In Scotland, the governing Scottish National Party passed a motion supporting basic income, and councillors in Fife and Glasgow are discussing local pilots.

In New Zealand, the opposition Labour Party has come out in favour of a basic income pilot. In the US, the District of Columbia city council has passed a motion calling for a pilot in Washington DC, San Francisco is investigating a pilot programme, and advocates have formed a political action committee, the National Campaign for Basic Income, to support initiatives at the local, state and national level. In December 2016, a group of US entrepreneurs, academics, activists and others launched the Economic Security Project with the stated aim of achieving the transition from 'conceptual discussion to meaningful action'. In Taiwan, a new political party, the Taiwan Republican Party, is promoting basic income. In South Korea, basic income is supported by several prominent liberal politicians, including presidential candidate Lee Jae-myung, mayor of Seongnam city.

In Iceland, the upstart Pirate Party, which came third in the October 2016 general election, supports holding a pilot, noting a severe poverty trap in the existing system. Germany's more marginal Pirate Party (2 per cent of votes in the 2013 federal elections) also favours basic income, while a new party, Bündnis Grundeinkommen (Basic Income League) was formed in September 2016 with the sole objective of introducing an unconditional basic income.

In Switzerland, the city of Lausanne passed a motion in April 2016 calling on the council to implement a basic income pilot. In France, the Senate has recommended trials, and there is a move to carry out a basic income experiment in the Aquitaine region.

In late 2016 in Italy, the port city of Livorno, run by the anti-establishment Five Star Movement, began a small-scale basic income experiment to give €500 a month, unconditionally, to 100 of the city's poorest families. It plans to extend the payments to more families in 2017. Two other Five Star municipalities, Ragusa in Sicily and Naples, are reported to be considering similar schemes.

And After Pilots?

Basic income pilots are primarily for testing behavioural claims and counter-claims and for helping to legitimize basic income as a practicable policy. But by definition a pilot is only a short-term change. This raises two questions. Would the effects be different if the change was a long-term 'permanent' one? And would the effects wear off and even be reversed after the end of the pilot?

There is relatively little empirical material to help answer these questions. And devoting resources to follow-up studies could simply result in more delay in pursuing desirable changes. Even so, there is some tentative evidence that even short-term basic income pilots can have lasting effects after they have ended. They may break taboos, which once broken cannot easily be resurrected. They may enable some people to break out of a financial stranglehold, as in the case of someone in debt bondage or in an abusive relationship. They may give some people the courage to take economic or social risks, emboldening them to continue.

In the Indian pilots mentioned in Chapter 10, a 'legacy survey' six months after the pilot had ended found that certain changes had persisted, most notably the emancipatory impact on young women. Several cash transfer schemes have found that positive economic effects continued subsequently, partly because people increased their earning opportunities by using the transfers to buy tools and equipment or livestock, but also because the schemes opened their minds to new possibilities that gave them hope for the future.[18] A study in Sri Lanka found that men's annual income five years after receiving transfers had increased by 64–94 per cent.[19] Another in Uganda found that four years after receiving one-off grants, youths were earning 41 per cent more on average than those who had not received grants.[20]

This prompts an idea. If short-term pilots do have positive effects, and if there is good reason for thinking that even basic incomes received for, say, eighteen months have lasting effects, then why not instigate a rolling series of localized schemes, moving from one or two regions to others selected randomly, and then continuing until the whole country is covered? No doubt some politicians would baulk at this. But at the least it would be fiscally easier to do.

Not every study has shown significant benefits persisting after payments cease, though in assessing longer-term outcomes the amount of the transfer and the length of time for which it was paid need to be taken into account. And some critics contend that short-term pilots of cash transfers do not succeed in the alleged aim of 'breaking the cycle of intergenerational poverty'. This may be setting the evaluation bar too high.

Conclusions

Pilots cannot test and evaluate the fundamental justifications for basic income – social justice, freedom and economic security – which is why some supporters of basic income think pilots are a waste of time and money. The question of whether a basic income should be introduced cannot be boiled down to an empirical test of observable behaviours. If basic income is considered a right, asking if it 'works' makes no sense, any more than the abolition of slavery. That said, properly designed, pilots can serve a useful purpose in evaluating competing claims and criticisms of basic income, gaining political acceptance and identifying potential issues arising from implementation.

Ideally, basic income pilots should be carried out by the state or local governments, in monetary form, and not by philanthropic bodies or in some unfamiliar and non-legitimized currency that cannot replicate reality. However, for all their limitations, the pilots already completed have demonstrated that the various aspects of a basic income have positive effects. As long as pilots are not used as an excuse for lack of political action, they should be a force for good, if only for showing or suggesting what other interventions would make a basic income optimally successful. The real challenge today is political will.

Perhaps the biggest danger in this fluid phase of basic income pilots is that they will evolve into social engineering, testing out morally dubious tactics derived from behavioural economics. The term 'basic income' could become a cover for something close to workfare, when pilots are presented as testing 'the incentive to work' (sic) and varieties of conditionality.

To be a proper test, any 'basic income' experiment must be consistent with the proper meaning of a basic income;

payment must be universal, unconditional and individual (see Appendix). What starts out as an incentive scheme can easily elide into one with all sorts of sanctions and disentitlement devices. Similarly, lottery and crowd-funding schemes may generate envy or resentment and divert attention from important community effects that are a hallmark of basic income.

The motivation for pilots should be to enhance freedom, social justice and economic security, while testing behavioural aspects that might need other interventions. If pilots compromise freedom, and offend principles of social justice and security, they should be resisted.

The Political Challenge – How to Get There from Here

'Our basic function is to develop alternatives to existing policy, to keep them alive and available until the politically impossible become the politically inevitable.'

MILTON FRIEDMAN

There is an oft-told story of a delegation going to the White House to present President Franklin D. Roosevelt with a policy proposal. After he had listened to them, he said, 'Okay, you have convinced me. Now go out and bring pressure on me to do it.' Fundamental social change rarely comes without sustained political pressure. And politicians are rarely intellectual or policy leaders, even though they will try to take the credit for something once it is up and running. Just occasionally, one emerges with the courage to lead.

Pressure matters. One lesson from the missed opportunity for advancing towards a basic income in the US in the early 1970s was that at a crucial moment the public pressure was released. As a result, the more conservative elements in the Democratic Party were able to stifle the initiative.

Today, the primary block to implementation of a basic income system is political, not economic or philosophical. However, this is changing rapidly. New political parties have embraced basic income in their manifestoes and some old established parties have moved towards including it in their party platforms or are committing themselves to conducting pilots. These include the British and New Zealand Labour Parties, the Scottish National Party, the Greens in most countries, including Britain, Canada, the Czech Republic, Finland, Ireland, Japan, the Netherlands, Norway and the United States, and the Pirate parties where they exist, most notably Iceland.

In Britain, although the Conservatives have shown no interest, both Jeremy Corbyn, the Labour Party leader, and Labour's Shadow Chancellor, John McDonnell, favour piloting the idea, as does Ed Miliband, Corbyn's predecessor as leader. Canada's governing Liberal Party has put basic income into its policy platform, and several provincial premiers have come out in support. As noted earlier, Finland's Prime Minister has put money aside for a pilot in his country. In France, senior politicians have spoken in favour of basic income, including former Prime Minister Manuel Valls, and the Socialist Party has chosen a basic income advocate, Benoît Hamon, as its candidate for the presidential election in April 2017. Basic income is demanded by some factions of Podemos in Spain, and by Alternativet in Denmark and Razem in Poland, new political parties formed to represent the precariat. All this reflects a new sense of legitimacy. Basic income can no longer be dismissed as unworldly utopianism.

Meanwhile, opinion polls reflect a spreading awareness of what basic income means, as a result of this more open political conversation. In 2016, a cross-EU opinion poll conducted by Berlin-based Dalia Research found over two-thirds of respondents in favour and only 24 per cent against, the remainder being undecided.

Above all, proposals for a basic income are moving up the political agenda because other policies supposedly offering social protection have been tried, have largely failed on their own terms, and have been unable to arrest growing inequality and economic insecurity. Rather, they have involved increasingly degrading interventions by the state, as exposed by various TV programmes and in harrowing films such as Ken Loach's *I, Daniel Blake*. Means testing, sanctions, demonizing the disadvantaged as 'shirkers' or worse, have not succeeded. Such policies shame us all.

The political parties that have promoted these illiberal policies are mostly on the defensive, discredited by their repeated failures and for offering at best prescriptions suited to twentieth-century problems, rather than policies to meet twenty-first century challenges.

They could get away with increasingly harsh sanctions, lack of due process, 'nudges' and workfare when, in the eyes of the majority, only a small minority of 'others' were the target. But the inadequacies and inequities are exposed when that minority becomes a large group, with many more people close to joining it or close to those who are.

The legitimacy of basic income as an idea may thus be greater now than at any time in the past, while the defence of existing policies and the trends they exhibit are at an ebb, swamped by the accumulation of negative evidence and imagery. These are two necessary conditions for progress, though far from a guarantee of it.

Transition Obstacles

'If I wanted to get there, I would not start from here.'
IRISH JOKE

Moving towards a basic income as the anchor of a new income distribution system must find a way of unravelling the complexity of the existing system which is the result of ad hoc tinkering over the past century or more. The US government, for example, administers 126 federal welfare programmes with no common rules on eligibility, conditionality, duration or rules for withdrawal, while the fifty states have additional programmes of their own. In the UK, the existing system was well described by the Scottish Nationalist MP Ronnie Cowan in a House of Commons debate on basic income in September 2016:

> If we were all given a blank sheet of paper and asked to design a welfare system, nobody – but nobody – would come up with the system we have now. They would need thousands of sheets of paper and would end up with a mishmash of abandoned projects, badly implemented and half-hearted ideas and a system so complicated that it lets down those who need it most.[1]

Untangling this mess requires a government with the political will to pursue a sustained strategy and weather inevitable setbacks. The travails of the hapless Iain Duncan Smith, Britain's former Secretary of State for Work and Pensions, in trying to simplify and consolidate several means-tested benefits into a single Universal Credit may hold some lessons on how best (or not) to move forward with a basic income.

Jurgen De Wispelaere and José Antonio Noguera have usefully broken down the political obstacles into three overlapping challenges.[2] First, there is the challenge of attaining *political* feasibility. Coalitions of support must be built. But these must be strong, rather than coalitions of convenience. Those supporting basic income must see it as part of their ideological or strategic agenda. And those in the coalition must have the capacity to engage in sustained political campaigning, perhaps suspending differences between themselves on design features or the phasing of reform. On basic income, libertarians might be advised to emphasize aspects that progressives, or egalitarians, would favour, and progressives to emphasize what libertarians as well as themselves would support.

Second, there is the challenge of demonstrating *institutional* feasibility. If implementing a basic income is perceived as risking administrative chaos, a bureaucracy intent on retaining its comfort zone could seize upon this to try to delegitimize the whole reform. The reformers must find ways of preventing that.

Third, there is the challenge of achieving *psychological* feasibility. Policymakers must secure a broad level of social acceptance of basic income among the public, or at least a willingness to give the reform a fair trial. This must mean, among other things, a sensitive campaign to explain the values and principles behind the reform. Reformers must be able to pre-empt the expected jibes over lack of 'reciprocity', affordability, inducement to laziness, 'something for nothing' and cash for the undeserving and unneedy.

Above all in this respect, reformers must confront the view that ordinary citizens would be taxed to help pay for some people to live at their expense. The right-wing media would seize upon any poor person they could display as enjoying life as proof that the basic income was encouraging debauchery, using 'taxpayers' money'. Sadly, statistical evidence would not be enough to curb such prejudiced journalism. Either a pre-emptive strategy would be required in which such incidents were built into the learning process. Or, better, the funding should be shown as coming from 'capital' or forms of rent, so the media could not present it as taxing Bill to pay Jack.

These challenges point to the political advantage of framing basic income as a social dividend, and as a matter of social justice, freedom and basic security, rather than as a better means of tackling poverty. Another rhetorical justification might be *strategic preparedness* for possible large-scale technological disruption of jobs and employment, analogous to military defence policy, disaster preparedness and measures to mitigate climate change. History is strewn with cases of politicians reacting too late. Here is an opportunity to take sensible action in advance.

Public Pressure

Moving the political debate forward also requires identification of groups most likely to support a basic income and those groups most likely to oppose it. The former have to be persuaded to give basic income priority in their public campaigns, and to coalesce with other supporters. Today they include non-governmental organizations representing the disabled, feminists, the homeless, various ecological interests, some trade unions, students and youth, artists and even medical organizations.

Opponents have included many social democrats, reformed

communists and traditional trade unionists, who continue to believe that the way to a better society is for everybody to have full-time jobs. They are suspicious of any policy that offers freedom from unwanted labour, suspecting that the advocates of basic income are motivated by a sinister desire to dismantle the welfare state, or what is left of it. This posture must be respected – and firmly rebutted, whatever the libertarian supporters of basic income might wish.

One response to their concern is to show them that the psychological basis of their worry is unfounded. If, as psychological experiments have shown, basic security encourages people to be more altruistic and solidaristic, a basic income system should strengthen public resolve to defend solidaristic social policies in general. Of course, that effect alone would not be enough. But specific public services or benefits should be defended on their own merits, independent of basic income. There is no reason to presume that people given basic income security would lose the will or desire to defend public services.

In the United States, a new phase in the public debate came with the establishment in June 2016 of the National Campaign for Basic Income (NCBI). Complementing the existing US Basic Income Guarantee Network (USBIG), which primarily promotes research and information, the NCBI has been set up as a '527' organization under the US tax code, which enables it to engage in direct political action with the aim of building political coalitions to influence elections and policymaking.[3]

The former US trade union leader Andy Stern has also mused that political pressure could be built up by the equivalent of the Townsend Clubs that mobilized support for Social Security in the 1930s.[4] And he hopes that some city mayors or state governors will ask for federal waivers to stage pilots. A report by the National League of Cities, which represents 19,000 US cities and towns, has recommended that cities investigate basic income.[5]

Meanwhile, a newly influential movement, Black Lives Matter, allying over fifty organizations, issued an 'official platform' in August 2016 that included a demand for a universal basic income (UBI). It also argued for an additional amount (a sort of UBI+) to be paid to black Americans as reparation for the harms of colonialism, slavery and the mass incarceration of mainly young black men in modern times. Without endorsing this specific demand, which would be hard to administer fairly, the essence of the platform is a demand for *reparation* for past injustices. The Middlesbrough tale of Chapter 2 is very much along the same lines.

In Europe, the scope for greater public pressure has been enhanced by the energies of new political parties, by national networks that are welcoming new members, and by new initiatives such as the annual Basic Income Week events. Unions and precariat groups are also starting to call for basic income. In September 2016, the Trades Union Congress (TUC), the UK's umbrella union body, voted in favour of the following motion endorsing the principles of basic income:

> Congress notes the growing popularity of the idea of a 'Universal Basic Income' with a variety of models being discussed here and around the world. Congress believes that the TUC should acknowledge Universal Basic Income and argue for a progressive

system that would be easier to administer, easier for people to navigate, paid individually and that is complementary to comprehensive public services and childcare provision. The transition from our current system to any new system that incorporates these principles should always leave people with lower incomes better off.

A motion included in the preliminary agenda for the Congress went further in calling for the TUC to 'argue for a progressive system that incorporates the basis of a Universal Basic Income system'. This was later subsumed into a composite motion containing the quoted paragraph.

While the voted motion stops short of a wholehearted endorsement, it indicates how a leading 'labourist' body is cautiously coming round to the cause of basic income, while correctly seeing the need to preserve other public services and income supplements. The TUC may not be the power in the land that it once was, but its conversion marks a welcome addition to the bodies advocating or supporting the principles behind a basic income in the UK.

I would urge anybody supporting basic income to join a pressure group that does so. A promising model may be the so-called 'Basisteams' in the Netherlands, local groups which undertake to inform their communities about basic income. What is not true is the claim that we lack knowledge. Finding the optimum justification out of the many rationales that have been cited in the preceding pages is the real challenge today, along with exercising the necessary public pressure. In that regard, there is one rationale that has never been a trump card before. It could be now.

The Political Imperative

'Nothing is more powerful than an idea whose
time has come.'

PARAPHRASED FROM VICTOR HUGO, *THE HISTORY OF A CRIME*

Something like a basic income has become a political imperative as never before. It is one policy that could reduce the
chronic economic and social insecurity at the heart of the
populist revolt behind Brexit, the election of Donald Trump
as US President and the rise of nationalist and far-right
movements in Europe and elsewhere. It may soon become
clear that nativist populism has no attractive answer for
these insecurities. Restricting migration and putting up trade
barriers will ultimately hurt the very people the populists
claim to represent.

That could open up new political possibilities for basic
income. So far, Third Way timidity has held up thinking. For
example, defeated Democrat candidate Hillary Clinton,
speaking before the US presidential election, said she was
'not ready to go there' on basic income. By contrast, Bernie
Sanders, whom she defeated for the Democratic nomination,
said he was 'absolutely sympathetic' to the idea.

Meanwhile, Donald Trump steamrollered his way to the
presidency by promising to bring jobs back to the US and
stop American firms from transferring jobs abroad. Yet with
the introduction of protectionist measures, production costs
will rise, automation will accelerate, and the next scapegoat
will be the robots 'taking American jobs from American

workers'. Then perhaps something like a basic income will creep back onto the policy table.

While there are reasons to be sceptical about the predicted technological dystopia that has prompted many high-tech plutocrats to come out in support of basic income, this may nevertheless be a strong factor in mobilizing public pressure and political action. Whether jobs are going to dry up or not, the march of the robots is undoubtedly accentuating insecurity and inequality. A basic income or social dividend system would provide at least a partial antidote to that, as more commentators now recognize.[6] For example, Klaus Schwab, founder and executive chairman of the World Economic Forum and author of *The Fourth Industrial Revolution*, has described basic income as a 'plausible' response to labour market disruption.[7]

President Barack Obama said in an interview shortly before the end of his presidency that universal basic income would be 'a debate that we'll be having over the next 10 or 20 years', noting: 'What is indisputable ... is that as AI [Artificial Intelligence] gets further incorporated, and the society potentially gets wealthier, the link between production and distribution, how much you work and how much you make, gets further and further attenuated.'[8]

The ethical and philosophical justifications for basic income – social justice, freedom and economic security – have been well established. They are embedded in the Enlightenment values of all civilized societies and are clearly interrelated, ultimately resting on the sentiment of empathy. This is the emotion that separates the progressive mind from the reactionary one. Empathy derives from a strong faith in the human condition. It is the ability to put oneself in another's shoes and to accept that people have the right to live as they wish, as long as they do no intentional or careless harm to others. Defending those values in the face of lurches to authoritarianism and paternalism may be very difficult in current circumstances. And we must recognize that this means a fundamental reform of 'rentier capitalism' arising from the policies and underlying ideology that have held sway since the 1980s.

In that context, one of the biggest challenges confronting any major social reform is identifying a feasible way of moving from the current situation to something very different. It requires a leap of imagination to postulate a better future. It is all too easy to see transitional drawbacks as impenetrable barriers. But before long the rising political anger in and around the precariat could make basic income a political imperative for any government keen to be re-elected. One may wish for a nobler motive, but expediency may prove significant.

Baby Steps?

So, how best to move from today's complex, mainly means-tested system, with its numerous behavioural conditionalities, to a system of social protection anchored by a basic income?[9] What is clear is that there is no ideal or optimum approach. In each society, it will depend in part on the structure of the economy and the structure of the old welfare system. Suggested approaches include building up 'partial basic incomes' for everybody, starting from a very low base, or introducing basic incomes for selected groups and gradually extending them to others.

The latter strategy was developed in detail for South Africa.[10] Sadly, the recommendations were not followed. It could be claimed that the cash transfer schemes in various Latin American countries have been doing the same implicitly, notably in Brazil through its *Bolsa Família*, which now reaches over 80 million people, and Mexico with *Oportunidades*. They have advanced the remit of non-contributory cash transfers and helped to legitimize giving cash rather than operating more paternalistic subsidy schemes.

More broadly, the main options are either to replace existing social protection schemes *in toto*, as advocated by some, particularly US libertarians, *or* to build up a basic income or 'social dividend' system alongside existing social security schemes, gradually integrating them into a multi-tiered social protection system in which basic income provides a floor.[11] The second probably offers the better prospect in industrialized countries.

Means-tested and behaviour-tested schemes would be phased out over time, and funds hitherto allocated to these schemes could then be paid into a basic income or social dividend fund. No one currently receiving benefits would be worse off than before; means-tested benefits would continue to be paid (though taking the social dividend into account would steadily reduce the number of households dependent on them) until the dividend reached a level at which they could be replaced.

Means-tested housing-related benefits might have to be continued in the UK and other countries with distorted housing markets, which should be tackled separately. However, behaviour testing for the unemployed, and fitness-for-work tests for those with disabilities, should be rapidly eliminated. Those with disabilities should receive a supplement based on their higher living costs and reduced earnings opportunities.

Launching a social dividend, at a very modest level to begin with, could be presented politically, drawing on Thomas Paine's argument, as a return on the social wealth generated by society and our ancestors, including part of the rental income from the private ownership or exploitation of assets – physical, financial and intellectual.

In a second tier, the social dividend could be topped up by a 'stabilization grant', which would fluctuate according to the state of the economy, paying more in times of recession and less in boom times, as outlined in Chapter 5.

The social dividend and the stabilization grant component could be adjusted by changes in national income and by the economic growth rate, with the level set by an Independent Basic Income Committee or Social Dividend Committee. Its members could be appointed from the mid-point of one parliament to the mid-point of another, which would insulate the social dividend policy from party politics and reduce the risk of it being used for party political ends.

A third tier would be a 'social insurance' layer of benefits for contingency risks such as sickness, involuntary unemployment and maternity. However, unlike today's contributory systems, the benefits paid would not be linked to contribution records. Instead, to regenerate an ethos of social solidarity, everyone above the basic income level (or a higher minimum level to be decided) would pay a certain percentage as social insurance contributions.

These could go into a social insurance fund as now, or into general taxation but shown as a separate item on tax statements. In this way, those having a relatively low probability of need would cross-subsidize those with a relatively high probability, the original concept behind social insurance schemes. And on top of that layer, there would be private, voluntary schemes, including company pension schemes, for people wanting to take out additional insurance.

This would be a coherent system, without being too radical or unwieldy, that would help combat the economic insecurity inevitable in an open market economy in the twenty-first century, buffeted by the pace and depth of technological change, that will otherwise be economically, socially and politically threatening.

Citizen Dividends . . . or Security Dividends?

The complexity of reform and the difficulty of overcoming prejudiced views on affordability and the impact on work and labour are two reasons why framing the idea of basic income as social dividends may offer the more politically feasible route forward. Introducing a universal social dividend scheme, with initial amounts set below those needed to meet most people's material needs, could not be dismissed as economically unfeasible and could allow time for a political consensus to emerge in favour of something more ambitious.

By itself, unlike means-tested benefits, the universality of a basic income could attract broad political support. It would still be *radical* in the best tradition of that word – aiming to reduce inequality, inequities and economic insecurity, while promoting republican freedom – in a way that a wide array of thinkers from very different philosophical traditions could share. It would also be *pragmatic* in leaving aside the eventual goals on which political and ideological thinking would differ. And it would sidestep the standard objections that persist in spite of repeated refutation, most notably that a basic income is unaffordable and would reduce labour and work.

Reformers could state their long-term ideal of moving towards a society that minimized economic insecurity, adding that the next steps would have to await a fresh electoral mandate. By this means they could counter the conservative or rather reactionary cry that it would be reckless and non-credible.

Taking the social dividend route would be strengthened by the establishment of democratic sovereign wealth or capital funds – a sort of partial socialization of capital, although to avoid raising ideological hackles another term might be found, such as a Commons Capital Depository.[12] This could be built up through taxation (or sharing) of rentier income, possibly augmented by a carbon tax, a financial transaction tax, other 'green' fiscal policies and so on. And alongside these two structural reforms, every citizen and entitled legal resident could be issued with a 'social dividend card'. At that point, we might wink to the spirit of William Morris, winning the objective with another name.

Politicians must find a way – or several ways for different groups – of framing basic income so as to outflank critics from the media and the establishment, most of whom have had more than the equivalent of a basic income from birth. Opponents will continue to use the sophistry of reciprocity – surely, you cannot want to give something for nothing – which they do not demand of inherited wealth.

They will continue to depict images of laziness, dependency, scrounging and such like while reporting gleefully on the frolicking of the indolent rich. And they will leap on any policy-maker or politician who suggests that, to finance a basic income, the affluent might need to pay more tax or lose certain tax privileges, while not questioning tax cuts for the wealthy at the expense of reduced social benefits and public services.

This double-standard treatment echoes the criticisms of previous socially progressive ideas. But advocates of basic income should accept the challenge with increasing confidence. Evolution rather than 'revolution' must be the message. Moreover, it is becoming ever clearer to everyone that the income distribution system of the twentieth century has broken down, and that unless something fundamental is changed, more and more people will face chronic social and economic insecurity, with all that implies for political instability and the drift to extremes.

Leaving aside instrumental reasons for supporting a basic income, the thrill lies in the potential to advance full freedom and social justice, and the values of work and leisure over the dictates of labour and consumption.

The times they are a-changin', sang Bob Dylan. And times do change the chances of success. As Thomas Paine so memorably put it in the introduction to his epochal *Common Sense* of 1776, 'Time makes more Converts than Reason.' For basic income or social dividends, the time is now.

How to Run a Basic Income Pilot

While some basic income advocates such as Philippe van Parijs regard pilots as unnecessary, they can be useful in many ways. These include assessing

a. the process of *implementation*,
b. the impact on *attitudes*,
c. the impact on *behaviour*, and
d. other *institutional or policy changes* that would strengthen positive effects and weaken or avoid possible negative ones.

To talk of 'evidence-based policy' is fair enough, but those designing, conducting and analysing the data from any experiment should have a sense of humility. Every pilot has limitations; no pilot is or can be ideal. And pilots should not become a barrier to reform. A pilot is better suited to uncovering *how* and *why* an intervention does or does not work, rather than whether or not it works.[1]

That danger is illustrated by a telling historical example. In the dying days of slavery in the nineteenth century, some apologists argued that there was no evidence that emancipation would lead to sustainable benefits for the economy, for production or for the slaves themselves. The answer blacks and abolitionists gave was that freedom should come first, and then resources should be made available to make emancipation work.

That said, each pilot should be judged on whether it can help support or refute hypotheses, prejudices and intuitions. And if pilots are to spread, they should adhere as closely as possible to objective principles. These may be summarized as follows:

THE PAYMENTS MUST BE PROPER BASIC INCOMES

For a pilot to test a true basic income, the payments should have the following features:

— The amount paid should be *basic*, sufficient to be meaningful for the recipient but not so high as to provide total security.

— The income should be paid in *cash*, or in a form easily convertible into cash, for example, via a bank account, smart card or mobile phone. It should be *regular*, *predictable* and *stable*, preferably paid monthly over a *sustained period*. It should not be paid as a lump sum, mainly because of the 'weakness of will' effect.

— The basic income should be *universal*, paid to all those usually resident in the pilot community at the outset. This will enable detection of community effects, including non-economic effects. It should also be *non-withdrawable*.

— It follows that there should be no *targeting*. The basic income should not be given only to those deemed to be 'poor', however poverty is defined. Basic income is intended to be a right and rights are universal. Moreover, means testing is unfair and prone to error, while targeting creates poverty traps.

— It also follows that there should be no *selectivity*. Giving to one 'deserving' group rather than another may put the selected group under pressure to share with others, diluting the effect of the basic income. Paying an income just to mothers risks generating tensions within households.

— The basic income should be *unconditional*, without requiring some pre-specified behaviour.

— The basic income should be paid *individually* and *equally* to each man and each woman. Basic income security is an individual right, and should not be applied to some notion of the 'family' or 'household', whose size and composition may be affected by the policy itself. For children, or adults unable to collect their own income because of disability or frailty, a *surrogate* (the mother in the case of children) can be designated to receive it on their behalf.

— No other *policy change* should be made at the start of or during the pilot, to ensure a fair assessment of its effects.

A basic income pilot that respected some but not all of these criteria might be acceptable to test the validity of certain features, perhaps because of resource constraints. But in evaluating the outcomes, researchers would need to recognize that the design was not a full or proper basic income.

THE PILOT DESIGN MUST BE CLEAR AND SUSTAINABLE

It is easy to overlook the need for clarity about the design and its sustainability – why a particular design is adopted rather than alternative feasible designs. This should apply to all aspects cited in the first principle, especially the amount of the basic income and the duration of the pilot. All the design features should be recorded at the outset. To ensure sustainability, there should be a clear workplan and proper budgeting.

THE DESIGN MUST BE KEPT CONSTANT

Once a pilot has been launched, its design should not be altered unless it becomes essential to do so.

THE PILOT MUST BE ADEQUATELY LARGE

A very large pilot cannot be sensibly managed, but if it is too small it fails to be a real basic income experiment. Behavioural and attitudinal changes may be *tendencies*; some people change, others hesitate, and others do not change. Often the hypothetical effects are relevant only to some of the people in the selected sample (teenagers, people with disabilities, etc.). It is essential to have enough people with the potential characteristics of interest for statisticians to estimate effects (or lack of them) with confidence. As a general rule, the minimum sample size should be 1,000 individuals, and a bigger sample would be preferable.

THE DURATION MUST BE LONG ENOUGH

Obviously, the duration of the pilot should not be very short, for then it would be merely a one-off capital grant. The effects of a basic income can be expected to manifest themselves over time, as people learn and adapt. There may be an *impact effect*, immediately after the grant is first received, and an *assimilation effect*, as individuals become used to receiving the basic income. There may also be a *wearing off* effect, in some respects, and a *learning effect* in others. For these reasons, the duration of the pilot should be more than a year. Two years is reasonable, though some would argue for longer.

One practical consideration is the *project fatigue* factor, easily ignored in the first flush of enthusiasm. However, any pilot scheme involves regular evaluation and the construction and maintenance of a team of researchers and fieldworkers. There is also *respondent fatigue*, since evaluating a pilot requires asking respondents questions or watching them in some way. In this respect, as in several others, the best may be the enemy of the good.

THE PILOT MUST BE REPLICABLE AND UP-SCALABLE

Pilots should be designed to be *replicable* and *up-scalable*. In other words, it should be possible to conduct a similar pilot somewhere else and it should be feasible in principle to scale up the pilot to a larger community and to national level.

RANDOM CONTROL GROUPS SHOULD BE USED

Determining the impact of a basic income requires comparing outcomes, both with the behaviour and attitudes of people beforehand (before the 'treatment' begins) and with 'control groups', otherwise similar, who do not receive the 'treatment' or come under the policy. The primary objective is to ensure outcomes are the result of the basic income and do not stem from a change coming from the outside.

While randomized controlled trials (RCTs) are currently

in vogue, they have severe limitations when it comes to evaluating basic income. The principle behind RCTs, as the name implies, is that those receiving the 'treatment' should be selected 'randomly' from a wider population, and the control group should also be selected 'randomly'. This would typically mean listing households in an area and drawing a sample, so that one family (or individual within a family) would receive the basic income while the family next door would not.

Apart from the risk of generating inter-community and inter-familial tensions, one likely outcome would be some sharing of the basic income between households and between family members, on a non-random basis. This would negate the universality of the basic income, dilute its impact and make it hard to evaluate outcomes. In the Indian pilot in Madhya Pradesh, twenty similar villages were selected randomly from a wide area: in eight of these, everyone received the basic income and in the remaining twelve villages no one did. It was thus possible to explore a range of effects, both at micro-level and community level, including attitudinal and behavioural changes.

THERE SHOULD BE BASELINE SURVEYS

For a proper evaluation, a *baseline census* or *survey* of the community is needed to provide detailed information on the prospective respondents, covering all aspects likely to be assessed by the pilot. (If a census is not practicable a large sample should be chosen.) This should be complemented by a *baseline community survey* that collects data on structural characteristics of the community – demographic breakdown, infrastructure, distance to schools and clinics and so on. The idea of both is to identify the conditions, behaviour and attitudes that exist before the impact of the basic income.

Preferably, the intended recipients of the cash transfers should not be informed of the plans at the time the baseline survey data are gathered – although of course cooperation in the survey is more likely if they do know!

Since the evaluators will not know in advance what effects the basic income will have, and cannot realistically anticipate all of them, the baseline surveys need to collect a rich array of data. They should be conducted about one month before the first grant pay-outs, so as to capture the patterns prevailing at the time of the launch.

One of the key decisions for the baseline census is the selection of respondent or respondents. Asking, say, the nominated 'household head' is likely to elicit different responses on some issues from those that would be given by another household member. Bearing in mind the individual nature of a basic income, responses can be expected to differ by gender, age and other personal factors.

Ideally, it would be desirable to collect background factual data on the household and individual data from each member separately. This may be impractical and too costly in terms of fieldwork and data processing. However, the number of women selected as respondents should be equal to the number of men. The Madhya Pradesh pilot interviewed one male and one female respondent per household.

After the baseline survey, it is advisable to conduct a public information campaign to explain what will happen in the course of the pilot, to overcome suspicions and to make sure respondents know what will be involved, including the fact that they will receive the payment regularly, without spending or behavioural conditions.

REGULAR EVALUATION SURVEYS MUST BE CONDUCTED

The idea of a pilot is to test effects, and to do so it should build in a series of surveys, starting with the baseline survey. Another survey should be conducted about six months after the start of the pilot, allowing enough time to detect an impact on behaviour and attitudes, and further interim surveys every six months or so, depending on the length of the pilot. At the end of the pilot, preferably within a month of the last cash transfer, there should be a final evaluation survey covering the same individuals and households questioned in the baseline survey. In each case, the questionnaire should be as close as possible to the one used in the baseline, with similar reference periods.

KEY INFORMANTS SHOULD BE USED

While the focus of attention should be on the individuals receiving the basic income, it is desirable to involve *key informants* in the evaluation process. Extra information should be collected from local authorities, local teachers and medical personnel, and others with knowledge of the community. They should be asked for information that is not available from recipients and for information on the way a basic income might influence behaviour. A good pilot evaluation should build on a structured questionnaire addressed to key informants with questions expressed in a neutral way.

If the pilot covers several communities, the areas chosen

need to be structurally similar, particularly for making comparisons between basic income areas and control areas. But the evaluation design should also take into account possible exogenous changes during the course of the pilot that may change the structure of a community so that it is no longer similar – the building of a new school, or the introduction of an irrigation scheme, for example. For this reason, it is desirable to have a simple community survey at each evaluation point to check on structural changes that may influence outcomes.

ANALYSIS SHOULD ADDRESS MULTI-LEVEL EFFECTS

The pilot should include adequate techniques to assess and evaluate effects on individuals, on households and families, and on the community, such as economic multiplier effects. Looking solely at effects on individuals can be misleading. (The most egregious example relates to labour subsidy schemes that look only at the effects on the person benefiting, without considering *deadweight* effects – the person could have obtained a job without the subsidy – and *displacement* effects – a subsidized person may displace a non-subsidized person.)

Some of the richest effects may be at the community level. If they are not studied at the same time, an evaluation may conclude that, because the effect at individual level was good or bad, basic income is good or bad. There may be *feedback effects* at community level on how individuals behave and interact with one another. One of the claims made by advocates of basic income is that it would foster altruism and social responsibility within communities.

EVALUATIONS SHOULD COVER BOTH
ATTITUDINAL AND BEHAVIOURAL EFFECTS

A basic income can be expected to affect behaviour, physical and emotional 'well-being' and attitudes. So a pilot must aim to look beyond directly measurable behavioural effects and include attitudinal questions, posed in as neutral a way as possible. To permit numerical evaluation, respondents should be asked to choose from a range of five possible answers on a *likert scale* (e.g. (1) strongly disagree, (2) disagree, (3) neither agree nor disagree, (4) agree, (5) strongly agree).

HYPOTHESES SHOULD BE EXPLICIT
BEFORE THE PILOT IS LAUNCHED

There should be a clear list of hypotheses to be tested, established *before* the pilot is launched and *before* the baseline survey is carried out. Too often pilot schemes are launched with only vague ideas of what to expect, perhaps because they are implemented under pressure or as a result of a conflicting array of claims and counter-claims. Another problem, less often noted, is when a pilot is launched with only one or two hypotheses to be tested, as has tended to be the case with RCTs.

Consider a few standard hypotheses:

a. A basic income enables the household or family to provide children with more food, and this induces better nutrition and better health.

b. A basic income reduces the pressure on the household to oblige children to labour and increases the probability of them attending school.

c. A basic income enables the household to pay off debt.

These hypotheses require *benchmark data*, from the baseline survey and baseline community survey.

Then consider another set of hypotheses:

d. A basic income granted to person X leads person Y to reduce the amount of time devoted to income-earning activity, and/or leads person Y to alter his/her consumption.

e. A basic income scheme leads to the establishment of a local group to advise recipients on how to spend their money.

f. A basic income leads to social community pressure on recipients to share with non-recipients outside the community.

These are indirect and external effects that may require information from the recipient, from the household and from outside the household. While this has implications for the design of a baseline household survey, it also requires a *community-level benchmark and monitoring survey*, and matching household and community *evaluation surveys* conducted over the period of the pilot.

Then there are hypotheses that relate to the effects on the local economy and local society, such as the following:

g. A basic income scheme leads to an improvement in income distribution, lessening income inequality, and it does so by more than a simple addition of the cash transfer.

h. A basic income leads to the establishment of local financial agencies, leading to a growth of financial intermediation.

i. A basic income scheme leads to the development of local businesses and more employment in the community.

Hypothesis (g), for instance, is crucial to a proper evaluation of a basic income system. If the pilot design was not able to measure the impact on income distribution, it would fail to evaluate a key aspect of basic income. However, if only a minority of the community were provided with the basic income, it would be impossible to test this crucial hypothesis altogether. Thus it is essential that the basic income is paid to all residents.

COST AND BUDGETING MUST BE REALISTIC

It is important to devise realistic cost estimates at the outset of the pilot. Proper evaluation requires decent funding and technical expertise. And besides costing for the basic incomes themselves, for administration and for the evaluation, some money must be set aside for contingencies. In any empirical study involving surveys, the only certain rule is that mistakes will occur, not necessarily because of errors in the design or conduct of the pilot but because inevitably there will be unexpected events and setbacks.

THE SAMPLE MUST BE AS CONSTANT AS POSSIBLE

It is an essential but hard-to-maintain principle of a basic income pilot that the sample must be as constant as possible.

However regrettable from a social point of view to deny a basic income to a newcomer, nobody not covered at the outset of the pilot should be subsequently included, with the exception of new babies. Migrants or returnees who enter the community after the start cannot be included. However, it is desirable to include them in the survey, since their presence may have effects on attitudes and behaviour that should be taken into account.

Out-migration is another issue. The solution will depend on the hypotheses to be tested. In the Madhya Pradesh pilot, people who moved away no longer received the basic income. However, the planned GiveDirectly pilot in Kenya will continue to pay the basic income to out-migrants present in the basic income villages at the start, because one hypothesis to be tested is the incentive to move to find paid work. Obviously, in a prolonged pilot there will also be some deaths. So keeping the sample constant will rarely be entirely maintained. The point is to try to come as close to it as possible.

THE TRANSFER MECHANISMS MUST BE MONITORED

One of the biggest challenges for any cash transfer scheme in developing countries is the lack of sophisticated financial institutions and widespread ignorance of banking. Cash transfers inevitably involve a learning function, and institutional failure can distort the effects on behaviour and attitudes (for example, if it is difficult to access cash paid into a bank account).

There are several methods for distributing cash transfers, none of which is entirely adequate. The important issue is to make sure people receive the money directly, without the

involvement of an intermediary. However, bearing in mind the
need for replicability and up-scaling, another question is: what
option would be the most desirable and replicable at national
level, in terms of cost, transparency and user-friendliness?[2]

While the method chosen will depend on local circumstances, most pilots will need to make provision for costs
and time involved in enabling people to receive the money,
by helping to set up bank accounts or by providing biometric
smart cards or even mobile phones, and by ensuring that
the money can be accessed locally quickly and easily. For
monitoring purposes, however, all transactions should
pass through the banking system, as may also be required
by law.

AGENCY OR 'VOICE' EFFECTS SHOULD BE CONSIDERED

No sensible advocate of basic income believes it to be a panacea. Many vulnerable people given a basic income would
remain vulnerable and liable to be oppressed or exploited. To
combat that vulnerability, they need *agency*, the capacity to
exercise effective 'Voice' in their defence. This writer has
long taken the view that basic income will work optimally
only if those receiving it have individual agency and some
form of collective Voice to defend their interests.

A pilot social policy project should always take account of
agency effects. Agency or Voice may exist prior to the experiment, or may emerge during and/or as a result of the intervention. In the Namibian basic income pilot, within months
of starting, the villagers formed a committee to advise on
good use of the money and to defend the more vulnerable
against anybody trying to take advantage of them. To what

extent did that affect the outcomes? The evaluation team had the strong impression that the impact was positive. But it was unable to tell how important it was.

Other pilot cash transfer schemes have picked up a positive effect of agency; a study in Nicaragua found that in areas with a relatively high proportion of 'community leaders', the effects of conditional cash transfers were stronger.[3] That is only one type of agency that could be measured in a pilot. Others should be taken into account in the selection of sampled areas and in the design of the evaluation instruments.

List of
BIEN-Affiliated
Organizations

INTERNATIONAL — Basic Income Earth Network (BIEN):
http://basicincome.org/

EUROPE — Unconditional Basic Income Europe (UBIE):
http://basicincome-europe.org/ubie/

SOUTHERN AFRICA — SADC*-wide Basic Income Grant Campaign
(SADC BIG): http://spii.org.za/sadcbigcampaign/

> (The Southern African Development Community covers 15 countries:
> Angola, Botswana, Democratic Republic of Congo, Lesotho, Madagascar,
> Malawi, Mauritius, Mozambique, Namibia, Seychelles, South Africa,
> Swaziland, Tanzania, Zambia and Zimbabwe.)

ARGENTINA — Red Argentina de Ingreso Ciudadano (RedAIC):
http://www.ingresociudadano.org.ar/

AUSTRALIA — Basic Income Guarantee Australia (BIGA):
http://www.basicincome.qut.edu.au/

AUSTRIA — Netzwerk Grundeinkommen und sozialer Zusam-
menhalt – BIEN Austria: http://www.grundeinkommen.at/

BELGIUM — Basic Income Belgium: https://basicincome.be/

BRAZIL — Rede Brasileira de Renda Básica de Cidadania:
http://eduardosuplicy.com.br/renda-basica-de-cidadania/

CANADA — Basic Income Canada Network/Réseau canadien
pour le revenu garanti: http://www.basicincomecanada.org/

CHINA — BIEN China : http://www.bienchina.com/

DENMARK — BIEN Danmark: http://basisindkomst.dk/

FINLAND — BIEN Finland: http://perustulo.org/

FRANCE — Mouvement français pour un revenu de base:
http://www.revenudebase.info/

GERMANY — Netzwerk Grundeinkommen:
https://www.grundeinkommen.de/

ICELAND — BIEN Ísland:
https://www.facebook.com/groups/1820421514854251/

INDIA — India Network for Basic Income (INBI):
http://basicincomeindia.weebly.com/

IRELAND — Basic Income Ireland:
http://www.basicincomeireland.com/

ITALY — Basic Income Network Italia (BIN Italia):
http://www.bin-italia.org/

JAPAN — BIEN Japan:
http://tyamamor.doshisha.ac.jp/bienj/bienj_top.html

MEXICO — Red Mexicana Ingreso Ciudadano Universal:
ingresociudadano@gmail.com

NAMIBIA — Basic Income Grant Coalition:
http://www.bignam.org/index.html

NETHERLANDS — Vereniging Basisinkomen:
http://basisinkomen.nl/

NEW ZEALAND — asic Income New Zealand (BINZ):
http://www.basicincomenz.net/

NORWAY — BIEN Norge: http://www.borgerlonn.no/

PORTUGAL — Rendimento Básico:
http://www.rendimentobasico.pt/

QUEBEC — Revenu de base Québec:
https://revenudebase.quebec/

SCOTLAND — Citizen's Basic Income Network (CBIN)
Scotland: https://cbin.scot/

SLOVENIA — Sekcija UTD: http://utd.zofijini.net/

SOUTH KOREA — Basic Income Korea Network (BIKN):
http://basicincomekorea.org/

SPAIN — Red Renta Básica: http://www.redrentabasica.org/rb/

SWITZERLAND — BIEN Switzerland (BIEN-CH): http://bien.ch/en

TAIWAN — Global Basic Income Social Welfare Promotion
Association: https://www.facebook.com/GBI.SWPA.TW/

UNITED KINGDOM — Citizen's Income Trust: http://
citizensincome.org/
— Basic Income UK: http://www.basicincome.org.uk/

UNITED STATES — U.S. Basic Income Guarantee (USBIG)
Network: http://www.usbig.net/index.php

ACKNOWLEDGEMENTS

At the risk of offending others who may have influenced me, I would like to mention some of the many who have been on the same basic income journey, in alphabetical order – David Casassas, Sarath Davala, Andrea Fumagalli, Louise Haagh, Seán Healy, Michael Howard, Renana Jhabvala, Bill Jordan, Annie Miller, Ingrid van Niekerk, Claus Offe, Philippe van Parijs, Brigid Reynolds, Alexander de Roo, Enno Schmidt (for his indefatigable efforts on the Swiss referendum), Eduardo Suplicy (not only for his many renditions of 'Blowin' in the Wind'), Malcolm Torry, Walter van Trier, Yannick Vanderborght, Robert van der Veen, Karl Widerquist, Frances Williams, Jurgen De Wispelaere and Toru Yamamori. Many, many thanks to them all.

Notes

CHAPTER 1: BASIC INCOME – ITS MEANING AND HISTORICAL ORIGINS

1. J. Cunliffe and G. Erreygers (eds.) (2004), *The Origins of Universal Grants: An Anthology of Historical Writings on Basic Capital and Basic Income.* Basingstoke: Palgrave Macmillan, p. xi.
2. B. Ackerman and A. Alstott (1999), *The Stakeholder Society.* New Haven: Yale University Press. B. Ackerman and A. Alstott (2006), 'Why stakeholding?', in E. O. Wright (ed.), *Redesigning Distribution: Basic Income and Stakeholder Grants as Cornerstones for an Egalitarian Capitalism.* London and New York: Verso, pp. 43–65.
3. G. Standing (2006), 'CIG, COAG and COG: A comment on a debate', in Wright (ed.), *Redesigning Distribution*, pp. 175–95.
4. L. Bershidsky (2016), 'Letting the hungry steal food is no solution', *Bloomberg*, 4 May.
5. T. Paine ([1795] 2005), 'Agrarian justice', in *Common Sense and Other Writings.* New York: Barnes & Noble, pp. 321–45.
6. B. Russell (1920), *Roads to Freedom: Socialism, Anarchism and Syndicalism.* London: Allen & Unwin. E. M. Milner and D. Milner (1918), *Scheme for a State Bonus.* London: Simpkin, Marshall & Co. B. Pickard (1919), *A Reasonable Revolution. Being a Discussion of the State Bonus Scheme – A Proposal for a National Minimum Income.* London: Allen & Unwin. G. D. H. Cole (1929), *The Next Ten Years in British Social and Economic Policy.* London: Macmillan.
7. W. van Trier (1995), 'Every One a King', PhD dissertation. Leuven: Département de Sociologie, Katholieke Universiteit Leuven.
8. Russell, *Roads to Freedom*, pp. 80–81, 127.
9. M. L. King (1967), *Where Do We Go From Here? Chaos or Community?* New York: Harper & Row.

10. For a selection of statements and analyses, see J. E. Meade (1972), 'Poverty in the welfare state', *Oxford Economic Papers*, 24(3), pp. 289–326. J. E. Meade (1989), *Agathotopia: The Economics of Partnership*. Aberdeen: Aberdeen University Press. J. Tobin (1966), 'The case for an income guarantee', *Public Interest*, 4 (Summer), pp. 31–41.

11. M. Samson and G. Standing (eds.) (2003), *A Basic Income Grant for South Africa*. Cape Town: University of Cape Town Press.

12. For example, A. Beattie (2016), 'A simple basic income delivers little benefit to complex lives', *Financial Times*, 3 June.

CHAPTER 2: BASIC INCOME AS SOCIAL JUSTICE

1. T. Paine ([1795] 2005), 'Agrarian justice', in *Common Sense and Other Writings*. New York: Barnes & Noble, p. 332.

2. Ibid., p. 334.

3. Ibid., p. 335.

4. Ibid., p. 339.

5. H. George (1879), *Progress and Poverty*. New York: Schalkenbach Foundation.

6. G. Standing (2016), *The Corruption of Capitalism: Why Rentiers Thrive and Work Does Not Pay*. London: Biteback.

7. Outlined in G. Standing (2014), *A Precariat Charter: From Denizens to Citizens*. London and New York: Bloomsbury.

8. T. Shildrick, R. MacDonald, C. Webster and K. Garthwaite (2012), *Poverty and Insecurity: Life in Low-Pay, No-Pay Britain*. Bristol: Policy Press.

9. Standing, *The Corruption of Capitalism*.

10. P. van Parijs (1995), *Real Freedom for All: What (If Anything) Can Justify Capitalism?* Oxford: Clarendon Press.

11. Besides the writer's arguments for this approach, see P. Barnes (2014), *With Liberty and Dividends for All: How to Save Our Middle Class When Jobs Don't Pay Enough*. San Francisco: Berrett-Koehler.

12. J. Rawls (1971), *A Theory of Justice*. Cambridge: Cambridge University Press.

13. N. Frohlich and J. A. Oppenheimer (1992), *Choosing Justice: An Experimental Approach to Ethical Theory*. Berkeley: University of California Press.

14. International Labour Organization (2004), *Economic Security for a Better World*. Geneva: ILO.

15. Citizens' Climate Lobby (2016), 'Carbon fee and dividend policy'. http://citizensclimatelobby.org/carbon-fee-and-dividend/.

16. T. Meireis (2004), '"Calling": A Christian argument for basic income', in G. Standing (ed.), *Promoting Income Security as a Right*. London: Anthem Press, pp. 147–64. M. Torry (2016), *Citizen's Basic Income: A Christian Social Policy*. London: Darton, Longman & Todd.

17. C. M. A. Clark (2006), 'Wealth as abundance and scarcity: Perspectives from Catholic social thought and economic theory', in H. Alford, C. M. A. Clark, S. A. Cortright and M. J. Naughton (eds.), *Rediscovering Abundance*. Notre Dame: University of Notre Dame Press, pp. 28–56.

18. Pope Francis (2015), 'Encyclical letter Laudato Si of the Holy Father Francis on care for our common home', Vatican, 24 May.

CHAPTER 3: BASIC INCOME AND FREEDOM

1. G. Standing (2014), *A Precariat Charter: From Denizens to Citizens*. London and New York: Bloomsbury.

2. R. Nozick (1974), *Anarchy, State and Utopia*. New York: Basic Books. C. Murray (2006), *In Our Hands: A Plan to Replace the Welfare State*. Washington, DC: AEI Press. C. Murray (2012), *Guaranteed Income as a Replacement for the Welfare State*. Oxford: The Foundation for Law, Justice and Society. P. van Parijs (1995), *Real Freedom for All: What (If Anything) Can Justify Capitalism?* Oxford: Clarendon Press. K. Widerquist (2006), 'Property and the Power to Say No: A Freedom-Based Argument for Basic Income', PhD dissertation. Oxford: University of Oxford.

3. E. Anderson (2001), 'Optional freedoms', in P. van Parijs (ed.), *What's Wrong With a Free Lunch?* Boston: Beacon Press, pp. 75–9.

4. M. Tanner (2015), *The Pros and Cons of a Guaranteed National Income*. Washington, DC: Cato Institute. M. Zwolinski (2015), 'Property rights, coercion and the welfare state: The libertarian case for a basic income for all', *Independent Review*, 19(4). J. Buchanan (1997), 'Can democracy promote the general welfare?', *Social Philosophy and Policy*, 14(2), pp. 165–79.

5. C. Murray (2014), 'Libertarian Charles Murray: The welfare state has denuded our civic culture', *PBS Newshour*, 10 April.

6. Murray, *Guaranteed Income*.

7. B. Linley (2016), 'Gary Johnson is open to universal basic income and that's not bad', *Libertarian Republic*, 20 July.

8. T. Prochazka (2016), 'US libertarian presidential candidate "open" to basic income', *Basic Income News*, 18 July.

9. Zwolinski, 'Property rights, coercion and the welfare state'.

10. Cited in interview, T. Prochazka (2016), 'Zwolinski: Basic income helps "protect freedom" ', *Basic Income News*, 24 August.

11. R. H. Thaler and C. R. Sunstein (2008), *Nudge: Improving Decisions about Health, Wealth and Happiness*. New Haven, CT: Yale University Press.

12. P. Pettit (1997), *Republicanism: A Theory of Freedom and Government*. Oxford: Oxford University Press. P. Pettit (2007), 'A republican right to basic income?', *Basic Income Studies*, 2(2), pp. 1–8. P. Pettit (2014), *Just Freedom: A Moral Compass for a Complex World*. New York: Norton. D. Raventos and D. Casassas (2005), 'Republicanism and basic income: The articulation of the public sphere from the repoliticization of the private sphere', in G. Standing (ed.), *Promoting Income Security as a Right*. London: Anthem Press, pp. 231–54.

13. D. Casassas (2016), 'Basic income and social emancipation: A new road to socialism', paper presented at the 16th BIEN Congress, Seoul, 7–9 July 2016.

14. K. Kipping (2016), 'Unconditional basic income as affixed rate of democracy: Safeguarding the social freedom and economic power of all people', paper presented at the 16th BIEN Congress, Seoul, 7–9 July.

15. For elaboration of this, see G. Standing (2009), *Work after Globalization: Building Occupational Citizenship*. Cheltenham: Elgar, Chapter 9.

16. S. Davala, R. Jhabvala, S. K. Mehta and G. Standing (2015), *Basic Income: A Transformative Policy for India*. London and New Delhi: Bloomsbury.

17. G. Standing (2015), 'Why basic income's emancipatory value exceeds its monetary value', *Basic Income Studies*, 10(2), pp. 1–31.

18. C. Pateman (2006), 'Democratizing citizenship: Some advantages of a basic income', in E. O. Wright (ed.), *Redesigning Distribution*. London and New York: Verso, pp. 101–19.

CHAPTER 4: REDUCING POVERTY, INEQUALITY AND INSECURITY

1. K. J. Edin and H. L. Schaefer (2015), *$2.00 a Day: Living on Almost Nothing in America*. Boston: Houghton Mifflin Harcourt.

2. A. Case and A. Deaton (2015), 'Rising morbidity and mortality in midlife among white non-Hispanic Americans in the 21st century', *Proceedings of the National Academy of Sciences of the United States of America (PNAS)*, 112(49), pp. 15078–83.

3. G. Standing (2011), *The Precariat: The New Dangerous Class*. London: Bloomsbury.

4. G. Standing (2014), *A Precariat Charter: From Denizens to Citizens*. London: Bloomsbury. G. Standing (2016), *The Corruption of Capitalism: Why Rentiers Thrive and Work Does Not Pay*. London: Biteback.

5. D. Calnitsky (2016), '"More normal than welfare": The Mincome experiment, stigma, and community experience', *Canadian Review of Sociology*, 53(1), pp. 26–71.

6. E. Martinson (2016), 'View from a *Reg* reader: My take on the basic income', *Register*, 29 December.

7. H. Reed and S. Lansley (2016), *Universal Basic Income: An Idea Whose Time Has Come?* London: Compass.

8. C. Blattman and P. Niehaus (2014), 'Show them the money: Why giving cash helps alleviate poverty', *Foreign Affairs*, May/June. https://www.foreignaffairs.com/articles/show-them-money.

9. *The Economist* (2010), 'Homelessness: Cutting out the middle men', *The Economist*, 4 November.

10. G. J. Whitehurst (2016), 'Family support or school readiness? Contrasting models of public spending on children's early care and learning', *Economic Studies at Brookings, Evidence Speaks Reports*, 1(16), 28 April.

11. J. Surowiecki (2014), 'Home free', *New Yorker*, 22 September.

12. J. Furman (2016), 'Is this time different? The opportunities and challenges of artificial intelligence', remarks by the Chairman of the Council of Economic Advisers at AI Now: The Social and Economic Implications of Artificial Intelligence Technologies in the Near Term, New York University, 7 July.

13. Remarks by Christopher Pissarides at the 2016 World Economic Forum meeting in Davos, January 2016. https://www.youtube.com/watch?v=UnNs2MYVQoE.

14. Standing, *A Precariat Charter*.

15. M. L. King (1967), *Where Do We Go From Here: Chaos or Community?* Boston: Beacon Press.

16. N. Gabler (2016), 'The secret shame of middle-class Americans', *The Atlantic*, May.

17. G. Tsipursky (2016), 'Free money is not so funny anymore: Confessions of a (former) skeptic of basic income', *Salon*, 21 August.

18. S. Mullainathan and E. Shafir (2013), *Scarcity: Why Having Too Little Means So Much*. London: Allen Lane.

19. World Bank (2015), *World Development Report 2015: Mind, Society and Behaviour*. Washington, DC: World Bank.

20. M. Velasquez-Manoff (2014), 'What happens when the poor receive a stipend', *New York Times*, 18 January.

21. N. N. Taleb (2012), *Antifragile: How to Live in a World We Don't Understand*. New York: Random House.

22. M. Abu Sharkh and I. Stepanikova (2005), *Ready to Mobilize? How Economic Security Fosters Pro-Activism Attitudes Instead of Apathy*. Socio-Economic Security Programme Working Paper; Geneva: International Labour Organization.

23. G. Herman (2016), 'Unions are changing and that should give us cause for hope', Union Solidarity International, 2016. https://usilive.org/opinions/36811/.

CHAPTER 5: THE ECONOMIC ARGUMENTS

1. G. Standing (2016), *The Corruption of Capitalism: Why Rentiers Thrive and Work Does Not Pay*. London: Biteback. G. Crocker (2015), *The Economic Necessity of Basic Income*. Mimeo. https://mpra.ub.uni-muenchen.de/62941/1/MPRA_paper_62941.pdf.

2. B. Nooteboom (1987), 'Basic income as a basis for small business', *International Small Business Journal*, 5(3), pp. 10–18.

3. M. Bianchi and M. Bobba (2013), 'Liquidity, risk, and occupational choices', *Review of Economic Studies*, 80(2), pp. 491–511. C. Blattman (2013), 'Can entrepreneurship transform the lives of the poor (and how)?', chrisblattman.com, 30 May.

4. S. Davala, R. Jhabvala, S. K. Mehta and G. Standing (2015), *Basic Income: A Transformative Policy for India*. London and New Delhi: Bloomsbury.

5. S. Sorenson and K. Garman (2013), 'How to tackle U.S. employees' stagnating engagement'. *Gallup*, 11 June.

6. G. Standing (2011), 'Responding to the crisis: Economic stabilization grants', *Policy & Politics*, 39(1), pp. 9–25.

7. T. McDonald and S. Morling (2011), 'The Australian economy and the global downturn. Part 1: Reasons for resilience', *Economic Roundup Issue 2*. Canberra: Treasury, Australian Government.

8. Standing, 'Responding to the crisis'. A. Kaletsky (2012), 'How about quantitative easing for the people?', *Reuters*, 1 August. G. Standing (2014), *A Precariat Charter: From Denizens to Citizens*. London: Bloomsbury. M. Blyth and E. Lonergan (2014), 'Print less but transfer more: Why central

banks should give money directly to the people', *Foreign Affairs*, September/October. V. Chick et al. (2015), 'Better ways to boost eurozone economy and employment', letter to *Financial Times*, 27 March. A. Turner (2015), *Between Debt and the Devil: Money, Credit, and Fixing Global Finance*. Princeton, NJ: Princeton University Press.

9. On the latter, see J. Authers and R. Wigglesworth (2016), 'Pensions: Low yields, high stress', *Financial Times*, 22 August. On the general failings of QE, see Standing, *The Corruption of Capitalism*, Chapter 3.

10. M. Friedman (1969), 'The optimum quantity of money', in *The Optimum Quantity of Money and Other Essays*. Chicago: Aldine, pp. 1–50.

11. P. van Parijs (2013), 'The Euro-Dividend', *Social Europe*, 3 July. https://www.socialeurope.eu/2013/07/the-euro-dividend.

12. M. Ford (2015), *Rise of the Robots: Technology and the Threat of a Jobless Future*. New York: Basic Books. N. Srnicek and A. Williams (2015), *Inventing the Future: Postcapitalism and a World without Work*. London: Verso. P. Mason (2015), *Postcapitalism: A Guide to Our Future*. London: Allen Lane.

13. B. Gross (2016), 'Culture clash', Investment Outlook, Janus Capital Group, 4 May.

14. N. Hines (2016), 'Robots could make universal basic income a necessity', *Inverse*, 11 August. J. Furman (2016), 'Is this time different? The opportunities and challenges of artificial intelligence', remarks by the Chairman of the Council of Economic Advisers at AI Now: The Social and Economic Implications of Artificial Intelligence Technologies in the Near Term, New York University, 7 July. Executive Office of the President (2016), *Artificial Intelligence, Automation, and the Economy*. Washington, DC: White House, December.

15. A. Stern (2016), *Raising the Floor: How a Universal Basic Income Can Renew Our Economy and Rebuild the American Dream*. New York: PublicAffairs.

16. Cited in N. Lee (2016), 'How will you survive when the robots take your job?', *Engadget*, 19 August.

17. C. B. Frey and M. A. Osborne (2013), 'The future of employment: How susceptible are jobs to computerization?' Oxford: University of Oxford. http://www.oxfordmartin.ox.ac.uk/downloads/academic/The_Future_of_Employment.pdf.

18. M. Arntz, T. Gregory and U. Zierahn (2016), 'The risk of automation for jobs in OECD countries: A comparative analysis'. OECD Social, Employment and Migration Working Papers No. 189. Paris: Organisation for Economic Co-operation and Development.

19. K. Schwab (2016), *The Fourth Industrial Revolution*. Geneva: World Economic Forum.

20. *The Economist* (2016), 'Basically flawed' and 'Sighing for paradise to come', *The Economist*, 4 June, pp. 12, 21–24.

21. Cited in Lee, 'How will you survive?'

22. C. Weller (2016), 'The inside story of one man's mission to give Americans unconditional free money', *Business Insider UK*, 27 June.

23. Standing, *The Corruption of Capitalism*.

24. T. Berners-Lee, interviewed by *The Economist* (2016), 'The *Economist* asks: Can the open web survive?', *Economist* podcast, 27 May.

25. A. C. Kaufman (2015), 'Stephen Hawking says we should really be scared of capitalism, not robots', *Huffington Post*, 8 October.

26. A. Berg, E. F. Buffie and L.-F. Zanna (2016), 'Robots, growth, and inequality', *Finance & Development*, 53(3).

27. N. Yeretsian (2016), 'New academic research shows that basic income improves health', *Basic Income News*, 11 November.

28. A. Aizer, S. Eli, J. Ferrie and A. Lleras-Muney (2016), 'The long-run impact of cash transfers to poor families', *American Economic Review*, 106(4), pp. 935–71.

29. E. L. Forget (2011), 'The town with no poverty: Using health administration data to revisit outcomes of a Canadian guaranteed annual income field experiment'. Winnipeg: University of Manitoba. https://public.econ.duke.edu~erw/197/forget-cea%20(2).pdf.

30. R. Akee, E. Simeonova, E. J. Costello and W. Copeland (2015), 'How does household income affect child personality traits and behaviors?'. NBER Working Paper No. 21562. Cambridge, MA: National Bureau of Economic Research. http://www.nber.org/papers/w21562.

CHAPTER 6: THE STANDARD OBJECTIONS

1. A. Hirschmann (1991), *The Rhetoric of Reaction: Perversity, Futility, Jeopardy*. Cambridge, MA: Harvard University Press.

2. Private communication (2016).

3. I. V. Sawhill (2016), 'Money for nothing: Why universal basic income is a step too far', *Brookings*, 15 June.

4. V. Navarro (2016), 'Is the nation-state and the welfare state dead? A critique of Varoufakis', *Social Europe*, 4 August.

5. W. Korpi and J. Palme (1998), 'The paradox of redistribution and strategies of equality: Welfare state institutions, inequality, and poverty in the Western countries', *American Sociological Review*, 63(5), pp. 661–87.

6. G. Standing (2016), *The Corruption of Capitalism: Why Rentiers Thrive and Work Does Not Pay*. London: Biteback.

7. K. Marx ([1844] 1970), *Economic and Philosophic Manuscripts of 1844*. London: Lawrence & Wishart, p. 149.

8. Kenya CT-OBC Evaluation Team (2012), 'The impact of the Kenya Cash Transfer Program for Orphans and Vulnerable Children on household spending', *Journal of Development Effectiveness*, 4(1), pp. 38–49.

9. S. Davala, R. Jhabvala, S. K. Mehta and G. Standing (2015), *Basic Income: A Transformative Policy for India*. London and New Delhi: Bloomsbury, pp. 96–7.

10. M. Friedman (1962), *Capitalism and Freedom*. Chicago: University of Chicago Press. H. L Minsky (1969), 'The macroeconomics of a negative income tax', in H. L. Minsky (2013), *Ending Poverty: Jobs, Not Welfare*. Annandale-on-Hudson, NY: Levy Economics Institute, Bard College.

11. Davala et al., *Basic Income*.

12. G. Crocker (2015), *The Economic Necessity of Basic Income*. Mimeo. https://mpra.ub.uni-muenchen.de/62941/1/MPRA_paper_62941.pdf.

13. G. Dench, K. Gavron and M. Young (2006), *The New East End: Kinship, Race and Conflict*. London: Profile Books.

14. T. Cowen (2016), 'My second thoughts about universal basic income', *Bloomberg*, 27 October.

15. A. Stern (2016), *Raising the Floor: How a Universal Basic Income Can Renew Our Economy and Rebuild the American Dream*. New York: PublicAffairs.

16. G. Standing (2014), *A Precariat Charter: From Denizens to Citizens*. London: Bloomsbury.

CHAPTER 7: THE AFFORDABILITY ISSUE

1. T. Harford (2016), 'Could an income for all provide the ultimate safety net?', *Financial Times*, 29 April.

2. J. Kay (2016), 'With a basic income, the numbers just do not add up', *Financial Times*, 31 May.

3. M. Sandbu (2016), 'Free lunch: An affordable utopia', *Financial Times*, 7 June.

4. *The Economist* (2016), 'Daily chart: Universal basic income in the OECD', *The Economist*, 3 June. http://www.economist.com/blogs/graphicdetail/2016/06/daily-chart-1.

5. K. Farnsworth (2015), 'The British corporate welfare state: Public provision for private businesses', SPERI Paper No. 24. Sheffield: University of Sheffield.

6. T. DeHaven (2012), 'Corporate welfare in the federal budget', Policy Analysis No. 703. Washington, DC: Cato Institute.

7. G. Standing (2016), *The Corruption of Capitalism: Why Rentiers Thrive and Work Does Not Pay*. London: Biteback.

8. *Guardian* (2017), 'The Guardian view on basic income: A worthwhile debate, not yet a policy', *Guardian*, 1 February.

9. Sandbu, 'Free lunch'.

10. Non-taxpayers with incomes below the tax threshold would be relatively likely to vote for 'left' parties. J. Gingrich (2014), 'Structuring the vote: Welfare institutions and value-based vote choices', in S. Kumlin and I. Stadelmann-Steffen (eds.), *How Welfare States Shape the Democratic Public: Policy Feedback, Participation, Voting and Attitudes*. Cheltenham: Elgar, p. 109.

11. V. Houlder (2016), 'Cost of UK tax breaks rises to £117bn', *Financial Times*, 10 January.

12. Congressional Budget Office (2013), 'The distribution of major tax expenditures in the individual income tax system', Congressional Budget Office, 29 May. A. Holt (2016), 'Critics of universal basic income just don't understand how the policy would actually work', *Quartz*, 6 June.

13. H. Parker (1989), *Instead of the Dole: An Enquiry into Integration of the Tax and Benefit System*. London: Routledge.

14. H. Reed and S. Lansley (2016), *Universal Basic Income: An Idea Whose Time Has Come?* London: Compass.

15. Sandbu, 'Free lunch'.

16. M. Torry (2015), 'Two Feasible Ways to Implement a Revenue Neutral Citizen's Income scheme', ISER Working Paper EM6/15. Colchester: Institute for Social and Economic Research, University of Essex, April. www.iser.essex.ac.uk/research/publications/working-papers/euromod/em6-15. M. Torry (2016), 'An Evaluation of a Strictly Revenue Neutral Citizen's Income Scheme', ISER Working Paper EM5/16. Colchester: Institute for Social and Economic Research, University of Essex, June. https://www.iser.essex.ac.uk/research/publications/working-papers/euromod/em5-16.

17. A. Painter and C. Thoung (2015), *Creative Citizen, Creative State – The Principled and Pragmatic Case for a Universal Basic Income*. London: Royal Society of Arts.

18. A. Painter (2015), 'In support of a universal basic income – Introducing the RSA basic income model', Royal Society of Arts blog, 16 December.

19. Reed and Lansley, *Universal Basic Income*.

20. J. Birch (2012), 'The problem of rent: Why Beveridge failed to tackle the cost of housing', *Guardian*, 22 November.

21. G. Morgan and S. Guthrie (2011), *The Big Kahuna: Turning Tax and Welfare in New Zealand on Its Head*. Auckland, New Zealand: Public Interest Publishing.

22. A. Stern (2016), *Raising the Floor: How a Universal Basic Income Can Renew Our Economy and Rebuild the American Dream*. New York: PublicAffairs.

23. C. Holtz (2016), 'The Panama Papers prove it: America can afford a universal basic income', *Guardian*, 8 April. http://www.theguardian.com/commentisfree/2016/apr/07/panama-papers-taxes-universal-basic-income-public-services.

24. J. S. Henry (2012), *The Price of Offshore Revisited*. Chesham, UK: Tax Justice Network.

25. G. Mankiw (2016), 'A quick note on a universal basic income', Greg Mankiw's Blog, 12 July. http://gregmankiw.blogspot.ch/2016/07/a-quick-note-on-universal-basic-income. html

26. A. Manning (2015), 'Top rate of income tax', Centre for Economic Performance Paper EA029. London: London School of Economics. http://cep.lse.ac.uk/pubs/download/EA029.pdf.

27. See, for example, J. Burke Murphy (2016), 'Basic income, sustainable consumption and the "degrowth" movement', *Basic Income News*, 13 August.

28. K. Ummel (2016), 'Impact of CCL's proposed carbon fee and dividend policy: A high-resolution analysis of the financial effect on U.S. households', Working Paper v1. 4. Coronado, CA: Citizens' Climate Lobby, April. https://citizensclimatelobby.org/wp-content/uploads/2016/05/Ummel-Impact-of-CCL-CFD-Policy-v1_4.pdf.

29. *The Economist* (2016), 'Sighing for paradise to come', *The Economist*, 4 June, p. 24.

30. C. Rhodes (2017), 'Funding basic income through data mining', *Basic Income News*, 29 January.

31. SamfundsTanken (2016), 'UBInow: Unconditional basic income implementation in Denmark', SamfundsTanken.dk.http://samfundstanken.dk/ubinow.pdf.

32. J. E. Meade (1989), *Agathotopia: The Economics of Partnership*. Aberdeen: Aberdeen University Press.

33. K. Widerquist and M. Howard (ed.) (2012), *Alaska's Permanent Fund Dividend: Examining Its Suitability as a Model*. New York and London: Palgrave Macmillan. K. Widerquist and M. Howard (ed.) (2012), *Exporting the Alaska Model: Adopting the Permanent Fund Dividend for Reform around the World*. New York and London: Palgrave Macmillan.

34. P. Barnes (2014), *Liberty and Dividends for All: How to Save Our Middle Class When Jobs Don't Pay Enough*. Oakland, CA: Berrett-Koehler.

35. S. Lansley (2015), 'Tackling the power of capital: The role of social wealth funds', Compass Thinkpiece No. 81. London: Compass.

36. S. Lansley (2016), *A Sharing Economy. How Social Wealth Funds Can Tackle Inequality and Balance the Books*. Bristol: Policy Press, Chapter 2.

37. Standing, *The Corruption of Capitalism*.

38. UK Treasury (2016), *Shale Wealth Fund: Consultation*. London: HM Treasury.

39. Standing, *The Corruption of Capitalism*.

CHAPTER 8: THE IMPLICATIONS FOR WORK AND LABOUR

1. M. Tanner (2015), *The Pros and Cons of a Guaranteed National Income*. Washington, DC: Cato Institute, p. 19.

2. Office for National Statistics (2016), 'Changes in the value and division of unpaid care work in the UK: 2000 to 2015', ONS, 10 November.

3. S. Green Carmichael (2015), 'The research is clear: Long hours backfire for people and for companies', *Harvard Business Review*, 19 August.

4. G. Burtless (1986), 'The work response to a guaranteed income: A survey of experimental evidence', in A. H. Munnell (ed.), *Lessons from the Income Maintenance Experiments*, Conference Series 30. Boston, MA: Federal Reserve Bank of Boston and Brookings Institution, pp. 22–59.

5. K. Widerquist (2005), 'What (if anything) can we learn from the Negative Income Tax experiments?', *Journal of Socio-Economics*, 34(1), pp. 49–81.

6. For example, Tanner, *Pros and Cons*.

7. S. Kennedy (2016), 'Are basic income proposals crazy?', Institute for Policy Studies, 8 September. http://inequality.org/basic-income-proposals-crazy/.

8. E. A. Hanushek (1987), 'Non-labor-supply responses to the income maintenance experiments', in Munnell (ed.), *Lessons from the Income Maintenance Experiments*, pp. 106–30.

9. N. Hines (2016), 'Robots could make universal basic income a necessity', *Inverse*, 11 August.

10. M. Naim (2016), 'As robots take our jobs, guaranteed income might ease the pain', *HuffPost*, 18 July.

11. P.-E. Gobry (2014), ' "Progressives" hot new poverty-fighting idea has just one basic problem: Science', *The Week*, 21 July.

12. B. R. Bergmann (2006), 'A Swedish-style welfare state or basic income: Which should have priority?', in E. O. Wright (ed.), *Redesigning Distribution: Basic Income and Stakeholder Grants as Cornerstones for an Egalitarian Capitalism.* London and New York: Verso, pp. 130–42.

13. R. Paulsen (2008), 'Economically forced to work: A critical reconsideration of the lottery question', *Basic Income Studies*, 3(2), pp. 1–20.

14. FERinfos (2016), 'Revenu de base inconditionnel: Les Suisses continueraient de travailler', *FERinfos*, February, p. 9.

15. Among others, N. Frohlich and J. A. Oppenheimer (1992), *Choosing Justice: An Experimental Approach to Ethical Theory.* Berkeley: University of California Press.

16. C. Haarmann, et al. (2008), *Towards a Basic Income Grant for All: Basic Income Pilot Project Assessment Report.* Windhoek: Basic Income Grant Coalition and Namibia NGO Forum.

17. S. Davala, R. Jhabvala, S. K. Mehta and G. Standing (2015), *Basic Income: A Transformative Policy for India.* London and New Delhi: Bloomsbury.

18. G. Standing (2016), *The Corruption of Capitalism: Why Rentiers Thrive and Work Does Not Pay.* London: Biteback.

19. V. Navarro (2016), 'Why the universal basic income is not the best public intervention to reduce poverty or income inequality', *Social Europe*, 24 May. V. Navarro (2016), 'Is the nation-state and its welfare state dead? A critique of Varoufakis', *Social Europe*, 4 August.

20. I. Robeyns (2000), 'Hush money or emancipation fee? A gender analysis of basic income', in R.-J. van der Veen and L. Groot (eds.), *Basic Income on the Agenda: Policy Objectives and Political Chances.* Amsterdam: Amsterdam University Press, pp. 121–36. Bergmann, 'A Swedish-style welfare state or basic income'.

21. C. Pateman (2006), 'Democratizing citizenship: Some advantages of a basic income', in Wright (ed.), *Redesigning Distribution*, pp. 101–19. A. McKay (2001), 'Why a citizen's basic income? A question of gender equality or gender bias', *Work, Employment and Society*, 21(2), pp. 337–48. A. Alstott (2001), 'Good for women', in P. van Parijs, J. Cohen and J. Rogers (eds.), *What's Wrong with a Free Lunch?* Boston: Beacon Press, pp. 75–9. K. Weeks

(2016), 'A feminist case for basic income: An interview with Kathi Weeks', *Critical Legal Thinking*, 27 August.

22. T. Yamamori (2016), 'What can we learn from a grassroots feminist UBI movement? Revisiting Keynes' prophecy', paper presented at the 16th BIEN Congress, Seoul, 7–9 July.

23. Among others: Pateman, 'Democratising citizenship'. R. Mulligan (2013), 'Universal basic income and recognition theory: A tangible step towards an ideal', *Basic Income Studies*, 8(2), pp. 153–72. T. Henderson (2016), 'Redistribution, recognition and emancipation: A feminist perspective on the case for basic income in Australia', paper presented at the 16th BIEN Congress, Seoul, 7–9 July.

24. IDHC (2004), *Charter of Emerging Human Rights*. Barcelona: Institut de Drets Humans de Catalunya.

25. G. Standing (2009), *Work after Globalization: Building Occupational Citizenship*. Cheltenham: Elgar.

26. A. B. Atkinson (1996), 'The case for a participation income', *Political Quarterly*, 67(1), pp. 67–70. A. B. Atkinson (2015), *Inequality: What Can Be Done?* Cambridge, MA, and London: Harvard University Press.

27. A. Gorz (1992), 'On the difference between society and community and why basic income cannot by itself confer full membership', in P. van Parijs (ed.), *Arguing for Basic Income*. London: Verso.

28. A. Painter (2015), 'In support of a universal basic income – Introducing the RSA basic income model', Royal Society of Arts blog, 16 December.

29. J. Dodge (2016), 'Universal basic income wouldn't make people lazy – it would change the nature of work', *Quartz*, 25 August.

30. M. Whitlock (2016), 'How Britain's Olympic success makes the case for a basic income', *Huffpost Sport UK*, 31 August.

31. J. O'Farrell (2016), 'A no-strings basic income? If it works for the royal family, it can work for us all', *Guardian*, 7 January.

32. E. Green (2016), 'What America lost as women entered the workforce', *Atlantic*, 19 September.

33. K. W. Knight, E. A. Rosa and J. B. Schor (2013), 'Could working less reduce pressures on the environment? A cross-national panel analysis of OECD countries, 1970–2007', *Global Environmental Change*, 23(4), pp. 691–700.

34. D. Graeber (2016), 'Why capitalism creates pointless jobs', *Evonomics*, 27 September.

35. J. Burke Murphy (2016), 'Basic income, sustainable consumption and the "DeGrowth" movement', *Basic Income News*, 13 August.

36. G. Standing (2014), *A Precariat Charter: From Denizens to Citizens*. London: Bloomsbury, Article 19.

37. Ibid, Article 1.

CHAPTER 9: THE ALTERNATIVES

1.   G. Standing (2016), *The Corruption of Capitalism: Why Rentiers Thrive and Work Does Not Pay*. London: Biteback.

2.   F. Lawrence (2016), 'Beyond parody: HMRC cleaners left worse off after introduction of the national living wage', *Guardian*, 28 July.

3.   L. M. Mead (1986), *Beyond Entitlement: The Social Obligations of Citizenship*. New York: Free Press.

4.   M. Torry (2016), *Citizen's Basic Income: A Christian Social Policy*. London: Darton, Longman & Todd, p. 44.

5.   Department for Work and Pensions (2016), 'Income-related benefits: Estimates of take-up', DWP, 28 June.

6.   D. Matthews (2014), '76 percent of people who qualify for housing aid don't get it', *Vox*, 31 May. http://www.vox.com/2014/5/31/5764262/76-percent-of-people-who-qualify-for-housing-aid-dont-get-it.

7.   Center on Budget and Policy Priorities (2016), 'Chart book: TANF at 20', cbbb.org, 5 August.

8.   G. Standing (2014), *A Precariat Charter: From Denizens to Citizens*. London: Bloomsbury.

9.   M. Tanner and C. Hughes (2013), 'The work versus welfare trade-off: 2013', Cato Institute White Paper, cato.org, 19 August. http://object.cato.org/sites/cato.org/files/pubs/pdf/the_work_versus_welfare_trade-off_2013_wp.pdf.

10. R. Berthoud (2007), *Work-Rich and Work-Poor: Three Decades of Change*. York: Joseph Rowntree Foundation.

11. J. Drèze and A. Sen (2014), *An Uncertain Glory: India and Its Contradictions*. Princeton, NJ: Princeton University Press. This argument can be dealt with through the provision of food buffer stocks, which could be released when prices rise due to temporary shortages. The danger is that they act as disincentives to local farm production.

12. D. K. Evans and A. Popova (2014), *Cash Transfers and Temptation Goods: A Review of the Global Evidence*. World Bank Policy Research Working Paper WPS6886, Washington, DC: World Bank.

13. S. Bailey and S. Pongracz (2015), *Humanitarian Cash Transfers: Cost, Value for Money and Economic Impact*. London: Overseas Development Institute.

14. S. S. Bhalla (2014), 'Dismantling the welfare state', *Livemint*, 11 June.

15. M. Hidrobo et al. (2014), 'Cash, food, or vouchers? Evidence from a randomized experiment in northern Ecuador', *Journal of Development Economics*, 107, March, pp. 144–56.

16. Bailey and Pongracz, *Humanitarian Cash Transfers*.

17. Hidrobo et al., 'Cash, food, or vouchers?'.

18. S. Santens (2016), 'The progressive case for replacing the welfare state with basic income', *TechCrunch*, 9 September.

19. S. Mathema (2013), 'Undue concentration of housing choice voucher holders: A literature review'. Poverty and Race Research Action Council (PRRAC). http://www.prrac.org/pdf/Undue_Concentration_of_Vouchers_-_lit_review_6-13.pdf.

20. Bhalla, 'Dismantling the welfare state'.

21. Hidrobo et al., 'Cash, food, or vouchers?'.

22. P. Gregg and R. Layard (2009), *A Job Guarantee*. London: Centre for Economic Performance Working Paper, London School of Economics. http://cep.lse.ac.uk/textonly/_new/staff/layard/pdf/001JGProposal-16-03-09.pdf.

23. P. Harvey (2005), 'The right to work and basic income guarantees: Competing or complementary goals?', *Rutgers Journal of Law and Urban Policy*, 2(1), pp. 8–59. P. Harvey (2013), 'More for less: The job guarantee strategy', *Basic Income Studies*, 7(2), pp. 3–18. W. Quigley (2003), *Ending Poverty as We Know It: Guaranteeing a Right to a Job at a Living Wage*. Philadelphia, PA: Temple University Press. H. L. Minsky (1969), 'The macroeconomics of a Negative Income Tax', in H. L. Minsky (2013), *Ending Poverty: Jobs, Not Welfare*. Annandale-on-Hudson, NY: Levy Economics Institute, Bard College.

24. K. McFarland (2016), 'Basic income, job guarantees and the non-monetary value of jobs: Response to Davenport and Kirby', *Basic Income News*, 5 September.

25. E. Mian (2016), 'Basic income is a terrible, inequitable solution to technological disruption', *TheLong+Short*, 21 July.

26. A. Coote and J. Franklin (eds.) (2013), *Time on Our Side: Why We All Need a Shorter Working Week*. London: New Economics Foundation.

27. G. Standing (1990), 'The road to workfare: Alternative to welfare or threat to occupation?', *International Labour Review*, 129(6), pp. 677–91. This is elaborated in Standing, *A Precariat Charter*, Article 20.

28. *The Economist* (2016), 'Welfare reform: A patchy record at 20', *The Economist*, 20 August, pp. 11–12.

29. J. L. Collins (2008), 'The specter of slavery: Workfare and the economic citizenship of poor women', in J. L. Collins, M. di Leonardo and B. Williams (eds.), *New Landscapes of Inequality: Neoliberalism and the Erosion of Democracy in America*. Santa Fe, NM: SAR Press, pp. 131–52.

30. J. Ferguson (2015), 'Prepare for tax hikes', *MoneyWeek*, 11 March.

31. A. Nichols and J. Rothstein (2016), 'The Earned Income Tax Credit (EITC)', in R. A. Moffitt (ed.), *Economics of Means-Tested Income Transfers*. Cambridge, MA: National Bureau of Economic Research, pp. 137–218. M. Brewer and J. Browne (2006), *The Effect of the Working Families' Tax Credit on Labour Market Participation*, Briefing Note No. 69. London: Institute for Fiscal Studies.

32. M. Tanner (2015), *The Pros and Cons of a Guaranteed National Income*. Washington, DC: Cato Institute, p. 17.

33. K. Rawlinson (2014), 'Thousands chased by HMRC debt collectors due to overpaid tax credits', *Guardian*, 30 May.

34. J. Rothstein (2009), *Is the EITC Equivalent to an NIT? Conditional Transfers and Tax Incidence*. Washington, DC: National Bureau of Economic Research, Working Paper No. 14966, May.

35. *The Economist* (2015), 'Credit where taxes are due', *The Economist*, 4 July.

36. For an excellent critique, see J. Millar and F. Bennett (2016), 'Universal credit: Assumptions, contradictions and virtual reality', *Social Policy and Society*, online 10 May. DOI: 10.1017/S1474746416000154.

37. Cited in A. Painter (2016), 'The age of insecurity is not coming. It's already here'. Royal Society of Arts blog, 2 May.

38. Department for Work and Pensions (2015), *Universal Credit at Work*. London: Department for Work and Pensions. https://www.gov.uk/government/uploads/system/uploads/attachment_data/file/483029/universal-credit-at-work-december-2015.pdf.

39. F. Field and A. Forsey (2016), *Fixing Broken Britain? An Audit of Working-Age Welfare Reform Since 2010*. London: Civitas, p. 73.

40. P. Harrison-Evans (2016), 'A universal basic income: What would it mean for charities?', *New Philanthropy Capital*, 16 August.

http://www.thinknpc.org/blog/a-universal-basic-income-what-would-it-mean-for-charities/.

41. Tanner, *Pros and Cons*, p. 14.

CHAPTER 10: BASIC INCOME AND DEVELOPMENT

1. World Bank (2015), *The State of Social Safety Nets 2015*. Washington, DC: World Bank.

2. G. Standing (2008), 'How cash transfers promote the case for basic income', *Basic Income Studies*, 3(1), pp. 1–30.

3. R. Jhabvala and G. Standing (2010), 'Targeting to the "poor": Clogged pipes and bureaucratic blinkers', *Economic and Political Weekly*, 45(26–7), 26 June, pp. 239–46.

4. Australian Agency for International Development (2011), *Targeting the Poorest: An Assessment of the Proxy Means Test Methodology*. Canberra: AusAID, Department of Foreign Affairs and Trade.

5. P. Bardhan (2016), 'Universal basic income for India', *Livemint*, 12 October.

6. P. Niehaus, A. Atanassova, M. Bertrand and S. Mullainathan (2013), 'Targeting with agents', *American Economic Journal: Economic Policy*, 5(1), pp. 206–38.

7. G. Standing, J. Unni, R. Jhabvala and U. Rani (2010), *Social Income and Insecurity: A Study in Gujarat*. New Delhi: Routledge.

8. N. Caldés, D. Coady and J. A. Maluccio (2004), 'The cost of poverty alleviation transfer programs: A comparative analysis of three programs in Latin America', FCND Discussion Paper No. 174. Washington, DC: Food Consumption and Nutrition Division, International Food Policy Research Institute.

9. K. Lindert, E. Skoufias and J. Shapiro (2006), 'Redistributing income to the poor and the rich: Public transfers in Latin America and the Caribbean'. Social Protection Discussion Paper No. 0605, Washington, DC: World Bank Institute. F. V. Soares, R. P. Ribas and R. G. Osório (2007), 'Evaluating the impact of Brazil's *Bolsa Família*: Cash transfer programmes in comparative perspective', IPC Evaluation Note No. 1. Brasilia: International Poverty Centre, United Nations Development Programme.

10. M. Ravallion (2007), 'How relevant is targeting to the success of an anti-poverty programme?', World Bank Policy Research Working Paper No. 4385. Washington, DC: World Bank.

11. World Bank, *The State of Social Safety Nets 2015*.

12. J. Hagen-Zanker, F. Bastagli, L. Harman, V. Barca, G. Sturge and T. Schmidt (2016), *Understanding the Impact of Cash Transfers: The Evidence*, ODI Briefing. London: Overseas Development Institute.

13. N. Benhassine, F. Devoto, E. Duflo, P. Dupas and V. Pouliquen (2015), 'Turning a shove into a nudge? A "labeled cash transfer" for education', *American Economic Journal: Economic Policy*, 7(3), pp. 86–125.

14. S. Baird, F. H. G. Ferreira, B. Özler and M. Woolcock (2014), 'Conditional, unconditional and everything in between: A systematic review of the effects of cash transfer programmes on schooling outcomes', *Journal of Development Effectiveness*, 6(1), pp. 1–43.

15. S. Baird, C. McIntosh and B. Özler (2011), 'Cash or condition? Evidence from a cash transfer experiment', *Quarterly Journal of Economics*, 126(4), pp. 1709–53.

16. F. Bastagli, J. Hagen-Zanker, L. Harman, G. Sturge, V. Barca, T. Schmidt and L. Pellerano (2016), *Cash Transfers: What Does the Evidence Say?* London: Overseas Development Institute.

17. D. K. Evans and A. Popova (2014), *Cash Transfers and Temptation Goods: A Review of the Global Evidence*, World Bank Policy Research Working Paper WPS6886. Washington, DC: World Bank. J. Haushofer and J. Shapiro (2013), *Household Response to Income Change: Evidence from an Unconditional Cash Transfer Program in Kenya*. Princeton, NJ: Department of Psychology and Public Affairs, Princeton University. Kenya CT-OBC Evaluation Team (2012), 'The impact of the Kenya Cash Transfer Program for Orphans and Vulnerable Children on household spending', *Journal of Development Effectiveness*, 4(1), pp. 9–37. J. Hoddinott, S. Sandström and J. Upton (2014), 'The impact of cash and food transfers: Evidence from a randomized intervention in Niger', IFPRI Discussion Paper 01341, Washington, DC: International Food Policy Research Institute.

18. C. Haarmann et al. (2008), *Towards a Basic Income Grant for All: Basic Income Grant Pilot Project Assessment Report*. Windhoek: Basic Income Grant Coalition and Namibia NGO forum. L. Chioda, J. M. P. De Mello and R. R. Soares (2013), 'Spillovers from conditional cash transfer programs: *Bolsa Família* and crime in urban Brazil'. http://siteresources.worldbank.org/INTRES/Resources/469232-1380041323304/Chioda_deMello_Soares_BolsaFamilia_April242013.pdf. Hagen-Zanker et al., *Understanding the Impact of Cash Transfers*. H. Mehlum, K. Moene and R. Torvik (2005), 'Crime induced poverty traps', *Journal of Development Economics*, 77, pp. 325–40.

19. J. M. Cunha, G. De Giorgi and S. Jayachandran (2011), 'The price effects of cash versus in-kind transfers'. NBER Working Paper No. 17456. Cambridge, MA: National Bureau of Economic Research.

20. O. Attanasio, E. Battistin, E. Fitzsimons, A. Mesnard and M. Vera-Hernandez (2005), 'How effective are conditional cash transfers? Evidence from Colombia'. IFS Briefing Note 54. London: Institute for Fiscal Studies.

21. R. Himaz (2008), 'Welfare grants and their impact on child health: The case of Sri Lanka', *World Development*, 36(10), pp. 1843–57.

22. C. Miller, M. Tsoka, and K. Reichert (2006), 'The impact of the social cash transfer scheme on food security in Malawi', *Food Policy*, 36(2), pp. 230–38.

23. F. Bastagli (2009), 'From social safety net to social policy? The role of conditional cash transfers in welfare state development in Latin America'. IPC-IG Working Paper No. 60. Brasilia: International Policy Centre for Inclusive Growth, United Nations Development Programme.

24. S. S. Lim, L. Dandona, J. A. Hoisington, S. L. James, M. C. Hogan and E. Gakidou (2010), 'India's *Janani Suraksha Yojana*, a conditional cash transfer programme to increase births in health facilities: An impact evaluation', *Lancet*, 375(9730), pp. 2009–23.

25. A number of countries operate targeted full or partial fee waiver schemes. For a review, see R. Bitrán and U. Giedion (2003), 'Waivers and exemptions for health services in developing countries'. Social Protection Discussion Paper Series No. 308. Washington, DC: World Bank.

26. J. M. Aguero, M. R. Carter and I. Woolard (2007), *The Impact of Unconditional Cash Transfers on Nutrition: The South African Child Support Grant*. Brasilia: International Poverty Centre.

27. M. Adato and L. Bassett (2009), 'Social protection to support vulnerable children and families: The potential of cash transfers to protect education, health and nutrition', *AIDS Care: Psychological and Socio-Medical Aspects of HIV-AIDS*, 21(1), Supplement 1, pp. 60–75.

28. A. Fiszbein and N. Schady (2009), *Conditional Cash Transfers: Reducing Present and Future Poverty*. Washington, DC: World Bank. R. Slavin (2010), 'Can financial incentives enhance educational outcomes? Evidence from international experiments', *Educational Research Review*, 5(1), pp. 68–80.

29. Baird, McIntosh and Özler ,'Cash or condition?'.

30. A. Case, V. Hosegood and F. Lund (2003), 'The reach of the South African child support grant: Evidence from Kwazulu-Natal', Centre for Social and Development Studies Working Paper 38. Durban: University of Natal. M. Samson, U. Lee, A. Ndlebe, K. MacQuene, I. van Niekerk, V. Gandhi, T. Harigaya and C. Abrahams (2004), 'The social and economic impact of

South Africa's social security system: Final report', EPRI Research Paper 37. Cape Town: Economic Policy Research Institute.

31. S. R. Khandker, M. Pitt and N. Fuwa (2003), 'Subsidy to promote girls' secondary education: The female stipend program in Bangladesh'. MPRA Paper No. 23688. Munich: Munich Personal RePEc Archive. http//mpra. ub.unimuenchen.de/23688. D. Filmer and N. Schady (2006), 'Getting girls into school: Evidence from a scholarship program in Cambodia', World Bank Policy Research Paper No. 3910. Washington, DC: World Bank.

32. S. Baird, C. McIntosh and B. Özler (2009), 'Designing cost-effective cash transfer programs to boost schooling among young women in Sub-Saharan Africa', World Bank Policy Research Working Paper No. 5090. Washington, DC: World Bank, p. 22.

33. Hagen-Zanker et al. (2016), *Understanding the Impact of Cash Transfers*. Baird et al., 'Conditional, unconditional and everything in between'.

34. Hagen-Zanker et al., *Understanding the Impact of Cash Transfers*.

35. See, for example, ibid. A. V. Banerjee, R. Hanna, G. Kreindler and B. A. Olken (2015), 'Debunking the stereotype of the lazy welfare recipient: Evidence from cash transfer programs worldwide'. HKS Working Paper No. 076. Cambridge, MA: Harvard Kennedy School.

36. A. de Janvry, E. Sadoulet and B. Davis (2011), 'Cash transfer programs with income multipliers: Procampa in Mexico', *World Development*, 29(6), pp. 1043–56.

37. P. J. Gertler, S. W. Martinez and M. Rubio-Codina (2012), 'Investing cash transfers to raise long-term living standards', *American Economic Journal: Applied Econometrics*, 4(1), pp. 164–92.

38. S. Handa, L. Natali, D. Seidenfeld, G. Tembo and B. Davis (2016), 'Can unconditional cash transfers lead to sustainable poverty reduction? Evidence from two government-led programmes in Zambia'. Innocenti Working Papers No. IWP_2016_21. Florence, Italy: UNICEF Office of Research – Innocenti.

39. M. Angelucci and G. De Giorgi (2009), 'Indirect effects of an aid program: How do cash transfers affect ineligibles' consumption?', *American Economic Review*, 99(1), pp. 486–508.

40. The author helped design the surveys for the first pilot, and helped write the first technical analysis.

41. Haarmann et al., *Towards a Basic Income Grant for All*.

42. The writer worked with SEWA at all stages of these pilots, including the technical analysis.

43. S. Davala, R. Jhabvala, S. K. Mehta and G. Standing (2015), *Basic Income: A Transformative Policy for India*. London and New Delhi: Bloomsbury.

44. G. Standing (2015), 'Why basic income's emancipatory value exceeds its monetary value', *Basic Income Studies*, 10(2), pp. 193–223.

45. IMF (2013), *Energy Subsidy Reform: Lessons and Implications*. Washington, DC: International Monetary Fund.

46. IMF (2010), *The Unequal Benefits of Fuel Subsidies: A Review of Evidence for Developing Countries*. Washington, DC: International Monetary Fund.

47. Bardhan, 'Universal basic income for India'.

48. F. Cheng (2016), 'China: Macao gives an annual state bonus to all citizens', *Basic Income News*, 31 August.

49. F. Cheng (2016), 'Cooperative society and basic income: A case from China', *Basic Income News*, 10 November.

50. H. Tabatabai (2011), 'The basic income road to reforming Iran's price subsidies', *Basic Income Studies*, 6(1), pp. 1–23. H. Tabatabai (2012), 'Iran: A bumpy road towards basic income', in R. K. Caputo (ed.), *Basic Income Guarantee and Politics*. New York: Palgrave Macmillan, pp. 285–300.

51. A. Demirguc-Kunt, L. Klapper, D. Singer and P. Van Oudheusden (2015), 'The global Findex database 2014: Measuring financial inclusion around the world'. Policy Research Working Paper 7255. Washington, DC: World Bank.

52. A. Enami, N. Lustig and A. Taqdiri (2016), 'The role of fiscal policy in fighting poverty and reducing inequality in Iran: An application of the Commitment to Equity (CEQ) Framework'. ERF Working Paper No. 1020. Giza, Egypt: Economic Research Forum.

53. G. Standing (2005), 'Tsunami recovery grants', *Economic and Political Weekly*, 40(6), 5 February, pp. 510–14.

54. J. Hoddinott, D. Gilligan, M. Hidrobo, A. Margolies, S. Roy, S. Sandström, B. Schwab and J. Upton (2013), *Enhancing WFP's Capacity and Experience to Design, Implement, Monitor, and Evaluate Vouchers and Cash Transfer Programmes: Study Summary*. Washington, DC: International Food Policy Research Institute.

55. C. Lehmann and D. T. R. Masterson (2014), *Emergency Economies: The Impact of Cash Assistance in Lebanon*. Beirut: International Rescue Committee.

56. UNHCR (2016), 'UNHCR to double funds for cash-based assistance to refugees by 2020'. Press Release, 31 October.

57. T. Cordella and H. Onder (2016), *Sharing Oil Rents and Political Violence*. Policy Research Working Paper 7869. Washington, DC: World Bank.

58. S. Devarajan and M. Giugale (2013), *The Case for Direct Transfers of Resource Revenues in Africa*. Working Paper 333. Washington, DC: Center for Global

Development. T. Moss, C. Lambert and S. Majerowicz (2015), *Oil-to-Cash: Fighting the Resource Curse through Cash Transfers*. Washington, DC: Center for Global Development.

59. A. R. Mishra (2017), 'Jammu and Kashmir commits to idea of universal basic income', *Livemint*, 12 January.

60. Ministry of Finance (2017), *Economic Survey 2016–17*. New Delhi: Government of India, January, Chapter 9.

CHAPTER 11: BASIC INCOME INITIATIVES AND PILOTS

1. For a set of the papers presented at the Geneva Congress of 2002, see G. Standing (ed.) (2004), *Promoting Income Security as a Right: Europe and North America*. London: Anthem Press. Other papers can be found on the BIEN website: http://basicincome.org/research/.

2. J. Thornhill and R. Atkins (2016), 'Universal basic income: Money for nothing', *Financial Times*, 26 May.

3. E. Forget (2011), 'The town with no poverty: The health effects of a Canadian guaranteed annual income field experiment', *Canadian Public Policy*, 37(3), pp. 283–305. D. Calnitsky (2016), '"More normal than welfare": The Mincome experiment, stigma, and community experience', *Canadian Review of Sociology*, 53(1), pp. 26–71.

4. T. Skocpol (1991), 'Targeting within universalism: Politically viable policies to combat poverty in the United States', in C. Jencks and P. E. Peterson (eds.), *The Urban Underclass*. Washington, DC: Brookings Institution, pp. 411–36.

5. Forget, 'The town with no poverty'.

6. Calnitsky, '"More normal than welfare"'.

7. R. Akee, E. Simeonova, E. J. Costello and W. Copeland (2015), 'How does household income affect child personality traits and behaviors?'. NBER Working Paper 21562. Cambridge, MA: National Bureau of Economic Research. http://www.nber.org/papers/w21562.

8. L. Kalliomaa-Puha, A.-K. Tuovinen and O. Kangas (2016), 'The basic income experiment in Finland', *Journal of Social Security Law*, 23(2), pp. 75–91.

9. O. Kangas (2016), *From Idea to Experiment: Report on Universal Basic Income Experiment in Finland*. KELA Working Paper 106. Helsinki: KELA.

10. L. Groot and T. Verlaat (2016), 'The rationale behind the Utrecht and Wagenengen experiments'. Utrecht: Utrecht University School of Economics, August.

11. Cited in F. Barnhoorn (2016), 'Netherlands: Design of BI experiments proposed', *Basic Income News*, 26 October.

12. H. D. Segal (2016), *Finding a Better Way: A Basic Income Pilot Project for Ontario – A Discussion Paper*. https://www.ontario.ca/page/finding-better-way-basic-income-pilot-project-ontario.

13. Government of Ontario (2016), *Consultation Guide for the Basic Income Pilot Project*. https://www.ontario.ca/page/consultation-guide-basic-income-pilot-project.

14. The writer has been invited to join the International Advisory Board for this project.

15. S. Altman (2016), 'Basic income', Y Combinator blog, 27 January. https://blog.ycombinator.com/basic-income/.

16. J. Haushofer and J. Shapiro (2016), 'The short-term impact of unconditional cash transfers to the poor: Experimental evidence from Kenya', *Quarterly Journal of Economics*, July.

17. K. McFarland (2016), 'Brazil: Basic income startup gives "lifetime basic incomes" to villagers', *Basic Income News*, 23 December.

18. *The Economist* (2012), 'Free exchange: Hope springs a trap', *The Economist*, 12 May.

19. S. De Mel, D. McKenzie and C. Woodruff (2012), 'One-time transfers of cash or capital have long-lasting effects on microenterprises in Sri Lanka', *Science*, 24 February.

20. C. Blattman, N. Fiala and S. Martinez (2013), 'The economic and social returns to cash transfers: Evidence from a Ugandan aid program'. CEGA Working Paper. Berkeley: Centre for Effective Global Action, University of California (Berkeley), April. http://cega.berkeley.edu/assets/cega_events/53/WGAPE_Sp2013_Blattman.pdf.

CHAPTER 12: THE POLITICAL CHALLENGE – HOW TO GET THERE FROM HERE

1. *Hansard*, 14 September 2016.

2. J. De Wispelaere and J. A. Noguera (2012), 'On the political feasibility of universal basic income: An analytic framework', in R. Caputo (ed.), *Basic Income Guarantee and Politics: International Experiences and Perspectives on the Viability of Income Guarantee*. New York and Basingstoke: Palgrave Macmillan, pp. 17–38.

3. Those interesting in joining can email: contact@nc4bi.org.

4. A. Stern (2016), *Raising the Floor: How a Universal Basic Income Can Renew Our Economy and Rebuild the American Dream*. New York: PublicAffairs.

5. N. DuPuis, B. Rainwater and E. Stahl (2016), *The Future of Work in Cities*. Washington, DC: National League of Cities Center for City Solutions and Applied Research.

6. M. Bittman (2015), 'Why not Utopia?', *New York Times, Sunday Review*, 20 March.

7. H. Koch and J. Quoos (2017), 'Schwab: "Gewinner müssen mit Verlierern solidarisch sein" ', *Hamburger Abendblatt*, 9 January.

8. S. Dadich (2016), 'Barack Obama, neural nets, self-driving cars and the future of the world', *Wired*, October. https://www.wired.com/2016/10/president-obama-mit-joi-ito-interview/.

9. The best general treatment is Caputo, *Basic Income Guarantee and Politics*.

10. V. Taylor et al. (2002), *Report of the Commission on the Comprehensive Reform of Social Security*. Cape Town: Department of Social Development, Government of South Africa. M. Samson and G. Standing (eds.) (2003), *A Basic Income Grant for South Africa*. Cape Town: University of Cape Town Press.

11. The Fabian Society in Britain has proposed gradually replacing the personal tax allowance with an individual credit, paid to all who fulfil certain conditions, that would run alongside the means-tested Universal Credit. Although the society has not endorsed universal and unconditional basic income, it acknowledged that this could be a possible route to its introduction. A. Harrop (2016), *For Us All: Redesigning Social Security for the 2020s*. London: Fabian Society.

12. Y. Varoufakis (2016), 'The universal right to capital income', *Project Syndicate*, 31 October. https://www.project-syndicate.org/print/basic-income-funded-by-capital-income-by-yanis-varoufakis-2016-10.

APPENDIX: HOW TO RUN A BASIC INCOME PILOT

1. This point is made forcefully by Angus Deaton in a critique of randomized controlled trials, and by Nobel Prize-winning economist Jim Heckman. A. Deaton (2008), 'Instruments of development: Randomization in the tropics, and the search for the elusive keys to economic development', The Keynes Lecture, British Academy, 9 October. J. J. Heckman and J. A. Smith (1995), 'Assessing the case for social experiment', *Journal of Economic Perspectives*, 9(2), pp. 85–115.

2. For a discussion of the technical issues, see D. Johnson (2008), 'Case study of the use of smartcards to deliver government benefits in Andra Pradesh, India'. Sri City, Andhra Pradesh, India: Institute for Financial Management and Research, Centre for Micro Finance.

3. K. Macours and R. Vakis (2009), *Changing Households' Investments and Aspirations Through Social Interactions: Evidence from a Randomized Transfer Program*. Policy Research Working Paper. Washington, DC: World Bank.

Index

The index covers the main text but not the Notes section. BI stands for basic income throughout.

Index of
Authors Cited

Authors whose works are cited in the Notes.